THE GREAT LEVEL

by the same author

The Great Ouse

THE GREAT LEVEL

A History of Drainage and Land Reclamation in the Fens

DOROTHY SUMMERS

With plates, maps and diagrams

DAVID & CHARLES
NEWTON ABBOT   LONDON
NORTH POMFRET (VT)   VANCOUVER

ISBN 0 7153 7041 3
Library of Congress Catalog Card Number 76-4363

© Dorothy Summers 1976

All rights reserved. No part of this publication may be reproduced, stored in a retrieval system, or transmitted, in any form or by any means, electronic, mechanical, photocopying, recording or otherwise, without the prior permission of David & Charles (Publishers) Limited

Set in 11 on 13pt Garamond
and printed in Great Britain
by Latimer Trend & Company Ltd Plymouth
for David & Charles (Publishers) Limited
Brunel House   Newton Abbot   Devon

Published in the United States of America
by David & Charles Inc
North Pomfret   Vermont 05053   USA

Published in Canada
by Douglas David & Charles Limited
1875 Welch Street   North Vancouver   BC

Contents

		page
1	THE GREAT EAST SWAMP A Deep and Horrible Fen – Two Powerful Enimies	9
2	THE FENLAND DURING THE MIDDLE AGES The Pre-drainage Economy – Early Attempts at Reclamation	30
3	THE START OF THE ENTERPRISE Initial Experiments in Draining – The Great Design	50
4	THE FOUNDATION OF THE BEDFORD LEVEL CORPORATION An Experiment in Centralisation – Financial Weaknesses	79
5	THE UNDERTAKING IN DIFFICULTIES The Sinking Land – The Clash with Vested Interests – The Bedford Level in Decay	92
6	THE TRIUMPH OF LOCALISM The New Drainage Authorities – Drainage Activity in the Northern Fenland	115
7	THE GREAT OUTFALL CONTROVERSY Moveable as the Winde and Sea – Outfall Projects	144
8	THE TURNING-POINT The Power of Steam – From Chaos Drear	162
9	THE POST-DRAINAGE ECONOMY OF THE FENLAND The Bedford Level: Patterns of Agriculture – Farming Activity in the Northern Fenland	183

CONTENTS

10 THE FINAL TRIUMPH? 211
From Steam to Diesel – Improvements in Drainage Administration – The Great Ouse and Welland Flood Protection Schemes

EPILOGUE – THE FENLAND PRESENT AND FUTURE 243
Administration: The Anglian Water Authority – The Wash: Estuary Storage Projects – Some Problems in Fenland Agriculture

Notes 259

Acknowledgements 285

Index 287

FOR
MY FATHER

Given that the lands are freed from the superfluous water, there remains to be described a vast number of benefits and advantages that would accrue to the Crown . . . the change will be so striking that it could not be greater in a work of this kind; a vague, deserted Empire without population turned into a fertile region; and wild and useless products therefrom into an abundance of grain and pasturage; humble huts into a beautiful and opulent city, together with various other benefits. With good regulation, the drained land will be a regal conquest, a new republic and complete state.

From Humphrey Bradley's *Treatise* (1589)

Grant them drained, and so continuing; as now the great fishes therein prey on the less, so the wealthy men would devour the poorer sort of people. Injurious partage would follow upon the enclosure, and rich men, to make room for themselves, would jostle the poor people out of their commons.

Thomas Fuller, *History of the University of Cambridge* (1655)

I

The Great East Swamp

A DEEP AND HORRIBLE FEN

WHEN the Saxon saint Guthlac – who subsequently achieved fame as the founder of Crowland Abbey – first took what proved to be his momentous decision to become a hermit, the Fenland of eastern England furnished him with a retreat sufficiently dismal and remote to satisfy even his exacting requirements. 'Comforted,' we are told, 'with divine support', and undeterred by tales of 'strange and uncouth monsters', he penetrated into the fastnesses of a strange land of 'fetid pools' and 'flowing rivers', finding a terrain grim enough to daunt all but the most intrepid settler.[1] St Guthlac had need of his much vaunted faith in God. The Fenland at this time – in the words of the eighth-century chronicler Felix of Crowland – was a trackless waste of 'immense marshes' and 'foul running streams'.[2] Because of its low-lying situation and the excessive damp the region was 'oft-times clouded with moist and dark vapours',[3] a circumstance which lent additional emphasis to rumours widely prevalent at the time that it was the favoured haunt of devils. Even so intrepid a man as St Guthlac was afflicted by moments of doubt, being 'greatly troubled within him about the undertaking he had begun, namely to dwell there alone in the wilderness'.[4] According to popular report the few scattered inhabitants almost certainly numbered amongst their ranks outlaws, bandits, and a half-savage race of fishers and wildfowlers. The latter are traditionally supposed to have led a semi-nomadic, amphibious life, rowing or wading from one patch of dry ground to another,[5] a misconception which may well have given rise to the universally held belief that fenmen had webbed feet. In fact the natives, far from being a race apart, were mostly ordinary farmers.

The pre-drainage Fenland came to be characterised by a unique organisation evolved from centuries of grappling with problems of enormous complexity. Because economic arrangements and modes of life tended to be widely at variance with those found in other parts of England, they were dubbed as strange and unorthodox, or in extreme cases as inferior, even repulsive. The Fenland inhabitants were regarded with something like horror; their habits were condemned as irregular and brutish, their mode of life seen as one of poverty-ridden squalor. Contemporaries depicted the fens before draining as a region of swamps and pools, their inhabitants crippled by ague, rheumatism and other disorders, prone to opium-eating, and eking out a precarious, wretched existence amidst thick fogs and a permanently moisture-laden atmosphere. Fen dwellers, on the other hand, seeing their fen lands through less prejudiced eyes and with a sympathy borne of long experience of their vagaries, held quite different opinions. To them the fens represented rich grazing lands and small but fertile arable fields, with abundant supplies of fish, wildfowl, sedge and turf, for food, building materials and fuel, thrown in as an additional bonus. The people themselves were certainly hardier than most, with a more sensitive awareness – fostered and nursed in a land of vast horizons – of the advantages of untrammelled freedom. The constant need to guard against land floods and encroachments of the sea made them alert, resourceful, enduring and courageous.

Certainly the later medieval Fenland economy was not as wasteful as some outsiders would have it believed. Then many fens, irrespective of what their earlier condition may have been, provided good grassland, whose lush growth was actually encouraged by the seasonal inundations so frequently deplored by the misinformed. The problem was how to turn to the best account both this and the rest of the local resources, and to do so, not merely in the summer months or at other favourable periods, but throughout the year and under a variety of conditions. A solution was found partly in the adoption of minute communal regulations, frequently imposed with considerable rigour, and partly by making animal husbandry the basis of Fenland life, with grain grown primarily as a fodder crop and for household use. The marshland, largely reclaimed from the sea, provided good pasture for horses and sheep. Cattle grazed in summer on the rich grass of the inland fens, being moved in winter into dry closes. The area then under water, far from being an unproductive waste, provided the local inhabitants with excellent fishing and fowling. There was almost certainly a thriving local trade in wares made from reeds, osiers and rushes.

But although much of the land was by no means valueless, the early pre-Norman Conquest sources are unanimous about the presence of much uninhabited wasteland in this sombre region. Dio Cassius may well have been referring to the Fenland when he recorded how the Romans 'wandered into the pathless marshes, and lost many of their soldiers'. In their subjugation of these regions the Romans encountered more than ordinary difficulty because the Britons were 'capable of enduring hunger and thirst, and hardships of every description . . . when hiding in the marshes they abide there many days with their heads only out of water'.[6] According to Bede the countryside around Ely during the late seventh century was 'on every side encompassed with the sea or marshes'. The Isle of Ely itself – 'environed with fens and reed-plecks unpassable, so that they feared not the invasion of the enemy' – functioned as a retreat for refugees and as a storehouse for valuables whenever times were especially turbulent.[7] Crowland, situated in the heart of the mist-enshrouded fens of Lincolnshire, was an obscure island, surrounded by bogs and pools, devoid of settled habitation 'on account of manifold horrors and fears, and the loneliness of the wide wilderness, so that no man could endure it'.[8] When speaking of St Guthlac and the foundation of Crowland Abbey it is not easy to divest the narrative of mysticism. St Guthlac found the Fenland haunted by devils 'in countenance horrible' – perhaps the Anglo-Saxon personification of ague and rheumatism – who 'came with such immoderate noises and immense horror, that it seemed to him that all between heaven and earth resounded with their dreadful cries'. They bound St Guthlac 'in all his limbs . . . and brought him to the black fen, and threw and sunk him into the muddy waters'.[9]

This picture of the early Fenland, however fantastic it may seem today, and however much it was derived from the hallucinations of high fever – for which the low-lying marshes formed a veritable breeding ground – yet has considerable significance in that it demonstrates the fears which the region generated in the minds of contemporaries. It is not surprising that the ingrained horror of the fens retained a profound hold on the Saxon mind, becoming so persistently rooted that it passed into tradition. But since these earlier times the foresight and efforts of a few men, successful drainage projects, and the tireless industry of local farmers and cultivators have converted this region, once known as the Great East Swamp, and described by William Elstobb as a 'deep and horrible fen',[10] into one of the most highly productive areas of England. Where formerly the Witham, Welland, Nene and Great Ouse rivers almost lost themselves in the encroaching bogs, the channels are now embanked and carry their waters direct to the sea. The entire country is intersected by artificial drains, whilst powerful engines pump surplus water into the arterial cuts. From lands which were once the haunt of many thousands of waterfowl, crops of corn, sugar beet, potatoes, celery and carrots are harvested every year. It is no exaggeration to say that the draining and reclamation of the fens represents a permanent and important influence on the social and economic history of England.

Paradoxically, now that the process of reclamation is virtually complete, drought frequently poses a far greater problem than flooding, especially in the peat lands. Water dries rapidly out of the surface peat, and during a dry spell can become inconveniently, sometimes drastically, scarce. Even during the Middle Ages drought had occasionally constituted a severe handicap as, for example, in 1353, when the sacrist of Ely received no returns from the fisheries or ferries belonging to the monastery.[11] In 1681 Thomas Baskerville recorded how the

> country from Milden Hall to Ely being nothing but turf or peat and is by its insufferable heat and dryth having exhausted all of the moisture out of the ditches, it was so suffocating hot by means of the brimstone and sulphury vapours we could hardly breathe or endure it, so that I verily think 'twas possible to have set the country on fire, the earth was then so dry.[12]

Almost 200 years later, in December 1874, S. B. J. Skertchly described how he 'walked dryshod along the bottoms of drains that ought to have had six feet of water in them, and saw pits sunk four feet below the bottom to obtain water, which then only filtered in slowly'.[13] Today the problem still remains; in fact it has assumed even greater significance. Dry peat soils are liable to erosion both by the action of strong winds and as a consequence of fires which are often started accidentally in summer. Peat fires are tenacious if not put out immediately, for once the fire has gained a hold on the dry peat between the surface and the ground water-table, it is difficult to extinguish and may burn slowly for weeks or months, extending laterally until stopped by a ditch. In one case a fire was known to burn for nearly two years. The surface foot or two of peat may thus be destroyed, as occurred over two fields in Waterbeach Level.

Its characteristic problems apart the Fenland, even today, remains a distinctive region. It forms a vast, extremely flat plain bordering the Wash, wedged between chalk highlands to the east and sandstone and limestone ridges to the west. The whole rests on a basic stratum of Oxford clay or glacial and interglacial sands and gravels. Extending into six counties, viz Lincoln, Northampton, Huntingdon, Cambridge, Suffolk and Norfolk, the region embraces an area of approximately 1,306 square miles, or about 700,000 acres. The extreme length of the Fenland between Lincoln and Quy is about 73 miles, its breadth from east to west, from Brandon in Suffolk across to Peterborough, is approximately 36 miles. On the north the Fenland boundary stretches from Lincoln to Burgh-le-Marsh, where it joins the marshland of the Lincolnshire coast, which is itself a continuation of the fens. Its western margin extends from Lincoln to Somersham via Bourne, Peterborough, Yaxley and Ramsey. The southern boundary of the fens runs from Somersham to Earith, Swaffham Prior and Mildenhall, while the eastern margin extends from Mildenhall to Lakenheath and Stoke Ferry; thence to King's Lynn and the sea via Downham Market in Norfolk, with an inflexion along the Nar valley.

To individual stretches of fen having a marked geographical entity special names have been given, for instance East, West and Wildmore Fens lying north and east of the Witham; Holland Fen to the west, and Deeping Fen bordering the Welland. The configuration of the fens to the south near Ely, Ramsey and Crowland is totally different. These are of varying size, more broken and irregular in shape than those lying to the north.

The Fenland as a whole has two principal characteristic features. In the first place it lies open to the sea, being conterminous with, or virtually an extension of, the Wash. Secondly it is intersected by many rivers, of which the major ones are the Witham, Welland, Nene and Great Ouse. These with their tributaries carry a colossal volume of drainage water from the surrounding highlands to the Wash, into which they collectively discharge the floodwaters of much of central England. They drain an area of some 6,000 square miles, a region almost five times the size of the Fenland itself.

The landscape of the fens has been modelled by the work of ice, rivers and the sea. Before the Glacial Period, or perhaps at its outset, the site of the Fenland basin presented an appearance far different from its modern aspect. Then the chalk uplands of Lincolnshire extended across what is now the mouth of the Wash to Hunstanton in Norfolk. To the west this chalk escarpment overlooked a low-lying plain, occupied by softer, and hence easily denuded, Oxford and Kimmeridge clays. Through gaps in this chalk barrier the ancestors of the present-day fen rivers (which contributed to the system of the combined Thames–Rhine) flowed eastwards to the sea. The ultimate reduction of this ridge to a mere line of isolated outliers may be attributed to the gradual enlargement of the river estuaries through normal erosive processes. Finally, with the submergence of the land, the sea broke through and destroyed the last remnants of the chalk barrier. The direct erosive action of the sea on the softer Kimmeridge and Oxford clays rapidly denuded the Fenland basin, scouring away the clays to the limits of the surrounding harder rocks, chalk to the north and south, and harder oolites on the west. A few places withstood the action of the sea, causing corrugations in the surface of the land. These frequently protruded sufficiently to form the present-day Fenland 'islands', which, together with the rest of eastern England were plastered with boulder clay during the advance of the Great Eastern Glacier. Boulder clay, occurring chiefly as remnants on plateaux and hills, represents an unstratified mass of lead-coloured clay, and includes fragments of chalk and limestone, as well as basalt, granite, sandstone and other formations not of Fenland origin. Many of these rocks are polished and scratched in a manner which seems clearly indicative of their early subjection to glacial action.

Three, or perhaps four, glaciations are believed to have affected East Anglia, but the last was less severe than the earlier ones and the ice is thought to have advanced only as far south as north Norfolk, many Fenland districts merely experiencing a cold climate and periglacial conditions during this period. With the retreat of the ice front for the last time there was apparently a relatively rapid eustatic rise in the sea level. The sea waters advanced into the area of the Wash and into much of the low-lying region of the present-day Fenland. Renewed denudation occurred, leaving the general terrain of the country in much the same condition as it is now. Subsequently the Fenland basin was filled during the course of varying processes of sedimentation under warmer post-glacial conditions, whilst the Wash as it exists today constitutes the remains of what was formerly a much larger coastal indentation. It should be noted that the marine transgression was gradual, and that the rivers maintained freshwater conditions over large areas of the landward part of the fens. These conditions were suitable for peat to form, and it began to accumulate before 3000 BC.

Nevertheless during much of the earlier post-glacial period many parts of the region were covered by salt-marsh vegetation and must, therefore, have lain slightly below high-tide levels. A change occurred with remarkable suddenness, and is probably accounted for by the fact that coarser silts, deposited by the sea, undoubtedly began to settle and increase in height along the seaward margin of the region. In places the silt lands were built up until they lay above the highest level of the spring tides, or about 20ft above low-water mark. The subsequent exclusion of the sea by this silt bar would quickly change conditions further inland from salt-marsh to fen. Peat formation, for the most part uninterrupted in the Cambridge area, became general.

The numerous large river systems entering the fens from the

surrounding uplands now assumed the dominant role, assisted by certain crucial factors, in creating an environment favourable to the development of great peat beds, often many feet thick. The blocking of the river outfalls by silt carried in from the Wash on every tide, coupled with the flat surface gradient of the land, which effectively diminished the rate of fall of the water draining to the sea, meant that floodwaters brought down by the rivers stagnated on the land. As the subsidence of the Fenland basin continued the rivers were increasingly obstructed in their passage out to sea; their currents became more sluggish so that high silt-laden tides from the Wash overrode them, and poured up the Fenland rivers, dropping silt in the channels. Here great silt banks were formed which further arrested the passage of the upland waters. Vast lakes took shape, which gradually became choked with rushes, sedge and waterweeds of every description. It was this accumulation of fresh water which encouraged the formation of peat soils, predominantly composed of organic matter derived from swamp vegetation. The peat fens themselves, by impeding the river courses, further assisted their own development. The rivers now pursued a winding, devious path across the flat country, spreading their waters far and wide, existing waterways being frequently abandoned when the rivers were compelled by obstructions in the marsh to cut a new channel. Today it is still possible to trace many of these extinct river courses or 'roddons', winding across the fen lands.[14]

Meanwhile the peat continued to grow, until the general level of the peat lands was even higher than that of the neighbouring silt lands, and well above high-tide level, a fact which ultimately misled some of the land drainers of the sixteenth and seventeenth centuries into making completely erroneous assessments of the ease with which the region could be drained. They assumed that the fens were high enough to drain themselves provided that the river outfalls were kept free from silt.[15] In fact, as we shall see, the surface peat of the fens has shrunk to a very marked degree since the completion of the major drainage projects, a circumstance which has posed seemingly insuperable obstacles. The disappearance of many feet of peat over a wide area of the fens during the last two or three centuries has many implications, not the least of these being the threatened gradual destruction of the entire peat surface.

Broadly speaking the surface of the Fenland at the present time is divided into three zones: a relatively narrow belt of salt-marsh bordering the Wash, a broader belt of silt land, and between this and the margin of older rocks, the peat fens. The relative surface extent of the peat and silt zones is by no means static. It has varied from time to time, and is subject to marginal admixture.[16] Furthermore these zones are purely superficial, representing the mere surface veneer of the alluvial deposits which fill the Fenland basin. During the period of Fenland formation there was never at any time a clearly defined boundary between fresh and salt water. Hence while the southern Fens have an overall peat surface and the northern Fens a predominantly silt one, the soil beneath is frequently composed of a series of layers which sometimes vary from field to field. These deposits consist of peat beds, marine clays and silts, and other alluvial deposits, which frequently run to a depth of 20 or 30ft. Moreover freshwater flooding had constituted a decisive factor throughout the entire Fenland even before the first inroads of the sea, and it is for this reason that peat beds cover large expanses of the clay or gravel floor of the Fenland, even to the coast and beyond.

The silt lands, including the coastal marshes, occupy the north and central portions of the Fenland, bordering virtually all three coasts of the Wash. In extent they are equal to rather more than one-half of the entire fen district, and are still in process of formation. The silt is brought in from the sea, being deposited mainly at the slack of high water along the coast. Mud-flats are formed, which are ultimately reclaimed for cultivation. Fairly reliable estimates, based on the position of works which the Romans are reputed to have carried out, indicate that there must have been an accretion to the land on the coastline of the Wash at the rate of somewhere between 10 and 11ft a year in the last 1,700 years. The receding water has stranded former coast towns and villages far inland. Wisbech, for example, is now 10 miles, and the harbours of Fleet and Bicker in Lincolnshire 6 miles or more, from the sea. The general elevation of the silt lands at the present day is several feet above the level of the peat fens, the rate of surface shrinkage

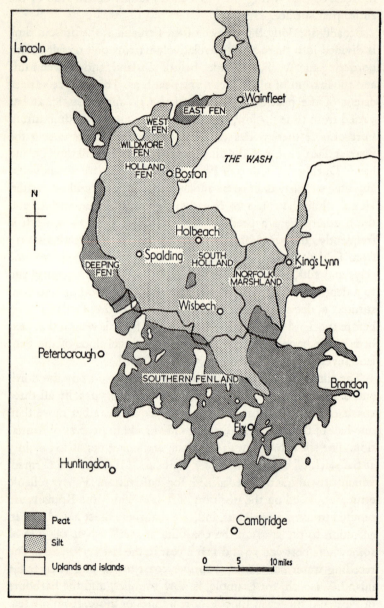

FIGURE 1. The fens: peat and silt zones

after draining having been less. Large areas, such as Norfolk Marshland, form broad, featureless tracts of fine-grained soils, easily worked and appreciated since the days of the Romans. Belloc describes Marshland thus: 'the dry land slips and wallows into a very quiet shallow water, confused with a yellow thickness, and brackish with the weight of inland water behind'. The surface of the land has no relief. Horizons are flat and hard. Even trees and farms seem foreign to the landscape. The skyline of the coastal marshes to seaward, as in Marshland, is flat and dull. The visitor receives an impression of desertion and loneliness. The Wootton marshes along the south-east coast of the Wash are fairly typical. Here there have been two stages of reclamation; the first has resulted in a belt along the landward slopes and presents a spidery network of ditches, the heritage of piecemeal reclamation in medieval times. The second, and much broader belt, dates from the beginning of the nineteenth century. It can be distinguished from the first by its rectangular, polder type drainage. Each field is surrounded by ditches. Beyond the last sea-dike lies the waterlogged samphire marsh veined by sea creeks.

The peat lands occupy almost the entire western edge of the Fenland, and the entire southern area. Whilst the acreage of the silt lands is expanding, that of the peat fens, due to decomposition and wastage through drying, is shrinking both in depth and surface extent. With the shrinkage the level of the land falls, so that large expanses of the peat fens have now sunk as much as 5ft below mean sea level and up to 17ft below the high-water level of the spring tides. A few elevations of from 20 to 100ft break the uniform flatness and low altitude of the plain, emerging out of the expanse of fen like islands out of the sea. Before the fens were drained places like Thorney, Whittlesey, Manea, Hilgay, Stuntney and Ely did actually form islands, havens of dry land rising out of a waste of water.

It is mainly in the region around the Isle of Ely and the Feltwell and Swaffham Fens where the peat lands today are the deepest and most extensive. The dominant features of the peat zone are the sparse distribution of houses – the peat affords no solid foundations on which to build – the perfect sea-like flatness of the landscape, and the absence over large areas of scattered trees and hedgerows. Whereas in the northern Fens the villages stand on their silt, there are almost no villages on the peat; most of the settlements are on islands. The region is indeed remarkable for its sparse habitation, and for its retention, especially in winter, of that same air of desolation which must have characterised large areas during the Middle Ages. It has been truly observed that whereas the silt-fen farmer settles on his land, the peat-fen farmer only visits his.[17] This is essentially an artificial countryside of straight field boundaries, drains and roads. It is this which helps to lend an aspect of rigid uniformity to the landscape.

The condition of the Fenland roads up to fairly recent times has constituted a major difficulty. For centuries routes across the fens were hazardous to all but the native population. Strangers seldom ventured without a regular guide. The almost total absence of stone posed a great problem, and fen roads had undergone little improvement as late as the first quarter of the nineteenth century, 'even the turnpike one from Downham to Wisbech, not excepted; the "mending" being only the silt, viz a sand formerly left by the sea, and not a stone amongst it'.[18] Up to the beginning of the present century secondary roads or 'droves' – as distinct from the main highways – were in an even more notoriously evil condition, being nothing more than broad, straight belts of uncultivated land. Although passable in summer Skertchly recorded how 'when the rains of winter fall vehicles sink to the axles in the spongy mass, and the roads become practically useless'. He continued:

> I have seen six horses try in vain to drag a loaded tumbril across a road; and have known a riding horse to be bogged and have to be shot to save it from death by cold and starvation . . . so rare are stones over this land that an occasional pebble or brickbat is a godsend to thrushes and blackbirds, and the broken snail-shells lying in profusion around show how alive the birds are to the value of this curiosity.[19]

Predictably inland navigation represented a major element in regional life. The rivers and their tributaries which intersect the region were for long the great highways, equally for the movement of heavy goods and for passenger transport. They provided a system of communications in many respects superior to that of the uplands, where even here roads were poor, impassable, or non-existent. It is not surprising to find many settlements from the earliest times concentrated on land adjacent to the rivers, assuming that the threat of flooding did not repel habitation; although in the peat zone the inherent instability of the peat has always rendered building impracticable on any large scale. A modern writer has described how he had

> been in many a lonely fenman's shack where not a wall, a floor, a door, a window but has sagged or sideslipped out of true. The brick floors of the living-rooms downstairs surge up and down. The front or the hind legs of the chairs will have been cut short to make them fit the floor, and the table too, unless it has bricks set underfoot to wedge it level. The stairway door swings back to meet you as the latch is lifted. The treads lead crazily upstairs. With the bedroom boards lurching over to a cock-eyed dormer window, the bed seems on the brink of sliding across to the wall. Only the great chimney that the cottage leans upon looks as if it might last a few years more ... such is the way of peat. The wise man spends his days upon it, tilling and tending, but at nightfall creeps out on to *terra firma* to sup and sleep.[20]

TWO POWERFUL ENIMIES

'It is a hard question,' observed Andrewes Burrell in 1642, 'whether the Sea or the Land Floods are the most potent enemies of the Fenns; but this is most certaine, that when the Sea floods and the Land floods meet, as they often times doe, halfe way betwixt the high Lands and the Sea, in that very place like two powerful enimies joyning in one, they doe over-run the Levell, and drowne it from one end unto the other.'[21] He meant that whenever an unusually heavy freshwater discharge happened to coincide with the period of spring tides the levels in the Fenland rivers rose, causing widespread flooding.

The story of fen drainage has been the transformation of river marsh and tidal silt into good arable and grazing land. Therefore the central theme of the Fenland story has been one of perpetual struggle with the freshwaters of the highlands and fens on the one hand, and the salt waters of the sea on the other. Fenland drainage has always been affected by two very differing sets of circumstances. The first is the large run-off water from the huge catchment area of almost 6,000 square miles, served by the rivers flowing through the fens. The second is the loose, sandy floor of the Wash into which the water discharges, a problem which has been considerably exacerbated by the nature of the tides.

The success of the rivers in discharging their waters into the sea has always represented a crucial factor in keeping the land free from floods. The Witham, Welland, Glen, Nene, Great Ouse, Cam, Lark, Little Ouse and Wissey are the important rivers flowing through the region, all of which, as the famous Dutch engineer Cornelius Vermuyden subsequently stressed 'do come out of divers vast and great countries which lye about it'.[22] In effect this meant that the autumn and winter floodwaters of half central England poured through the fens on their journey to the sea. It was due to this that some of the more prominent difficulties associated with the region were eventually encountered. Cornelius Vermuyden drew attention to a further problem:

> The level is broad, and of great extent, and flat, with little or no descent of its own, and grown full of hassacks, sedge and reed; and the rivers full of weeds; and the waters go slowly away from the lands and out of the rivers, and they come swift into and upon it out of the Upland Counties, where the rivers have a great fall.[23]

In times of heavy rainfall the capacity of the Fenland rivers, choked as they were by slime, mud and weeds, proved totally unable to cope with the colossal volume of water pouring into the fens from the higher catchment areas, where the rivers had a superior gradient and hence a swifter current. The effects of long continued rainfall could be disastrous. As the rivers entered the flat country their currents, deprived of their velocity, lost their power to dredge the obstructed river-beds and to maintain stable channels. Consequently these river-beds displayed a uniform tendency to be exceptionally winding, shallow and wide. Also the Fenland rivers lay for the most part 'common with the land, without separation by banks ... and for this reason, and for want of a sufficient passage for the waters that come by the rivers, all the lands are overflown'.[24] The waters spread themselves over the flat surface of the fens, almost losing their identity in meres and morasses, ultimately stagnating on the land without hope of finding a direct passage out to sea. It is not surprising to find Daniel Defoe, at a much later date, describing the Fenland as 'the sink of no less than thirteen Counties'.[25] When the rivers were overcharged with rain-water it will be seen that the problem of how to carry them safely, at an almost negligible gradient, across the level plain into the sea without flooding the surrounding area, was an overriding one. There was the added problem of the rain which fell on the Fenland itself, and which could not drain off. A complex network of drains has had to be established to carry this local water into the main rivers. Every difficulty has been thrown into sharper relief by the shrinking surface of the land after drainage improvement, with the corresponding rise in the river levels making the adoption of some form of pumping system essential. There was, however, at least one outstanding solution to the problem of conveying upland water to the sea. This was to block its entrance into the Fenland altogether by catchwater drains, a system which seems to have undergone experiment initially by the Romans before being shelved for many centuries.

The condition of the Fenland during the Roman Occupation has been productive of innumerable theories and considerable speculation. The extent to which the Romans drained the fens, indeed the extent to which the fens required draining at this time has been much debated. Nevertheless there seems little reason to suppose that the peat fens were anything but a partial swamp when the Romans took over the administration. The flat gradient of the land, choked outfalls, and the difficulties which the rivers experienced in gaining a passage out to sea admit of no other conclusion. Indeed to the period from 500 BC onwards has been traced the formation of such shallow lakes as Whittlesey and Ugg Meres, which owed their immediate origin to obstructions in the watercourses.[26] In these circumstances it seems almost certain that the Romans, to prevent the highland waters from overflowing the fens, caused a long cut, some 60ft wide, to be made. This was the Cardyke, running from Ramsey to Lincoln, and which may even have started near Cambridge. Although it is sometimes considered that this was constructed primarily for navigation purposes, it undoubtedly functioned as a catchwater for the highland waters by conveying them seaward in a channel skirting the western edge of the region, and by this means arresting their progress through the Fenland itself. It is interesting that the plan of surrounding the highlands with a catchwater, as the most feasible means of maintaining the fens in a condition fit for occupation, has now gained general acceptance. In this sense the Cardyke, although what now remains of it is hardly more than a ditch, ranks as one of the greatest monuments to Fenland drainage in existence. It is evident that the Romans themselves attached the utmost importance to this work from the fact that they erected seven forts along its course, at Northborough, Braceborough, Billingborough, Garrick, Walcot, Linwood and Washingborough.

But although the rivers, swollen with rain-water, often caused serious flood problems especially during the autumn and winter months, the effects of very low water in the Fenland rivers during a dry summer did nothing to alleviate the situation. A dry summer meant that the water flowing down from the uplands was insufficient to keep the channels and estuaries silt-free. These became so blocked that the first floods of winter, balked in their efforts to grind a passage out to sea, ran instead over the lands. The drier the summer the more acute the problem became in winter. In the seventeenth century William Dodson drew attention to 'the want of freshes in the summer, which doth not onely make the countrey, and the cattle miserable, but the out-falls will be destroyed for want of water to scour them in dry summers'.[27] But the outfall channels were not simply prone to constant silting, but also to incessant variation of course, due to the inability of the weak currents to maintain a permanent channel. Hence Skertchly, as late as 1877, commented how 'the channels are so variable that boats carry sounding poles and use them daily. A fisherman would not think of going down certain channels from which he had been absent a week or two without sounding.'[28]

The situation was further complicated by the nature of tidal action in the Wash. Although a certain amount of silt was brought down by the rivers from the upland counties, especially by floods, it was the 'ill disposition of the Sea in those parts, which being troubled by stormy windes, doe carry such abundance of silt or sand into the Outfalls'.[29] The tides on this part of the coast were exceptionally strong, and the immense quantities of sand and silt which they tore up from the sea bed were carried into the rivers and deposited there. If we remember that the spring tides penetrated many miles inland, for example almost up to Peterborough in the Nene and as far as Earith in the Great Ouse, the gravity of this particular problem will be obvious. But there was another problem apart from silting. The weak flow in the Fenland rivers was checked and even for a short time actually reversed by tidal action, so that the freshwater discharge was interrupted for several hours. The long, slow ebb of the tide dammed up the freshwater currents in their passage to the sea, making the deposition and accumulation of silt in the rivers inevitable, and rendering them increasingly unable to discharge the rainfall of the district.

But the Fenland is not only subject to tidal flooding along the tidal length of the rivers, but also along the low-lying parts of the coast. Large tracts would be constantly overflown were it not for the erection of great embankments or 'sea-walls' along much of the coastline of Lincolnshire and west Norfolk. A high tide, especially if swollen by floods and whipped up by strong winds, can rise as much as 24ft above low-water mark. In the past salt water has poured up the rivers, flooding the surrounding lands, whilst an actual breach in the sea-walls could bring disaster to thousands of acres. The conditions prevailing in Norfolk Marshland during the early seventeenth century illustrate with particular clarity the difficulties which the Fenland has had to combat at every stage of its history.

Marshland lies in the silt zone bordering the Wash, with the Great Ouse constituting its eastern, and the New Podyke its southern boundary. William Camden gives a graphic description of the region during the pre-General Drainage era:

> Over against *Linne*, on the farther side of the River [Ouse] lieth *Mershland*, a little moist mersh country, as the name implieth, divided and parted every where with ditches, trenches and furrowes to draine and draw the waters away . . . so subject to the beating and overflowing of the roaring maine Sea, which very often breaketh, teareth, and troubleth it so grievously, that hardly it can be holden off with chargeable wals and workes.[30]

The vital importance, then as now, of maintaining the sea-walls in an adequate state of repair requires little emphasis.

To the Romans are often attributed the great banks – forerunners of the present system – which protected 150 miles of the ancient coastline from King's Lynn to present-day Skegness and beyond. Remains of these old sea-walls, equipped with mounds which may well have served as watch-towers, have been discovered along what was apparently the former shore of the Wash. These, although considered by some authorities to be of more recent date,[31] may very likely have had as their nucleus walls built originally by the Romans. It has been suggested that during the Occupation the silt lands were sufficiently elevated above sea-level to make their defence against inroads of the sea, with anything more than a 3ft sea-bank, unnecessary, and that the banks were subsequently raised 8 or 9ft higher – piecemeal and at intervals, as the situation demanded – during the Middle Ages, probably by the Anglo-Saxons.[32] The subject of the sea banks is so fraught with uncertainty that it is impossible to reach any definite conclusion, although an Anglo-Saxon origin seems unlikely. In the absence of more conclusive evidence it may well be stressed that a work of such dimensions – it has been estimated that not less than 11 million tons of earth were used to construct the banks[33] – obviously demanded the efforts of skilled engineers and land surveyors of the calibre for which the Romans were justifiably famous. William Dugdale considered that no major drainage works could be attributed either to the Britons or to the Saxons: 'the first of these, being a people so rude and barbarous, as they were not versed in any arts; and the latter so illiterate, for the most part, as that little of invention can justly be ascribed to them'.[34] This, in many respects, is a somewhat facile conclusion; witness the great linear earthworks of the Cambridge region, notably the Devil's Dyke, extending for a distance of over 7 miles from Wood Ditton across Newmarket Heath to the fen at Reach. It is commonly accepted that this and a number of presumed contemporary parallel earthworks as the Fleam Dyke and the Bran and Brent Ditches, are Anglo-Saxon, probably constructed during the early wars between Mercia and East Anglia (c665). The construction of the Devil's Dyke in particular called for considerable surveying skill. Even so such a work as the sea-banks – noting the considerable difference between 150 and 7½ miles – implies a highly organised, stable and disciplined environment, similar to that which the Romans invariably created within their subject provinces, and of a kind for which the early Middle Ages were not conspicuously noteworthy. In this context it seems relevant to mention that the Devil's Dyke, along with other similar earthworks of the region, was probably constructed for purposes of frontier defence, or to hinder communication along the open chalk downland with a view to preventing cattle raids, continual warfare of one kind or another being an outstanding characteristic of this earlier period.[35]

Another major drawback in attributing the sea-banks to the Anglo-Saxons is the condition of the Fenland during the early Middle Ages. We know that the region as a whole deteriorated after the departure of the Romans, and that this deterioration was accompanied by a general abandonment of land hitherto under cultivation. There seems little reason to suppose that the Saxons had sufficient incentive or interest to undertake massive drainage works; if they did they accomplished surprisingly little. Even the fen islands were regarded in the seventh and eighth centuries as being unfit for normal settlement, hence their relegation, for the most part, to hermits and ascetics. Nothing provides a more marked contrast to the prosperous conditions which archaeology and aerial photography have revealed of the Roman Occupation than the picture of St Guthlac's life at Crowland, 'among the murky thickets of the more inaccessible solitude'; of his wretched living conditions, his frame racked by rheumatism and fever, and his incessant struggles with demons.[36] It seems probable that the drainage system surviving from the earlier period fell, for one reason or another, into increasing decrepitude, providing yet another indication of the breakdown of a civilisation after the departure of the Romans. Archaeological finds and aerial photography indicate that the Romans inhabited and cultivated areas which ultimately (either from subsequent neglect of their drainage works, or through some slight change in the relative levels of land and sea) degenerated into the swamps eventually made famous by St Guthlac's biographer, and which today, through a variety of causes, can be kept free from floods only by extensive drainage works.

The Romans were in possession of England for approximately 400 years, and it would have been very surprising had so enterprising a people overlooked the agricultural potential of the fens and East Anglia. In fact at some point in the Roman Occupation there took place a movement of population into the fens, and more particularly into the relatively higher silt lands, on such a scale as to leave little room for doubt that it was directed by the central government as deliberate policy.[37] We know that the main colonisation of the Fenland took place during the first half of the second century, although the origin of the settlers is uncertain. The colonisation may have resulted from land hunger or displacement elsewhere. Some of the colonists may even have been brought over from the continent. On the other hand after the Boudiccan revolt a proportion of the East Anglian population was transported, and it may have been then that the original settlements took place. The drainage of the Fenland area by the Romans seems to have gained momentum during the second century, involving the cutting of several major waterways to facilitate the clearance of the upland waters to the sea, and was clearly more than could have been undertaken by private enterprise. Therefore it follows that it was carried out by government initiative, and hence that the area reclaimed for cultivation would have been regarded as an imperial estate, its settlers being state tenants or *coloni*. Consequently it is a safe assumption that at least a section of the Fenland was under full cultivation at this period, even less favoured parts of the region supporting some small communities. Aerial photography has revealed traces of close settlement during the Roman Occupation, in the form of enclosures, field systems crossed by frequent dykes, droveways and groups of habitations, and all quite different from those favoured by the Anglo-Saxons. Roman pottery and coin hoards have been unearthed in a number of places. It would appear that during the Roman era the Fenland was a fairly important corn-growing and cattle-raising area, this being made possible not only by the Roman engineering works but also by the less spectacular but equally important efforts of the immigrant settlers who, where necessary, dug a network of ditches and minor waterways to drain their lands. It has even been suggested that the Fenland was specifically earmarked for provisioning the armies in the north, and that the bulk of its produce was transported in barges to the military capital at York.[38] The digging of the Cardyke during the late first or early second century lends weight to this theory. Besides functioning as a catchwater drain it seems likely that the Cardyke was also a transport canal, whose extensions linked the fens with Lincoln, the Trent, and ultimately the Humber. This being so, it seems not unreasonable to suggest that several major drainage works may well trace their origin to the Romans who, in the circumstances, would certainly consider it of the utmost importance to defend so vital a region from inundation by sea and land floods.

2

The Fenland during the Middle Ages

THE PRE-DRAINAGE ECONOMY

In some parts of the Fenland the number of farms, invariably supporting a mixed livestock and arable economy, doubled during the second century, but between the end of the third century and the fifth conditions in the locality seem to have deteriorated so drastically that a large-scale abandonment of the district followed as an inevitable consequence of the disaster. Much of the land that had been well drained reverted to primeval swamp,[1] and even as late as the eleventh century no general major increase in population was apparent. The Domesday survey records that settlement in the peat fens was confined to the islands. Apart from these, only in the silt areas bordering the Wash, and on the Fenland margins, where the lands had a better drainage and where the soil composition afforded a more solid foundation for building, was any form of continuous settlement recorded. Even here there was a relatively low population density. Although more prosperous than the peat zone to the south, the silt belt was still a poor country at the time of the Domesday survey. The wapentake of Skirbeck, to the north of Boston, was one of the most intensively occupied regions, and even its prosperity has been compared to that of the average infertile upland area.[2]

It was round the fen margins, on ground which ultimately became the frontier zone between the conflicting territorial interests of Mercia, East Anglia and Northumbria that the first Anglo-Saxon communities were located. The earliest settlers lacked stable institutions and a central government; no annals have recorded their history. Even the names of their more prominent tribes have been preserved by later writers. A twelfth-century chronicler of Ely mentions the Gyrwe, a people blanketed in a cloud of obscurity so dense as to be well nigh impenetrable. The Gyrwe, we are told, were 'all the southern Angles that inhabit the great marsh in which the island of Ely is situated'.[3] According to William Camden, in his *Britannia* of 1586, 'They that inhabit the fennish country ... were even in the Saxon times called Girvij, that is, as some interpret it, Fen-men or Fen-dwellers. A kind of people according to the nature of the place where they dwell, rude, uncivil and envious to all others whom they call Upland Men; who stalking on high upon stilts apply their minds to grazing, fishing and fowling.' Briefly, the known facts about the Gyrwe are that they were grouped into northern and southern provinces, that they probably inhabited the fen margins and islands, and that the southern Gyrwe may have consisted of 600 families.[4] The exact extent of their territory, or what constituted the boundary between the northern and southern groups, is not known. In addition to the Isle of Ely their territory may well have included parts of Lincolnshire and perhaps Northamptonshire, although this cannot be stated with any absolute degree of certainty.[5]

The fact that Anglo-Saxon settlements totally avoided large sections of the Fenland is in itself a circumstance of more than ordinary significance. It seems unlikely that the Anglo-Saxons would deliberately have shunned areas which had formerly been successfully cultivated, unless these had deteriorated in the meantime to an extent where cultivation had become impracticable or impossible. A number of causes have been suggested to account for the seemingly abrupt deterioration of the Fenland during the early Middle Ages. The increasing difficulties confronting the Romans and their subsequent abandonment of the region undoubtedly led to a neglect of their drainage works; alternatively it may have been the result of a slight subsidence of the entire Fenland basin. In fact archaeological evidence for the Wash indicates a considerable variation in land level, with a fall in late Roman times being succeeded by a steady rise which culminated in Norman times, only to be followed by a rapid subsidence by the fourteenth and fifteenth centuries.

To attempt a reconstruction of the medieval Fenland economy

during the pre-Norman era is impossible due to the dearth of evidence. Those Saxons who were intrepid enough to settle in this forbidding region undoubtedly utilised any natural advantages which existed locally. From the numerous grants of salt-pans contained in Saxon documents it is evident that they had acquired the art of evaporating salt from the sea-water of the estuaries, whilst fishing became a prominent and highly organised local industry. The silt lands were imperfectly drained and prone to flooding by the sea. The peat fens were subject to inundations by the rivers, contained many large meres, and were always more or less flooded in winter. These marshes and fens afforded valuable summer grazing for livestock. There was a dearth of arable land. Even as late as the eleventh century the low density of plough teams listed for the Fenland in Domesday Book seems to indicate a sparse area of existing or potentially cultivable land. However some wheat and barley could be grown on the higher grounds.

Very little was accomplished in the way of draining the fens during the earlier Middle Ages. Such drainage as the Fenland had at this time was by means of the natural streams and the remains of the works executed by the Romans. The Cardyke to the west partially intercepted and carried off the water from the numerous highland brooks and streams between Lincoln and Ramsey, and the river Witham fulfilled a similar function on the eastern side of the Lincolnshire Fens. Deeping Fen was hardly better than a lake all the winter, but had an outlet, however unsatisfactory, into the river Welland. Nevertheless there is evidence of a continuous process which involved bringing into cultivation small pieces of fen, chiefly by the monastic houses, although the fenmen themselves were continually trying to win portions which they might use for pasture or even arable.

Actuated as they always were by the desire to plant their settlements where an abundance of hard work could purify the celibate life, the religious orders made the low-lying fens and marshes their especial province. From the seventh century onwards the Fenland became a favoured place for the location of monastic sites, the marshes affording 'to not a few congregations of monks, desirable havens of lonely life where the solitude could not fail the hermits'.⁶ Dugdale mentions the islands 'which God of purpose raised . . . to be habitations for his servants, who chose to dwell there'. Hence the Isle of Ely was 'made choice of for a place of voluntary retirement, by those who, out of great piety, forsaking the vanities of this transitory world, betook themselves wholly to the service of God, in devout prayers, frequent watchings, and strict abstinence'.⁷ Religious foundations were established at Peterborough (c657), Thorney (662), Ely (673), and Crowland (716). Others followed, for example at Chatteris, Denny, Ramsey, Boston, Kyme, Bardney, Spalding and Sempringham, the Norman Conquest providing a further impetus to the movement. On the banks of the river Witham twelve monastic houses were erected within a space of 20 miles. The monasteries became the principal landowners in the fens, and considerable local effort in draining marshes and bringing wasteland into cultivation is indicated. Abbot Egelric is stated to have so improved a portion of the marshes belonging to the monastery of Crowland that they were ultimately ploughed and sown with corn.⁸

Inquisitions taken at Fleet in Lincolnshire towards the close of the fourteenth century are vividly illustrative of the grip which the monastic foundations ultimately acquired over the region. When listing the obligations of the various landowners to maintain drains and banks in the locality there is constant reference to the Prior of Spalding and the Abbot of Crowland.⁹ However there were secular owners also. For example after the Norman Conquest the Wake and the de Albini families held great lordships in the stretch of Fenland lying between the Welland and the Glen. These and the religious houses were constantly contending with one another, for pasture, turf-cutting, and other fen rights and profits. The reason is not hard to seek. The space of arable land occupied by fen villages, especially on the smaller islands, was often so restricted that the maintenance of rights in the adjacent fen became a matter of prime importance. Often entire villages were totally dependent on the fen for a means of existence, having little land of their own. It is significant that the prosperity of the Fenland seems to have increased steadily during the later Middle Ages, although local attempts at drainage were of varying

B

seriousness and met with varying degrees of success. In 1334 the tax assessment per acre of the Lincolnshire Fenland was the fourth highest in England.[10] The monks were generally efficient farmers, and deliberately set about the task of improving the value of the land round their monasteries. Local disasters still occurred, but at many periods and in many localities the course of the waters was well controlled. Because the prosperity of the fen villages was to a degree determined by the extent of safe stretches of pasture this was a matter of vital importance.

From the earliest times Fenland life, occupations, customs and economy were all moulded by the distinctive nature of the terrain. But to portray the fenmen as a race devoted exclusively to fishing and wildfowling, with each man pursuing his own interests regardless of those of his neighbours, would be a dangerous oversimplification. In fact the local inhabitants were in many respects highly organised, because the very nature of fen life made some form of organised effort essential. A complex system of communal regulations, designed to ensure a careful utilisation of the land at all times, gradually evolved.

The activities of the region fell into three main groups, each being determined by the extent of drainage. In those areas which were almost perpetually flooded, fishing, fowling, gathering reeds and rushes, and making salt were the chief occupations. On the so-called 'half-lands', ie flooded only during the winter season or for a part of the year, the production of hay, livestock grazing, and turf-cutting were the predominant activities. Where the land was permanently drained, as on the higher lands and the islands, arable cultivation was frequently possible.

Fishing developed into a major local industry, with important centres at Doddington, Littleport, Soham, Stuntney, Wisbech, Spalding and Bourne. According to Dugdale it was the ease of fishing which had been a vital factor in attracting early monastic foundations to the area.[11] No less than seventy-seven fisheries are mentioned in Domesday Book as paying rents in the Lincolnshire Fenland, the rents varying from 8d and upwards a year. The town of Crowland paid the relatively massive sum of £300 annually to the Abbot in return for fishing concessions. About 1125 William of Malmesbury commented on the abundance of fish, which were so numerous 'as to cause astonishment in strangers'.[12] This applied in particular to eels, and it was common for rents, tithes, even debts, to be paid with eels in lieu of money. Hence Ramsey paid annually to Peterborough Abbey 4,000 eels in return for freestone from the neighbouring quarries at Barnack.[13] Large quantities of fish were exported from the fens to London. The important part played by fishing in the medieval economy of the Fenland can be assessed from the stringency of the regulations laid down relative to fishing rights. Acrimonious disputes erupted over the vexed question of the separation of private from public fisheries. 'Fishing by night in the fisheries of others' was a common offence.[14] At Littleport it was found that John Beystens 'drew the pools at Wellenheath by night and carried thence fish, price 6d, and that he ought to be removed from out of the vill'.[15]

Reeds and sedge represented other vital products of the undrained fen, being used throughout the region for thatching. Reed-cutting, like fishing, was subject to minute regulation, and could only take place at 'competent and reasonable times of the year'.[16] Fines and even severer penalties were imposed for trespassing and over-cutting. In 1304 Aylward le Turnere was expelled from the manor of Ramsey 'for waste of the fen'.[17] At Littleport John Bantelig and John Herring were presented at the Manor Court, the former for mowing sedge 'before the feast of S. John against the general ordinance'; the latter for employing 'two men mowing in the fen where he should have but one'.[18]

The production of salt also merits especial mention. This was obtained by evaporating the salt water, and perhaps as far back as the days of the Roman Occupation large quantities of 'bay salt' had been manufactured along the Fenland coasts. At the time of the Domesday survey there were twenty-two salt-pans (apart from one which was derelict) in the Lincolnshire parish of Bicker Haven alone, whilst Leake boasted forty-one and Donington twenty-seven. The method of procuring salt was relatively simple, the salt water being run through three pits. After remaining in the first pit for a sufficient length of time for the mud and sand to settle, it was allowed to flow into the second until it became brine. This was then run into a third pit where it remained exposed to the sun until the water had evaporated and the salt crystals were formed. Salt-pans were an important factor in the medieval economy of the silt zone.

So much for the marsh itself. So far as the 'half-lands' or meadows were concerned some of these were surrounded with water and were reached by boat; to others the cattle were driven along paths. Many meadows were dry only in summer; others, apart from exceptionally wet seasons, during the greater part of the year. Some were actually flooded in summer as, for example, at Wistow in 1324, when an account roll recorded: 'For the sale of hay nothing through floods.'[19] But normally the meadows were dry in summer, whilst the winter floods, provided they were not of too long standing, constituted an advantage rather than otherwise in that they enriched the land. After the Norman Conquest there seems to have been a steady increase in the extent of meadowland in the fens, with references to meadows becoming increasingly frequent in contemporary documents. Livestock grazing embodied a central feature of the Fenland economy, certainly from about the twelfth century onwards.

The system of intercommoning was very widely prevalent, ie a group of towns and villages shared grazing rights in the adjoining fens, which meant in effect that one tract of land served as common pasture for the livestock of several townships. Tilney Smeeth in Norfolk Marshland, a vast acreage said to be capable of supporting 'at least thirty thousand sheep',[20] was intercommoned by the villages of Wiggenhall, Terrington, Walpole, Walton, Tilney, Walsoken, Emneth, Outwell and Clenchwarton, whilst the circle of towns and villages intercommoning in Deeping Fen included Spalding, Pinchbeck, Boston, Langtoft, Market Deeping and Crowland. Holland Fen, an expanse of 21,463 acres, belonged to eleven villages in Kirton and Skirbeck, whilst on the East, West and Wildmore Fens the villagers of Skirbeck and the sokes of Bolingbroke and Horncastle grazed their stock. Ely represented the nucleus of a group of villages and hamlets, all with grazing rights in the adjoining fens, a circumstance which ensured a considerable degree of social coherence throughout the Isle. The system had its less salutary aspects, however, in that it bred interminable disputes. Also this type of organisation – to avoid general confusion and the dangers of over-stocking – entailed a considerable amount of detailed regulation under the supervision of fen reeves and overseers. In some fens livestock was pastured without payment with no limit of time or number. In other fens the number of beasts which each commoner could pasture was specifically defined and rigorously controlled. In many places cattle were excluded from the fens for several months, commencing in early spring. But despite restrictions the practice of intercommoning was so profitable that any attempts at enclosure were fiercely resisted. That enclosure was fairly common, especially from the thirteenth century onwards, is nevertheless apparent from the frequency of the complaints lodged against it.[21]

In addition to livestock grazing, by about the twelfth century turf-cutting had developed as another characteristic occupation of the half-lands. Due to the dearth of trees throughout the Fenland the inhabitants had recourse to turf as an alternative fuel to wood. Also turf had other uses, being employed for building houses as well as for repairing the drainage embankments. Either the peat was sold when dug, after it had been dried and stacked, or else great stretches of moor itself were sold or leased. Turf-cutting, in common with most other Fenland activities, was subject to stringent regulations, being allowed only in certain parts of the fen at stated times of the year.

On the higher lands, possessed of an efficient natural drainage, arable cultivation was fairly common. At Ramsey during the twelfth century the fertility of the soil was 'such that the land converted to tillage bears corn plentifully; nor is it less profitable otherwise, being full of fair gardens, rich pastures, shady groves, and rich meadows; which in the springtime look most beautiful'.[22] William of Malmesbury's description of early twelfth-century Thorney emphasises the absence of waste-land: 'in some parts there are apple trees, in others, vines which either spread upon poles or run along the ground'.[23] The existence of a surplus in grain production in at least some areas is indicated by the evidence for the grain-feeding of pigs. The Abbot of Peterborough, as early as the eleventh century, was fattening '60 pigs with corn' on his Huntingdonshire lands. In Norfolk Marshland oats, barley and flax were being widely grown during the thirteenth and fourteenth centuries. In the Lincolnshire Fens crops played an important, howbeit a subsidiary role, with some winter fodder being grown, as well as wheat and barley for domestic consumption. During the thirteenth century Matthew Paris recorded that land in the fens, formerly 'accessible neither for man nor for beast, affording only deep mud with sedge and reeds, and inhabited by birds, indeed more likely by devils' was 'now changed into delightful meadows and also arable ground'.[24] The great Abbey of Crowland owned acres of fen land and was famous for cattle rearing and sheep farming. Here there arose a two-way passage of fat cattle from the meadow granges to the mother house, and of corn from the arable farms to the cattle estates. The cattle were stocked not only for the Abbey, but to provide dairy produce, and cheese became an 'export' of the fen country.

But despite very considerable pockets of prosperity still no major attempt had been made to drain the fens as a whole, although local efforts to drain specific localities became increasingly more numerous. During the Middle Ages there was no general demand for a systematic reclamation, probably because there was no great need. The population – doubtless partly due to expansionist tendencies having been in some measure checked by the Black Death – was not increasing to that extent where it imposed any undue pressure on native resources, and the Fenland inhabitants themselves, by adapting their mode of life to local conditions, were able to survive well enough. It is true that arable land was relatively scarce, but meadowland, even if only partially unflooded, was much more highly prized than arable at this period.[25]

Meanwhile fen farmers waged an intermittent battle against the ravages caused by upland floodwaters and inroads of the sea. In this connection it was unfortunate that the Great Ouse was allowed to hollow out for itself a wide estuary, in which the stream lost much of its force. The river at King's Lynn was 40 perches wide, 'every perch being reckoned at sixteen feet'.[26] The inevitable silting of Lynn Haven further obstructed the run-off of water out of the fens. Another consequence of this widening of the Great Ouse was that the buildings adjacent to the river were washed away. Thus the church of West Lynn was swallowed up by the waters. Tilney lost its church, parsonage, manor house, several cottages and a hundred acres of land between 1277 and 1337. Wiggenhall was scarcely more fortunate, losing a great deal of property, especially in 1337.

The other Fenland rivers were in an equally unsatisfactory condition. In 1365 it was presented at the Court of King's Bench that the channel of the Witham 'in Wildemore, near Coningesby, was bending and defective . . . so that the marshes of Wildemore and Bolingbroke were overflowed and drowned thereby'.[27] By 1382 the river was 'choaked up with mud, and obstructed with the planting of trees'.[28] In the Welland region during the fourteenth century 'there was so much water in winter time that it covered the ground an ell and a half in depth and in a tempestuous wind two ells'.[29] By 1395 the estuary was so choked with tidal silt that 'the water of Welland cannot have his course into the sea, by reason whereof divers of the lands and tenements in Holland be drowned'.[30] According to Ingulph the flooding of the South Holland district was so severe by 1467 that 'there was scarcely a house or building, but what the streams of water made their way and flowed through it'.[31]

Flooding by high tides, when they breached the sea-walls, also caused great damage. The tide was unpredictable but fortunately major inundations from this source did not happen every year. Dugdale thought that 'these irruptions of the sea' were 'casual' and 'not frequent'.[32] However when the sea broke through conditions were disastrous enough. The banks of the Great Ouse between Tilney and King's Lynn 'were, through the extraordinary raging of the sea' so miserably 'broken and torn' that all the neighbouring towns were flooded.[33] Norfolk Marshland suffered badly; on occasions the sea wreaked such havoc in this highly vulnerable region that even the higher corn lands were not immune from disaster. In 1337,

> Upon Monday next after the feast of St Hillary preceding, the same bank was so broken, by the raging of the sea, in no less than five places, that the town of Tilney was overflowed with the seawater, and the lands, meadows, and pastures belonging thereto, continually drowned for the space of seven days, by which means their winter-corn, then sowed upon the ground, was destroyed, as also much of the corn and hay in their barns; with an hundred

muttons and sixty ewes to the damage of eccl unto the said town.[34]

Between 1250 and 1350 Norfolk Marshland was flooded twelve times, Wiggenhall, Emneth, Walsoken, Walpole, Terrington and West Walton all suffering serious damage. Kesteven and Holland further to the north were also implicated in this catalogue of disasters. According to Stowe's *Chronicle*, through the force of the wind and violence of the sea the monastery of Spalding and many churches were destroyed in 1287: 'All the whole country in the parts of Holland was for the most part turned into a standing pool, so that an intolerable multitude of men, women and children were overwhelmed with the water, especially in the town of Boston, a great part whereof was destroyed.' In 1351 the boundary which separated the province of Holland from that of Kesteven was completely obliterated by the floods, 'insomuch as great controversies and debates were occasioned betwixt the inhabitants in those parts, upon the execution of the King's writs, and otherwise'.[35]

But damaging as these floods most certainly were, earlier writers – who for the most part lived outside the area – gave publicity to what was terrifying and disastrous, making it possible for subsequent generations to gain a somewhat distorted picture of the true situation in the later medieval Fenland. The sensational accounts have almost certainly had a tendency to obscure a steady and continuous development in many localities, which the floods temporarily disrupted but never wholly checked. Indeed farming was sufficiently profitable to justify the constant effort expended on stemming back the waters, even though this made the imposition of heavy taxes for the defence of the land a prime necessity. The duty of maintaining the sea-walls along the coast, and the dykes and drains which intersected the region was apportioned among the intercommoning villages. In the East Fen of Lincolnshire 3s 4d was usually levied from the inhabitants of Hareby, Kirkby, Wainfleet, Thorpe, Holton and Toynton for the repair of the common sewers. The commoners of Holland Fen were responsible for the maintenance of a bank some 20 miles in circumference. The great fen dyke, the 'fossatum marisci', dividing

Lincolnshire from Cambridgeshire, was upkept by Wisbech, Upwell, Tydd St Giles, Newton, Outwell, Elm and Leverington. The great importance of maintaining this work was made abundantly clear during the reign of Henry VI. On St Wulfstan's day, 1439, through the default of Thomas Flower of Okeham, who had failed to repair his portion of the 'fossatum marisci', the waters broke in flooding a total of 12,400 acres in Wisbech, Leverington, Newton and Tydd.[36]

Walls between the townships of the Wisbech Hundred had to be kept 16ft high to exclude the waters of one town from another. In Norfolk Marshland each township had its own 'indike' surrounding it, ie a wall to serve as its special defence against the floods. During the later Middle Ages Terrington set aside the profits from a certain portion of pasture for repairing its indikes and two great walls 'armed and defended' against the sea with piles of 'wood-shoves'.[37] An inlet of the sea penetrated up to Wiggenhall, which had to be protected by two sea-walls, one 6 miles, the other 3 miles long. Tilney, following a great flood during the reign of Edward III, was compelled to maintain 2 miles of sea-bank; on one occasion repairs cost £65.[38] Walpole and Walsoken each maintained 3 miles of sea-bank, and West Walton 5½ miles. Wiggenhall was burdened with the upkeep of 7 miles of Ouse embankment.

Some instances have survived of the method of apportioning the burden of drainage maintenance. In Walsoken and West Walton every acre committed its owner to repairing between 4ft and 6ft of sea-bank.[39] Heavy fines were imposed for neglect to maintain a vital work, ie 12d for every perch of sea-wall unrepaired; 6d for every perch of freshwater bank, and 3d for every perch of ditch or gutter. These fines could be doubled or even trebled in cases of persistent default by the landowners responsible. With the passage of time taxes became increasingly burdensome. Ultimately tax assessments which had originally been based on ownership of anciently arable land within each township were extended to include land reclaimed from the waste, with all rights of common being in the end also taken into account as a basis of assessment. Hence the great bank which ran from Guyhirne to the sea was repaired by all the inhabitants of the Hundred of Wisbech, the amounts in each case being assessed according to individual acreages held, or on the extent of common pasture, fishing or turf-cutting. Taxes were in part remitted to those towns throughout the Fenland which were particularly hard-pressed, and there is no doubt that many local inhabitants did find the taxes oppressive. In 1423 we find the Bishop of Ely's tenants at Sutton complaining how

> the most parte of this londe thus charged with the grete habondance of water that has falne in the said partes is suroundyd and drownde so that it may nother be tillyd ner sawne ... at this tyme men may rowe in a bote, in ccc acres of londe for the which the tenants er chargyd for every acre yerely sum xxxd, sum iiis, sum iis to thare utter destruccion.[40]

There are even instances of conditions becoming so bad that entire localities had to be abandoned.[41]

In this difficult region dyke reeves held offices of much importance, being responsible for enforcing the 'custom of the fen', ie collecting fines for neglect to repair the works, preventing pigs from feeding and rooting near the banks and persons from digging near the walls, and taking measures to halt drifts of beasts along the sea-banks. A major problem was the neglect on the part of many individuals to clean their channels, which consequently became obstructed and incapable of functioning efficiently. The upkeep of such a vast network of banks and small drains created problems of considerable complexity. Ownership of land frequently changed; worse, the channels themselves were always changing, with new ones constantly being dug, and others just as constantly filled in. It sometimes proved difficult to define responsibility for their maintenance, whilst agreements were often so vaguely worded as to make misinterpretation inevitable and evasion easy. There were continual complaints and presentments about floods caused by the neglect of those responsible for maintaining the drains 'according to the custom of the fen'. Internecine feuds were waged between the monastic foundations, with disputes dragging on literally for years. There was incessant controversy involving rights and obligations. Individuals were frequently found guilty of obstructing drains for their own private benefit, irrespective of any damage this might cause to the lands of their neighbours. In a region where co-operation was essential individual acts of lawlessness could have a dire effect, as when Guy Bullok of Holbeach 'on 1 February, 1396, by force of arms narrowed the common river of Holbeach at Holbeach weir to the damage of the whole community'.[42] Channels sometimes interfered with the passage of livestock on their way to the common pastures. Hence in 1294 the Bishop of Ely had found it expedient to enter into an agreement with the Abbot of Ramsey that 'the lode which leads from Needingworth to the great bank shall not be so deep but that the cattle of the bishop and his men, and the other commoners, may cross it to their pasture towards Holywell without damage'.[43] Fishing rights, too, frequently presented acute problems, and the complaint that Thomas Halmere and Simon Malle of Spalding and John Hare of Weston had 'by force of arms and with dogs' impeded the common sewer in Weston with nets and other fishing contrivances to the hurt of the entire community, is a fairly typical one.[44] Although the duty of repairing the banks and sluices which protected the land from inundations of the sea, and also of maintaining the channels of the waterways in good order, devolved upon the individual owners of the adjoining lands according to 'antient and approved customs', no really competent authority existed for superintending the works and ensuring their maintenance in a reasonable condition. This was a great drawback throughout the Fenland at this period.

EARLY ATTEMPTS AT RECLAMATION

In the medieval Fenland large-scale drainage works constituted an extreme rarity, although the region was not altogether devoid of achievements in this field. During the eleventh century we read of an attempt by Richard de Rulos, Chamberlain of William the Conqueror, to drain Deeping Fen in Lincolnshire. He was supposed to have enclosed much of the common fen, converting it into meadow and pasture. According to William Dugdale (who followed the account given by Ingulph, a former Abbot of Crowland) he defended the whole of his land from the Welland waters with 'a mighty bank; because every year, almost all his meadows, lying near unto that stream, were overflowed with the continual inundations thereof . . . And by thus banking the said river, reduced those low grounds, which were before that time deep lakes and unpassable fens, into most fruitful fields and pastures'.[45] There was undoubtedly some germ of truth in these claims, although the extent to which they are absolutely accurate in detail remains uncertain.[46]

But there were other works, whose existence is more firmly rooted in historical fact. In 1223 a bank called the Old Podyke was erected by the inhabitants of Norfolk Marshland as a defence against the torrents of water pouring down from the uplands during wet seasons. However, resulting from a succession of breaches, it became 'broken and ruinous', so that the countryside for miles around was flooded. By 1422 the inevitable conclusion had been reached that further repairs were impossible, due to the growing instability of the ground on which it stood. Its successor, the New Podyke, was made, extending from Upwell to Downham, all the landowners and towns of Norfolk Marshland who benefited from its construction contributing to its cost.[47] It was between 5 and 6ft high, 18ft wide at the base, and 12ft at the top. On its south side no digging was allowed within 40ft, and upon it no pasturage or passage of livestock was permitted.

But possibly the most important drainage work to come out of the Middle Ages was the cut, 12 miles long and 40ft wide, running from Stanground near Peterborough to Guyhirne. It was constructed by John Morton, Bishop of Ely, during the closing years of the fifteenth century, with a sluice erected at Stanground to divert the river Nene waters into the new cut as far as Guyhirne; thence direct to Wisbech and out to sea. Morton's Leam is of major significance, in that its originator pioneered the system of running off surplus water from the Fenland by the agency of a straight cut, designed to increase the velocity of the current and hence its scouring action. But the work had a less salutory aspect, for we find Richard Atkyns complaining that 'then was the fall of the waters in Wisbech so great, as no man would venture under the bridge with a boat, but by veering through'.[48] However this had nothing to do with drainage, and it was unfortunate that Morton's Leam was allowed to fall into ruin, by the late sixteenth century, standing, according to William Camden in the *Britannia*, 'in no great steed'.[49]

Apart from these projects attempts at reclamation were almost entirely confined to monastic and local effort, although this movement seems to have been very widespread throughout the fens. The evidence, although somewhat patchy, still gives an overall picture of continuous effort. In 1189 Richard I granted permission to the inhabitants of Holland and Kesteven 'to build upon the said marshes, and till the same and to enjoy all their easements upon the same'.[50] In the Norfolk silt zone towards the close of the twelfth century

> There was neither any habitation, nor ground that yielded profit, within that part of Wigenhale ... except the monastery of Crabhous, with some lands belonging thereto; all being then waste and in the nature of a fen: But afterwards the inhabitants of that place, and of divers others, came; and, with draining and banking, won as much thereof, by their industry, as they could.[51]

In 1196 we find the Abbot of Ramsey leasing Staplewere Fen for twelve years, with the proviso that it should be returned at the termination of the lease 'with any improvements which shall be made in that fen'.[52] Also significant in this context, we learn of a messuage in Ely which Alan, the parson of Bassingbourn had, at some time during the early thirteenth century, 'raised from the marsh at his own expense'.[53] More than 30 acres of meadow belonging to the episcopal manor of Ely were described, about 1250, as having been recently reclaimed,[54] whilst a considerable acreage of land at Littleport seems to have been taken in from the fen by the closing years of the thirteenth century.[55] Individual monastic expansion entailed the constant piecemeal acquisition of both large and small portions of land. Sometimes very large areas were reclaimed, although these were not necessarily of the most fertile, and were often held on a somewhat precarious tenure due to the continued threat of flooding. Nevertheless it is interesting to observe that the estates of the Bishop of Ely underwent considerable expansion during the twelfth and thirteenth centuries, the most spectacular gains being made in the Fenland.[56] Similarly at Thorney: between 1305 and 1322 the Abbot, William Clopton, built and enclosed with ditches, a house and appurtenances in the middle of Thorney Fen, simultaneously enclosing a 'large part of the fen to have as arable land or meadow'.[57] Partial attempts at the reclamation of the Holland Fens were made from time to time, and by about the beginning of the fourteenth century the marshes in the vicinity of Crowland seem to have been brought into cultivation.[58]

Up to the mid-thirteenth century, as we have seen, the continuous duty of draining and protecting those fen lands under cultivation was the responsibility of each local community. Here the efforts of the religious houses were particularly noteworthy. The monasteries carefully safeguarded their Fenland estates, liability for the maintenance of banks and drains being minutely apportioned between the tenants of adjoining lands. Growing concern over drainage may well have been a partial consequence of the Black Death. Some connection was probably seen between visitations of the plague and the stagnant ditches and drains, leading to increasing insistence on their proper maintenance. On the other hand the decimation of entire localities would make upkeep singularly difficult due to labour shortages, whilst land passed so rapidly from hand to hand as a result of the disaster that it was difficult to determine legal ownership and hence liability for the upkeep of the drains. Such a situation would of course be eminently favourable to those wishing to evade responsibility. Also it was unfortunate that, although the monasteries were 'very assiduous to maintain and improve their several properties and interest . . . many contentions and disputes relating to their rights, properties, and grants . . . arose between them'.[59] Indeed local effort as a whole had proved altogether too haphazard a means of coping with the growing complexities of the situation, and an alternative arrangement had to be sought.

From the mid-thirteenth century the responsibility for land drainage and for dealing with inroads of the sea devolved mainly upon successive Commissions of Sewers, the term 'sewer' in this connection being applied to watercourses and streams in general. The appointment of these commissions – which superseded the earlier commissions to sheriffs and itinerant justices – constituted the central government's remedy for supplementing the inadequacies of local organisation. They were established, not to inaugurate new administrative methods, but to enforce customs and practices of long standing which had shown a tendency to lapse in the absence of any official machinery of coercion; in a word to superimpose some sort of order on the administrative chaos prevailing in the region. The commission issued to Henry de Bathe in 1258 is generally considered to represent the first of a regular series.[60] The immediate reason for its creation was the urgent need to deal with the crisis that had arisen through inundations of the sea in several parts of Holland in Lincolnshire. Henry de Bathe was instructed to 'provide and ordain' with the sheriff of Lincoln 'to distrain all persons having lands and tenements in those parts who ought to repair and keep up the dikes, bridges and walls of the sea and marsh there . . .'[61] The efforts of the commission apparently met with reasonable success as the appointment of others quickly followed. These appointments became increasingly frequent towards the latter end of the thirteenth century.

Although a detailed analysis of the intricacies and ramifications of the sewer commissions does not fall within the scope of this work, something needs to be said about their general duties.[62] The commissioners combined in themselves judicial, executive and legislative powers, exercised through the medium of the so-called Courts of Sewers. Briefly, it was their responsibility to make provisions against inroads of the sea; to maintain a clear passage in all waterways by the removal of obstructions which impeded the free flow of the current, and to repair the banks, bridges and causeways. By the verdict of a jury they determined what essential repairs should be undertaken and at whose expense. They were empowered to levy taxes and fines from defaulters, besides being given considerable scope to make ordinances for the protection and maintenance of the works.

From the extant records of the commissioners' proceedings it would appear that no general routine plan of drainage maintenance, involving the systematic dredging of waterways and the upkeep of banks, was adopted, procedure being predominantly a matter of dealing with each crisis as it arose. There is a strong element of truth in the assertion that 'hardly anything was done to keep up the embankments and cleanse the watercourses, till the work was forced upon the liable parties by losses and drownings'.[63] This was a definite weakness of the commissions; there were a number of others.

The Commissions of Sewers were not, strictly speaking, permanently constituted bodies with a continuous policy. Although the life span of each individual commission was ultimately extended from ten to twenty-five years,[64] so that a certain continuity of activity and policy became possible, the fact remains that, however long the period of each commission might be, during the probable time-lag between the expiry of one commission and the appointment of another, almost any disaster might occur. Another serious weakness was that, whatever the emergency, the commissioners were prevented from taking prompt action to deal with the situation by the necessity, implicit in their constitution, of having first to summon a jury of local men, and of having to obtain presentments of that jury.[65] But, above all, the commissions were hampered by the lack of any specific authority to construct new works. Their essential terms of reference were rigidly confined to the maintenance and improvement of existing ones. This thorny point was variously argued by many people at different times, and at considerable length by Robert Callis during the seventeenth century. Upon examination of the evidence he concluded that the commissioners had power to execute new works 'upon urgent necessity in defence of the country or for the safety thereof'.[66] The situation had always been extremely controversial, and there is no doubt that new works were in fact undertaken during the medieval period. For example an inquisition taken at Fleet in Lincolnshire in 1395 found that

> a certeine porc'on of lands of the townes of Quapload, Holbech, Fleete, Gedney, Sutton, and Tydd, called the Fenn Ends ... be so lowe and deepe ... wherupon they are yearely drowned; and therefore it is necessary that a newe sewer be made.

Then followed detailed specifications of the proposed new project.[67]

The work of the sewer commissions was also obstructed by individual acts of carelessness. An instance of 1439 is a typical one. Due to neglect on the part of several landholders Wisbech

Fen, the property of the Bishop of Ely, was completely devastated by floods, 'so that the said Bishop and his tenants of Wisebech hundred could not receive any benefit in the same'.[68] Yet even though the efforts of the commissioners were attended by only partial success this is not to imply that they were devoid of any great value. Without the commissioners the general condition of the Fenland could well have been much worse. However, as we shall see, the seventeenth century saw the balance of responsibility for maintaining the drainage of much of the Fenland shifted from the old fen landowners to a new class of adventurers; this by virtue of the fact that these latter were risking their capital in what was essentially a large-scale commercial enterprise to drain the region which later became known as the 'Bedford Level'.

3

The Start of the Enterprise

INITIAL EXPERIMENTS IN DRAINING

As we have seen the monastic system had constituted a central feature of Fenland administration during the Middle Ages. Nevertheless the repercussions exerted by the Dissolution of the Monasteries in 1536 and 1539 upon the agrarian economy and drainage of the region have sometimes been questioned.[1] Yet there is no doubt that in some places a concentrated blow was dealt at vital points in the drainage network. So close were the ties which bound the Fenland economy to the monastic houses that some disruption must have been an unavoidable consequence of their severance. Also the Dissolution had the important effect of throwing a great quantity of land on to the market. The large estates, hitherto administered by single owners, were now subject to considerable division and subdivision. There was a sharp increase in the number of landowners and consequently of the interests involved in the drainage. In this respect the Dissolution bred a crop of administrative problems which had at least some repercussions on the upkeep of the banks and watercourses. In many localities it was even more difficult than formerly to assess liability for repairs. In the prevailing chaos opportunities to evade obligations arose on every side, and it proved a relatively simple matter for proprietors to shuffle off their responsibilities on to other shoulders, equally reluctant or incompetent. It became increasingly impossible for the already hard-pressed sewer commissions to function effectively. Therefore although no comprehensive drainage system fell into decay throughout the Fenland at this period – simply because none existed – and although there is no evidence to indicate any widespread or continuous inundation traceable directly to this cause, there is no doubt that the Dissolution caused inconvenience, muddle, uncertainty and actual hardship in some places. Certainly Thorney underwent considerable deterioration during the reign of Queen Elizabeth I. Lands formerly owned by the monastery which 'in memory' had been 'dry and firm lye now surrounded (for the most part) in water, by reason of the drains, ever sithence uncast, and other the infinite watercourses suffered to grow up'.[2]

To sketch a really clear picture of Fenland agriculture during the sixteenth century would be a virtually impossible task. Conditions were subject to constant, often violent, usually unforeseen, fluctuation, not merely from year to year but also from locality to locality. However contemporary sources are almost unanimous in their agreement that conditions in the Fenland evinced signs of a deterioration, which became more strongly pronounced as the century moved on.

The fens continued to be swamped by floods from the upland counties and battered by inroads of the sea, seemingly to a greater extent than formerly. It was not unusual for much of the region to remain under water throughout the winter. Walter Graves found conditions unbearably rigorous, and in 1535 wrote to Cromwell complaining that he had been 'nearly two years teaching youth at Crowland where the climate is so unwholesome that he would rather die than pass a third summer there'.[3] According to William Camden's account in *Britannia* it was even worse in winter: 'wholly in manner overcovered with water, farther every way than a man is able to Ken', resembling 'in some sort a very sea'.[4] In their distress the local inhabitants, 'verie greatly impoverished and like to be overthrowne and utterly undone', appealed to the Privy Council for help in 1596, pointing out the serious losses they had sustained 'by the outragious inundations and overflowings of waters descendinge from the higher parts'.[5]

Isaac Casaubon, a continental scholar, who journeyed through the countryside around Ely during August and September 1611, found these areas quite useless for anything except grazing. Arable cultivation in any form was out of the question. Some places resembled a marsh, 'where nothing grows except reeds'. In the vicinity of Crowland the ground was 'so rotten and moorish, that a man may thrust a pole downe right thirty foote deepe; and round about it every way is nothing but a plot of reeds'.[6] Another writer, who in 1629 urged the need to drain the fens upon the government, painted a singularly unpleasant picture of the region:

> The Aer Nebulous, Grosse, and full of rotten Harres; the Water putred and muddy, yea, full of loathsome Vermine; the Earth spuing, unfast, and boggie; the Fire noysome turfe and hassocks; such are the inconveniences of the Drownings.[7]

But even at this period the poor state of the peat fens should not be too much exaggerated. Land adjacent to the rivers in Cambridgeshire and the Isle of Ely was reputedly 'a very rich soyle and well inhabited'.[8] There were many areas which remained dry throughout the winter, and these supported large herds of livestock, predominantly cattle and sheep. Provided that a spring were sufficiently dry to give the winter rains a chance to drain from the land, the herds could even be driven into the lower parts of the fens. In this context the remarks of the inhabitants of Methwold and adjacent towns at the beginning of the seventeenth century are significant. They had

> sheep walks for one thousand, seven hundred sheep, which fed winter and summer, upon their common fens; . . . when any floods happened they came by wind-catches, and run over but some part of their grounds, and continued not long, so that they were not damaged, but made better by such overflowings; and on those grounds they kept three or four hundred milch cows . . . and fed their working horses, and bred store of young cattle, which were kept on the common in winter, time out of mind.[9]

The inhabitants of Lakenheath and other Fenland communities painted a similar picture.

If conditions in the peat zone were uncertain, they were almost equally so on the silt lands, where the ever-present threat of 'a mighty confluence of waters from out of the higher Counties' hung suspended over the heads of the local populace like the proverbial sword of Damocles. This threat was 'in such sort that all the Winter quarter the people of the country are faine to keepe watch and ward continually, and hardly with all the bankes and dammes that they make against the waters are able to defend themselves from the great violence and outrage thereof'.[10] Inroads of the sea still constituted a periodical menace. In October 1570 the sea broke into the region between Wisbech and Walsoken, flooding much of Norfolk Marshland. At Mumby Chapel in Lincolnshire almost the entire town was flooded. In one place a ship was driven upon a house: 'the sailors thought they had bin upon a rocke and committed themselves to God'.[11] Three saved themselves by clinging to the roof. In 1613, on the Feast of All Saints, another catastrophe occurred. Again the sea flooded Norfolk Marshland and the region around Wisbech. On this occasion it was Terrington that bore the brunt of the inundation. The inhabitants fled to the church

> for refuge; some to hay-stacks; some to the baulks in the houses, till they were near famished; poor women leaving their children swimming in their beds, till good people adventuring their lives, went up to the breast in the waters to fetch them out at the windows.

Fortunately it 'pleased God to move the hearts of the mayor and aldermen of King's Lynn with compassion'. They promptly despatched food supplies by boat for the relief of the flood victims, 'which boats came the direct away over the soil from Lynne to Terrington'.[12]

There were other hazards. In 1607 the jurors of Gedney had emphasised the acute risks involved in pasturing animals on the salt marshes where they were exposed to constant threat from the tides:

> the numbringe of the acres is a verie uncertaine thinge for us to doe for there wilbe sometymes a hundrethe acres of marsh ground; and within three howers space the best of it wilbe overflowed with the sea above six foote deepe.[13]

Fortunately experienced shepherds knew when the high tides threatened, and complaints of serious livestock losses by drowning were rare.

But although drainage in the silt zone seems to have deteriorated, in a number of localities many areas retained a high level of prosperity. Hence the resources of the Holland Fens in the sixteenth century enabled them to support at least as great a population as any other part of Lincolnshire. It is true that the dangers of flooding and difficult climatic conditions prohibited any wide choice in the location of village sites, but this circumstance simply encouraged the establishment of larger, if fewer, communities.[14] That the Lincolnshire Fenland as a whole was far from being a poverty-stricken region is evident from the stocks of cattle, sheep and horses which it maintained.

The decay of the drainage in some localities at this period has been attributed to a variety of factors: to the careless manner in which the sea-walls were maintained, to the intense localism which was a distinguishing feature of drainage maintenance, and to the neglect of the river outfalls which, due to silting, were daily growing less capable of discharging their waters. Two reports compiled on the major Fenland rivers during the early years of the seventeenth century – one by Richard Atkyns, the other by Sir Clement Edmonds – give a unanimous verdict on the worst outfall complications.[15] The river Welland was almost silted up from Spalding seawards 'for want of dykeing, and a current of fresh water to scower the channel'. Sir Clement Edmonds observed boats being carried down the river by cart due to the insufficient depth of water, whilst the Spalding inhabitants complained about having 'no water in the river to serve the necessary use of the towne, but such as was unwholesome by reason of the shallowness thereof'. The Nene outfall below Wisbech 'wanteth much depth and is grown up and choaked with silt'; the river bed was 'six foot or more higher than it was before', and water which had formerly passed via this outfall to the sea 'turneth away and seeketh his course where it may, and much of it passeth about 50 miles before it can recover an outfall, drowning yearly by the way many thousand acres'. Meanwhile the Great Ouse outfall at King's Lynn was so shallow and wide that when 'the Sea cometh in with such tide, especially if a northerly wind meet with a land flood . . . divers townes in Marshland are in danger to be overflowed and surrounded'. The solution here advocated was to straighten, deepen and confine the estuary not only 'to keep out the Sea', but also to improve the current to facilitate the clearance of silt.

Increasingly closer attention was being directed at these problems, for during the sixteenth century, despite the obvious difficulties, there had developed a growing conviction that the recovery of the fens, from summer floods at least, would constitute a sound economic proposition. William Dugdale drew attention to the remarkable fertility of the soil 'gained from the waters, doth it not, for the most part, exceed the high grounds thereon bordering . . . And do we not see, that in the marshes beyond Waynfleete in Lincolnshire, where the grounds are severed and trenched, it is hard to find a poor man, though they sit at great rents?'[16] The example of Holland, where large drainage works had been undertaken with outstanding success, lent added emphasis to the arguments. The Netherlands revolt against Spain at the close of Elizabeth's reign gave to many Englishmen an opportunity of studying these works at close quarters. Also many Dutch refugees fled to England. One small colony became established near Thorney, and with typical native enterprise proceeded to reclaim part of the area.

There can be no doubt of the vital importance attached to draining the fens. Apart from any other considerations it would add hundreds of thousands of acres of exceptionally rich land to the arable, at a time when the advantages to be derived from bringing such an acreage into full cultivation were becoming increasingly apparent. For important as the reclamation of the fens was, the subject acquires an added interest from being seen in its wider setting. In this context the story of fen drainage reflects the main elements of the national movement towards land reclamation, increasingly prominent from the beginning of the seventeenth century. Extension of the area under cultivation was a natural response to the pressure of an increasing demand for food, demonstrated by the fact that after about the mid-sixteenth century grain prices in England began to rise. Growing demand was largely related to the increase in population, from approximately three million at the beginning of the sixteenth century to over five million by the end of the seventeenth, the rapid growth of London being especially significant in this context. To feed its expanding population food had to be drawn from the surrounding counties. To meet the needs of the time, therefore, land was reclaimed not, as hitherto, largely without cost, or automatically through the gradual diminution of woodlands, but at vast expense, with the deliberate object of employing it in cultivation. This was especially true of the fens. The relative proximity of the region to London cannot have been overlooked; neither can the existence of the navigable rivers, by means of which the products of the Fenland could be shipped, not only to the metropolis, but to such northern industrial centres as Newcastle, Blyth and Sunderland via the ports of King's Lynn, Wisbech and Boston.

During the sixteenth century there had been a universal quickening of economic activity with boom conditions accompanied by rising prices. Growing pressure on food resources coupled with price inflation ensured that demand for land, particularly on the part of wealthy landowners and merchants, was always ahead of supply. Land was synonymous with wealth and the resulting spate of land dealing and speculation pushed up values all round, giving a decisive impetus to reclamation. The inflated price levels of the sixteenth and early seventeenth centuries provided an incentive for the investment of capital in new ventures by holding out the prospect of a higher return on capital expenditure. In a period when soaring grain prices promised the cereal farmer handsome returns it was natural that speculators should eye with disfavour the existence of so vast a tract of non-arable fenland. These circumstances aroused a fever of intense speculation, particularly from the reign of James I onwards. So obvious were the advantages of reclaiming the fens that the matter could not fail to attract the attention of the central government, coming to the forefront as a project of increasingly national importance. A great step forward was achieved by the passage of the General Draining Act of Elizabeth I, as this fully acknowledged the benefits to be derived from a comprehensive drainage project for the fens throughout England.[17] The Waldersea Draining Act further stressed the 'great benefit' that would accrue to the nation as a whole, even from such a relatively limited undertaking as that of draining the fens around the Isle of Ely.[18] The enormous potential was too obvious to be ignored by James I and his successor who, confronted with the prospect of a decisive enrichment of the royal purse, were eager in return to grant drainage concessions, or even to undertake the work themselves. Until 1630, when the vital decision to 'lay dry' the southern Fenland was taken, there was no fully adequate appreciation of the need for a unified drainage system, and certainly the capital necessary to finance such a venture had not been forthcoming. This is not to suggest, however, that the idea of draining the fens failed to gain at least a measure of practical support before the seventeenth century. Some progress had been made at an earlier date, although there had been many difficulties. Early schemes were often impracticable, taking no account of the magnitude of the task, the expense, or the technical difficulties involved. A sluice at the Horseshoe below Wisbech, 'erected at . . . great charge', was so imperfectly constructed that it 'stood not seven days, but was broken and blown up by the tyde'.[19] In 1596 the land surveyor Ralph Agas complained to Lord Burghley that 'almost as mainie errours are comitted as there are operacions undertaken'.[20] The severe dearth of capital was a principal stumbling block, whilst the absence of large estates in the Fenland served to make the problem more acute. Such phrases as 'they cannot agree where to lay the charge'; 'sticketh upon the charge'; 'the commoners in respect of their poverty are unable to pay the great charges' are frequent enough in contemporary documents. The opposition of landowners and commoners was another obstacle needing to be overcome. They feared the partial or complete loss of their existing rights in the area, and when Lord Chief Justice Popham was declared undertaker in 1606 for draining a part of the Fenland an anonymous writer warned King James that the 'covetous bloodie Popham' would ruin many poor men in the locality.[21] But despite the difficulties there was a great deal of activity in connection with draining the Fenland from the second quarter of the sixteenth century onwards, not all of it limited to theoretical discussion.

At the close of the sixteenth century we find Sir William Russell – ultimately Baron Thornhaugh – the father of Francis, fourth Earl of Bedford, examining the possibilities of draining his own Fenland estate of Thorney which, as it stood, was 'more charge than profit'. Sir William had fought with distinction in the Netherlands campaign against Spain, eventually succeeding

Sir Philip Sidney as Governor of Flushing, a post which he retained for rather more than two years. This was not long but, military affairs apart, it gave him ample time whilst in the Low Countries to study the efforts made by the Dutch in reclaiming their lands from flooding by sea and rivers. He was sufficiently impressed by what he saw to bring three Dutchmen over to England in 1590 to survey the Thorney estate, apparently with the object of ascertaining the possibilities of draining it. That their verdict was favourable seems obvious from Sir William's subsequent action in requesting the Privy Council for permission to drain Thorney with the aid of Dutch settlers. This project was, of course, a relatively minor one, and in fact nothing tangible was accomplished at this period. Its importance lies in the fact that it furnished yet another stepping-stone in the direction of a wider drainage. Probably the important decision of the fourth Earl of Bedford in 1629–30 to head the Bedford Level drainage venture may be attributed in some measure to his father's influence.

Throughout the closing years of Elizabeth's reign the widespread interest in fen reclamation, both on the part of private individuals and of the Crown, continued to be expressed in varying forms. In 1592 Guillaume Mostart, who had undertaken to drain the fens to the south of Wisbech, wrote to Lord Burghley, Elizabeth's shrewd minister. At great expense he had perfected an engine, such 'as was never seen in the Kingdom before', and he now petitioned that no activity on the part of others should be allowed to interfere with his own project.[22] In 1593 Humphrey Bradley likewise submitted proposals to Lord Burghley, on this occasion for draining the entire Fenland.[23] His claims that he could accomplish the task with a labour-force of 700 to 800 men, at a modest cost of £5,000, the greater part of the work to be accomplished within six months seem to have been based more on optimism than on sound practical reasoning. His calculation of the probable annual income to be received by the Crown was hardly so modest. This was estimated at not less than £40,000, and he informed Lord Burghley that if neither he nor the Queen were prepared to entertain the proposition he, Bradley, would 'bring the names of certain gentlemen of wealth who were willing to perform it upon reasonable conditions'. Lord Burghley was not apparently as impressed by these suggestions as had been hoped, and no action was taken. But there was much activity in other directions. In 1597 the interest of the mercantile class in the fen project was demonstrated by 'certaine merchantes of London' who outlined proposals for draining land around Upwell, Outwell and Denver.[24] In the same year a patent was issued to Captain Thomas Lovell for draining marshes with the aid of inventions perfected overseas. During the ensuing year a group of Lincolnshire landowners petitioned for help in draining their 'fenny tracts'.[25]

With the accession of James I in 1603 the campaign for a general drainage received fresh impetus. The Crown held many estates in the region and so had a vested interest in the project. But although James' reign witnessed considerable activity there was still no record of any permanent achievement. The efforts of Thomas Lovell in Deeping, Spalding, Bourne and Crowland Fens in Lincolnshire met with scant success. In 1604 Richard Atkyns was commissioned to survey the Fenland, whilst James himself instituted preliminary inquiries with a view to compiling a list of those who might be willing to surrender a portion of their flooded lands to anyone willing to undertake a general drainage.[26] It is unlikely that his list was a very long one. In 1605 the Lord Chief Justice, Sir John Popham, and a group of undertakers attempted to drain lands near Upwell. In return for maintaining the draining works they were to receive 130,000 acres of the poorest land. The undertaking probably encountered technical or financial difficulties, as it was completely abandoned after three years. Popham's Eau, a straight cut running from the Nene near March into Well Creek at Nordelph, alone remained to commemorate their efforts.

In 1607, under a local act, was attempted the reclamation of about 6,000 acres in the Isle of Ely,[27] whilst at the same period a group of Londoners drained about 3,000 acres near Upwell. The work cost 'great sums of money' and remained intact until the closing years of James I's reign, when the fen waters 'broke their banks, and drowned all again'.[28] Proposals from a group of French contractors met with considerable opposition from the towns and villages of west Cambridgeshire. The inhabitants requested that their own lands should be excluded from any such project, 'as they need not the help of foreign undertakers'.[29] However one fitful ray of hope appeared on the Fenland horizon. In 1618 the Commissioners of Sewers representing Lincolnshire, Northamptonshire, Norfolk, Cambridgeshire and the Isle of Ely, and Huntingdonshire met at Wisbech: 'soe great an assembly ... as hath seldome been seene togeather att any one tyme before.'[30] A comprehensive survey of rivers, drains and outfalls throughout the Fenland was undertaken, and resolutions were passed to dredge the Welland, Nene, Great Ouse and Cam, and several major drains, and to remove impediments from their channels. Responsibility for the work was minutely defined, divided between the landowners concerned, time limits imposed, and severe penalties drawn up in cases of default. Two drains in the Littleport area, 'being very crooked and narrow . . . allmost utterly growne upp . . . insufficient and unprofitable' were to be replaced by two new drains. There were to be 'cutt more large and lyne streight than the former'. The work was begun, but predictably did not proceed without disturbance, being hindered by 'a few quarellous, and contentious and refractory persons, making question of the power of the . . . Commissioners in this behalfe, and bringing severall acc'ons against theire officers and ministers for the taxes assessed for the . . . workes'. Undeterred for once by the opposition the commissioners pushed forward with the project 'with as much speed as conveniently may bee' and ignoring the popular demonstrations. It is doubtful whether very much was accomplished throughout the Fenland as a whole; the proceedings are significant only in so far as they represent the beginnings of a real unanimity of purpose, with decisions being taken which related to a large part of the region. Opposition from the local inhabitants was still constituting a major obstacle. Disputes about the power of the sewer commissions to make new drains proliferated, especially amongst the residents of the Isle of Ely, who were implacably opposed to drainage innovations of any kind.[31]

A venture of 1619 represented a further addition to the steadily lengthening catalogue of failures. The Earl of Arundel, Sir William Ayloffe and Anthony Thomas, having carried out an inspection of the Great Level of the Fens on behalf of the Privy Council, and having 'the Assistance of some rare Engineers', conceived the idea of draining the region themselves, 'by God's Help', but at 'their own and their Friends' Charges and Expences'.[32] James I seems to have inclined a favourable ear to their proposals, for he instructed the council to come to terms with them. He was doubtless impressed by their guarantee that no taxes would be levied on any of the local people, or on his subjects at large, to finance the undertaking. However no agreement was reached and in November 1620 Ayloffe and Thomas were bitterly complaining that

> they are not allowed to see the Commissioners' valuations of the lands, which are greatly over estimated; that their reward is to be at the disposal of the Commissioners for seven years; that the security is insufficient, and that the general dealings of the Commissioners are unfair . . . Have ridden 10,000 miles, and spent 2,400l., and yet find the country averse to their undertaking, and plotting to compel them to desist.[33]

They encountered antagonism from local landowners, Cambridge university, and the Wash ports. Opposition from such prominent figures as the Bishops of Ely and Peterborough hardly assisted their cause.[34] One very weak point was the heavy expense always associated with any large-scale drainage project, and a principal stumbling block was the lack of security which could be offered to would-be undertakers apart from a portion of the lands to be drained. The Commissioners of Sewers argued that they had no power to give the undertakers any man's land without his voluntary consent, and so the debates went on. One anonymous critic pointed out that the Earl of Exeter had reduced the value of 1,000 acres in Deeping Fen by draining: moreover, 'The people think the undertakers will work by witchcraft, no persons of experience supposing their designs possible.'[35]

A deadlock seems to have been reached, principally because the undertakers refused to begin work until their profits were guaranteed, whilst the commissioners refused to discuss the question of remuneration until the work had been completed. There seems to have been some element of opportunism in the approach of Ayloffe and Thomas; it is doubtful whether they had any sound plan on which to work, and there are reasons for concluding that their chief concern was the monetary gain, without much heed for the technical and financial problems involved. Not surprisingly James seems to have lost all patience with the incessant procrastination, for he ordered them to 'exhibit in writing what it was they promised to effect: Secondly, To specify what they demanded as Recompence for their labour'.[36] But Ayloffe and Thomas were unable or unwilling to do this, so James, who 'for the Honour of this Kingdom . . . would not suffer any longer, the said Land to bee abandoned to the will of the Waters, nor to let it lye wast and unprofitable' declared that he himself would execute the works, taking care to reserve for himself the generous recompense of 120,000 acres. Devoid alike of technical knowledge and financial resources, he overcame the first handicap by inviting the Dutch engineer Cornelius Vermuyden to direct the undertaking. The financial problem still awaited a solution, but by reason of 'his Majesties great occasions and the time' nothing was done.[37] James died in 1625, leaving the matter in the hands of his successor, who at first seemed disinclined to intervene in the project.

Meanwhile in 1626 the drainage of Hatfield Chase, Ditchmarsh, and of all the lands adjacent to the rivers Idle, Aire and Don was commenced by Vermuyden, pioneering the way for the much greater task of draining the Great Level. In 1630 the local gentry, who formed the Commissioners of Sewers, contracted with Vermuyden – now Sir Cornelius, and fresh from his Hatfield Chase triumph – to execute this work. However the question of remuneration seems to have posed an insurmountable obstacle; it was felt that Vermuyden's demand for 95,000 acres of the drained lands was excessive, whilst his foreign birth posed a considerable difficulty. Therefore the commissioners approached the Earl of Bedford with the suggestion that he should seek the King's approval as undertaker, at the same time guaranteeing their support. The venture gained strong backing – moral if not material; Charles was as usual short of funds – from the Crown. It was, in fact, Charles I who had in some measure precipitated the outcome. It had become increasingly clear that the lone efforts of the sewer commissions would accomplish nothing of lasting value, and we find the King penning an irascible letter to the commissioners of Lincolnshire: he had

> found from them no respect nor conformity to his pleasure, but rather such a proceeding as could not but induce distraction and the overthrow of the business. Requires them to conclude... such a bargain as the undertakers may be encouraged to proceed with the work. Advises them not to stop upon unnecessary difficulties, nor to give ear to froward men... Expects them to comply with his pleasure, and that he be not constrained to interpose his regal power.[38]

There was a threat implicit in the last sentence and the work proceeded vigorously enough.

THE GREAT DESIGN

By the so-called Lynn Law of 1630 Francis, the fourth Earl of Bedford, contracted to drain, within six years, that entire expanse of the southern Fenland ultimately known as the Bedford Level.[39] The Russell reward was to be 95,000 acres – despite the fact that Vermuyden had recently been refused this figure – out of which the tax revenue from 40,000 acres was to be appropriated to meet the costs of maintaining the drainage works and 12,000 acres were to be allotted to the Crown. Subsequently the entire 95,000 acres were taxed for the support of the works, presumably because the revenue from 40,000 acres was found to be inadequate. So far as the enterprise itself was concerned the earl was given a free hand, apart from being bound by the proviso not to interfere with navigation. He was fortunate in securing the services of Vermuyden, who possessed much of the technical knowledge that he lacked. Without Vermuyden, unpopular but indispensable, the entire undertaking would have been doomed to the ignominious failure hitherto associated with almost every fen drainage project.

There is no doubt that the fourth earl had been endowed with considerable energy and much shrewdness. He seems to have undertaken the work of draining primarily because he considered that the 'Fen business' was 'feasible' and would prove 'profitable'. On this account he was willing to venture 'some of his own shrunk fortune'.[40] The owner of 20,000 acres of land at Thorney and Whittlesey in the Isle of Ely, he could be expected to take an added interest in a project from which he would derive so great a personal advantage. It soon became clear that the financial profits of the fen venture would be considerable, and the increased income from the Thorney estate after draining was undoubtedly a major factor in enabling Francis' son William, the fifth earl and first duke, to consolidate his position and pay off his debts. However, when Francis decided to involve himself actively in the drainage of the southern Fens there is almost certainly more than an element of truth in the statement that 'he gave his thoughts to an undertaking highly patriotic in its principle, and vast in its design'.[41] Although it remains true to say that Thorney – from the Russells' point of view at least – had been the primary concern during the earlier stages of the enterprise, its importance became merely incidental as the work of draining progressed. But a consideration of the true motives for the Russells' involvement in the fens is somewhat irrelevant to the main issue, which is the extent of their contribution to the work of draining the Bedford Level. The House of Russell was to prove the 'uniform, constant and strenuous supporter of the interests of the Fens'.[42] A large proportion of the capital required for draining was provided by the fourth and fifth earls. On numerous occasions when ready money was required Francis paid his drainage taxes in advance. He furnished much of the security for the colossal sums borrowed by his fellow undertakers, and actually lent them money. Between 1631 and 1637 he appears to have expended not less than £93,000 on the drainage works out of his own resources.[43]

However Francis at no time entertained the idea of shouldering the entire financial burden himself. The Russells, although extremely wealthy, seem to have lacked sufficient hard cash to see the project through. Their wealth was principally tied up in family estates, and borrowing on their security was no simple matter during the seventeenth century. Therefore the earl, we are told, 'undertook so great a work upon the confidence he had of the aid and assistance therein from divers other gentlemen, who by his good example and encouragement would become adventurers with him'.[44] In 1631 he was joined by thirteen co-adventurers, in effect speculators, who shared the risks equally with the profits of the undertaking according to the size of their initial investment. The enterprise, by a contract known as the 'Indenture of Fourteen Parts', was now divided into twenty transferable shares, each representing 4,000 acres of the land to be drained.[45] Each share committed its owner to sustaining one-twentieth part of the expenses of the project with an initial minimum outlay of £500 per share, ie £10,000 in all. It will be realised that some of these original adventurers took up more than one share. Provision was made for additional sums to be raised from time to time as the need arose. As it was recognised that a large capital would be required, the adventurers agreed that any share where the required payments had not been met within ten days was subject to forfeiture. This could then be reissued, provided that the person or persons taking it up paid any outstanding sums due.[46] Therefore although the total number of shares issued remained fixed at twenty the amount paid on each share could increase indefinitely, and this is in fact what happened. Also each adventurer could assign part of his share, subject only to the conditions laid down in the original contract. As the need for new capital became steadily more pressing this became common practice, so that the number of undertakers eventually increased from the original fourteen to more than two hundred.

It should be stressed that, although the original impetus for the general draining of the southern Fens came from the Fenland itself, enthusiasm for the undertaking was in no sense confined to a handful of landowners within the area. The drainage project attracted the interest of land speculators in all parts of England, and this soon reached fever pitch. The demand for shares in the venture was expected to be so great that when Sir John Carleton advised his uncle Lord Dorchester to 'have thereout 3,000 acres' he warned him that in the event of his failure to 'get a grant of the King immediately he will be prevented by others'.[47] In November 1630 Thomas Blechendon wrote to Sir Henry Vane, the ambassador at the Hague: 'the business of draining is now conceived so feasible that the Earl of Bedford will have sharers sufficient in England to carry him through the vast undertaking'.[48] In connection with the early relative popularity of investment in the fen venture it is interesting to note a 'Report of the Committee

C

appointed by Parliament to enquire into the state and condition of the family of Gualter Frost, late Secretary to the Council of State'. His investments included: '£2,000 in the excise, which will not come in for some years; £2,000 in the East India Company; £1,100 in the Guinea Company, and £800 in the Fens'.[49]

In fact there was a striking dearth of large estates in the Fenland, whilst those who held common rights were unable 'in respect of their poverty' to meet the heavy costs of reclamation.[50] Since few people could command such personal financial resources as the Earl of Bedford only a percentage of the total capital required could be raised from within the Fenland itself. Therefore it was imperative to seek it elsewhere. In these circumstances to offer a portion of the land to be reclaimed to any who were willing to venture their capital in the project was an obvious solution to the problem of furnishing security and an adequate remuneration. It was inevitable that an enterprise demanding such a heavy capital expenditure should draw its finance from over a wide area. Of the fourteen original adventurers only five, if we include the Earl of Bedford, could definitely be termed local men. The remainder originated from counties as far afield as Buckingham, Kent and Yorkshire, as well as from London.[51]

Once the financial preliminaries were settled work could begin. The project was of enormous magnitude, especially when we remember that all drains had to be manually excavated. Spades, wheelbarrows and horses constituted the only equipment; the ground was swampy, the natives hostile, and financial difficulties pressing. Up to this time considerable effort had been concentrated on the task of draining the silt lands, but the Earl of Bedford's venture undertook to drain the more difficult peat fens. The work was accomplished in two stages, the first of these falling into the period 1630-7, whilst the second half of the project was completed during the period 1649-53 after the Civil War, with William, the fifth Earl of Bedford, now heading the venture. The task called for a considerable labour force, a problem which the fourth earl partially solved by employing a number of Dutch refugees, and the fifth earl by using Scottish prisoners captured after Cromwell's victory at Dunbar.

It was an unfortunate oversight that the Lynn Law, whilst

stating that the drainage works were to be completed within six years, gave no very precise stipulation of the exact degree of draining to be aimed at, hence furnishing a fruitful source of future controversy. It merely stated:

> That Francis Earl of Bedford would do his best endeavour at his own charge to drain the said marsh, waste, fenny and surrounded grounds, in such manner as they shall be fit for meadow or pasture, or arable ... overflowings by sudden waters which shall not lie longer upon the lands than in convenient time the same may pass away again, shall not be esteemed a not draining thereof.[52]

The drainers seem to have interpreted this to mean that their liability was confined to the production of 'summer grounds' only, ie land free from water in summer but liable to flooding during the winter season.

The aims having been established discussion followed about the best methods of draining to be employed. There were two main schools of thought, both of which attracted a host of supporters. Each group recognised that the principal objective was to run surplus water out to sea with all possible speed, to prevent its accumulation in the rivers with the ultimate danger of overflowing the surrounding lands. Both sides undoubtedly realised that the more rapid discharge of the main rivers could only be achieved if the outfalls were clear, but so far as the interior work on the rivers was concerned their ideas were completely divergent.

One view, of which a foremost advocate was the Dutchman, Jan Barents Westerdyke, was that existing waterways should be deepened and embanked to confine the flow of water within defined limits, so increasing its velocity and enabling the land waters to be discharged more quickly. He favoured a free tidal influx into the rivers, arguing that this, by lending weight to the ebb current, assisted in grinding out and maintaining deep channels. Subsequent centuries were to gain many adherents for this latter part at least of his theory.

Conversely Vermuyden's scheme, whilst favouring a free tidal influx into the Fenland rivers, relied, as those of Bishop Morton and Lord Chief Justice Popham before him had done, on the principle of straightening the rivers by artificial cuts in order to shorten their course to the sea thereby increasing the fall per mile.[53] He was particularly concerned to augment the discharge capacity of the Great Ouse by a straight cut between Earith and Salter's Lode, concluding that this would go a long way towards solving the problems associated with the region around Ely.

Much can be said in favour of both Vermuyden's and Westerdyke's proposals, but in a general sense it was unfortunate that Westerdyke's views could not have been adopted. They had the enormous advantage of simplicity, and in the long run might have been much cheaper to effect. The foremost objection lodged against them at the time was that the embankment of all the major rivers of the southern Fenland would have been difficult due to the extreme local scarcity of suitable material for embankment purposes; it was argued that the costs of importing such material into the area would have been prohibitive. Vermuyden ultimately stressed in his *Discourse* that one of his major objectives was 'to avoid multiplicity of banks, which are very chargeable both in their making and maintaining'.[54] Needless to say Vermuyden's scheme did not turn out to be particularly cheap – quite the reverse – whilst over it, for many centuries, was to hang the stigma of failure.

It was probably the considerable prestige which Vermuyden had acquired from his recent drainage successes at Hatfield Chase which ensured that his plans would be accepted in preference to those of Westerdyke. At his instigation several major cuts were made, one or two existing drains were enlarged, and a number of sluices built. The chief works undertaken at this period were:

1 The Bedford river (later called the Old Bedford river). This was cut from Earith to Salter's Lode, 70ft wide and 21 miles long. It was the most important work executed at this period
2 Sam's Cut from Feltwell in Norfolk to the Great Ouse
3 Sandy's (or Sandall's) Cut near Ely, 40ft wide and 2 miles long
4 Bevill's Leam from Whittlesey Mere to Guyhirne, 40ft wide and 2 miles long
5 Morton's Leam from Peterborough to Guyhirne, improved and re-made

6 Peakirk Drain from Peterborough Great Fen to Guyhirne, 17ft wide, 10 miles long
7 New South Eau from Crowland to Clough's Cross
8 Shire Drain from Clough's Cross to Tydd and out to sea, this representing an enlargement of an existing drain.[55]

The work proceeded in the teeth of turmoil and opposition. Antagonism was directed at the works themselves and at the foreigners who were employed. Vermuyden himself was the source of considerable discontent, and besides Vermuyden there were many other foreigners – protestant refugees from the continent who had settled in the region to join in the work. That the opposition of the local inhabitants was formidable is apparent from an order of 1 May 1637 addressed to the Justices of the Peace 'to suppress these tumults'. Orders were given to bind over or imprison offenders where necessary, 'providing by the most effectual means you can to quiet the country'.[56] Meanwhile towns like Cambridge and Wisbech complained that the rivers were no longer navigable and that their trade was declining.

But despite repeated setbacks and difficulty the works appear to have been completed within three years and according to the terms of the original contract; at all events a Session of Sewers held at St Ives in Huntingdonshire on 12 October 1637 adjudged the 'late surrounded grounds' to have been drained according to the 'true intent' of the Lynn Law.[57] A schedule was drawn up of the 95,000 acres to be allotted to the earl and his co-adventurers, and the work of separating these from the rest of the fen by enclosures commenced.

But if the adventurers had hoped to sit back and reap a rich harvest of profits from their venture they were doomed to bitter disappointment. It is not clear precisely what went wrong. It could not be expected that Vermuyden's scheme would be adequate to reclaim the entire Bedford Level for winter pasture, though it was undoubtedly sufficient, at least for the time being, to ensure that the fens were inundated in summer only in exceptional circumstances. In view of the general provisions set out in the Lynn Law it was irrational to expect anything more than this. Vermuyden's own verdict was that 'the lands can yield little or no

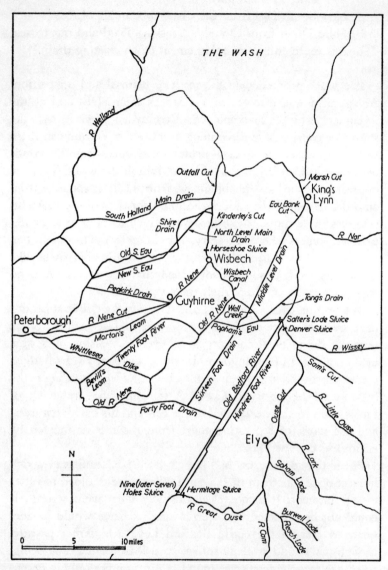

FIGURE 2. The southern Fenland: drainage system

profit, being subject to inundation still (though not so familiarly)' and suggested that the adventurers became 'frustrate of their expectation', which seems to imply that they had not achieved all their original objectives.[58] Also the people whose lands were supposed to have been reclaimed were far from satisfied. They had expected more and the Privy Council was showered with petitions and complaints. Many places had 'received no benefit by the draining'.[59] Another sore point was that the local inhabitants considered they were being unfairly dispossessed of their lands by the grant of 95,000 acres to the Earl of Bedford. Following the outcries against the commissioners' decision Charles himself intervened, whether because he saw an opportunity to exploit the general discontent to his own advantage, or out of a genuine desire to redress the grievances of his subjects is not clear. Undoubtedly his motives were mixed. At a Session of Sewers held at Huntingdon in April 1638 the decision of the St Ives Commission was reversed, and the earl's enterprise judged to be defective. Shortly afterwards the King himself was officially declared undertaker to make the fens 'winter grounds', in return for a grant of 57,000 acres of the drained land. The Earl of Bedford and his associates were given 40,000 acres as compensation for what they had done. In view of the universal discontent they could probably count themselves fortunate to have received any return on their capital at all.

King Charles, having re-engaged Vermuyden, lost no time in pressing forward with his own project, at least at the theoretical level. He seems to have plunged headlong into the venture without first taking even a cursory assessment of the financial and technical problems involved, but doubtless relying on Vermuyden to pull him somehow through the morass of difficulties likely to beset the enterprise. His aims were grandiose enough:

> [to] enrich these countries by several new plantations, and divers ample privileges: Amongst which his royal intentions, that of the building an eminent town in the midst of the Level, at a little village called Manea, and to have called it Charlemont, was one; the design whereof he drew himself, intending to have made a navigable stream from thence to the river of Ouse.[60]

In 1638 Vermuyden prepared for the King's guidance *A Dis-*

course Touching the Draining of the Great Fennes lying within the several Counties of Lincoln, Northampton, Huntington, Norfolke, Suffolke, Cambridge, and the Isle of Ely, etc, although this was not published until 1642. The work includes a review of the general condition of the Level, and a statement of how Vermuyden proposed to effect its improvement. His suggestions, although widely accepted, did not entirely escape criticism. According to Andrewes Burrell Charles I was 'misinformed and abused', the *Discourse* lacking 'all the essential parts of a Designe'.[61] In fact Vermuyden produced a scheme for draining the fens which has been largely vindicated by many people in recent years.[62] He remained firmly opposed to the principle of embanking all the Fenland rivers: 'For then a multitude of banks must be made, about 70,000 rods in length, on a level and moorish ground, and far distant from the falls.'[63] A central feature of his plan, apart from additional straight cuts to shorten the natural course of the rivers, was the establishment of a number of 'washes' or 'washlands'. These were strips of land separating the rivers from their main banks 'for the water in time of extremity to bed on upon all occasions of floods, and so to keep the waters at a lesser height by far against the banks'.[64] Moreover the washlands had other uses, apart from acting as reservoirs for floodwater. During the summer months or dry seasons they would furnish good grazing land, whilst providing space in which the embankments could be widened and raised. Thus Vermuyden clearly set out his arguments in favour of washes. More explicitly he emphasised the need for the banks to be set 'a great distance the one from the other, so that the water, in time of extremity, may go in a large room to keep it from rising too high'.[65] Again and again he hammered home this point: 'for if the water be pent into a narrow room, then the water in that narrow room must be higher, and so rise over the banks. But if it shall lye on a wide bed, then it lyeth broader.'[66]

Vermuyden had a clear appreciation of the existing outfall difficulties associated with the Welland and Nene which, he predicted, would deteriorate with the passage of time. He found the Great Ouse in a somewhat better condition, having 'sufficient water to keep open his channel, and although in the summer the sands in Lynn haven overcome the ebbs somewhat, yet they do not lye long, but the first land waters or next spring tides carry them away again'.[67] For technical and administrative convenience he found it 'the fittest way' to divide the Level into three sections:

1. The area extending north of Morton's Leam up to the river Glen
2. The region between Morton's Leam and the Old Bedford river
3. The district lying south of the Old Bedford river.

These divisions were ultimately known as the North, Middle and South Levels respectively.

But Vermuyden's scheme had as its true centrepiece – based on the same principle as that of the Roman Cardyke – the conveyance seawards of the upland waters of the Lark, Little Ouse and Wissey by a catchwater channel skirting the eastern edge of the fens.[68] This would have been successful, as it would have relieved the Ouse from too great an overcharge of water by these tributaries during times of high flood. Unfortunately the catchwater project was abandoned because of the crippling expense, and the rest of Vermuyden's work, with this essential key omitted, was to prove in many respects a failure.

The outbreak of the Civil War abruptly terminated any further designs, whilst the existing drainage works were abandoned to increasing decrepitude. But the idea of draining the southern Fenland was never wholly renounced, even during this turbulent period. In 1645 Oliver Cromwell, a local man and therefore possessing an intimate knowledge of Fenland problems, was appointed governor of the Isle of Ely. He formed a committee with a view to devising ways and means of completing the drainage of the area. The committee, with a life span of four years, and constantly running up against the hurdle of inadequate finance, accomplished little beyond the production of one or two reports. Nevertheless its activities kept the idea of draining the fens at the forefront of men's minds, and in 1649 an act was passed authorising William, the fifth Earl and first Duke of Bedford, and his associates to drain the land sufficiently to make it fit for permanent agricultural use.[69] Vermuyden was for a third time put in charge of the works, still considered to be the only man with sufficient technical ability to carry the plan forward. The Russells, the sole family possessing large estates in the fens, combined with adequate capital and influence to prevail against opponents, were equally indispensable. The preamble of the 1649 Act fully stressed the vital importance of the venture, as contemporaries saw it, and very little need be added to the points which it enumerates. The lands, once recovered, would

> be fit to bear coleseed and rapeseed in great abundance, which is of singular use to make soap and oils within this nation, to the advancement of the trade of clothing and spinning of wool, and much of it will be improved into good pasture for feeding and breeding of cattle, and of tillage to be sown with corn and grain, and for hemp and flax in great quantity, for making all sorts of linen cloth and cordage for shipping within this nation; which will increase manufactures, commerce, and trading at home and abroad, will relieve the poor by setting them on work, and will many other ways redound to the great advantage and strengthening of the nation.

The more ambitious aim of this second stage of the fen project was to transform the lands into 'winter ground', ie free from flooding throughout the year. With this end in view several major works were undertaken. The New Bedford or Hundred Foot river was cut to the east of the Old Bedford river and running roughly parallel to it. The old course of the Ouse was sluiced at Earith in order to divert all the upland waters into this new drain. The river Ouse between Earith and Denver now figured solely as a land drain for the South Level, and conveyed seaward the water of the tributaries on its eastern flank. Just above Downham, across the Great Ouse near its junction with the Hundred Foot river, the controversial Denver sluice was built, effectively excluding the tides from the river and diverting them along the much shallower, higher situated Hundred Foot.

In view of Vermuyden's previous emphasis on the desirability of encouraging a free tidal influx into the Fenland rivers to augment the scouring action of the ebb, it seems permissible to question his reasons for constructing not only a sluice at Denver but also the Hundred Foot in its existing dimensions, both of which considerably reduced tidal penetration in the area.[70] It was argued by many that because the bed of the Hundred Foot river was higher than that of the Ouse, much tidal volume was lost. Also the tide began to ebb in the Hundred Foot river at least an hour sooner than it had formerly done in the old river, and before the water-level below Denver sluice had fallen; therefore 'it lost its Property of grinding' and was 'almost a dead Water'.[71] Vermuyden had recommended the avoidance of sluices on tidal rivers wherever possible, 'because they are both chargeable and dangerous in the makeing and maintaining'.[72] Why then did he build Denver sluice, especially after stressing, before its construction, that the channel of the Ouse was of 'a great wideness and depth'?[73] There is no hint in the *Discourse* of the intention to build a sluice at Denver, and it would appear that the expedient was forced on him initially by his appalling error in cutting the Hundred Foot river with its bed elevated 8ft above that of the Great Ouse. The consequences should have been foreseeable. Much of the upland floodwater, pouring down the Hundred Foot, turned at the junction of the two rivers at Denver and, instead of passing out to sea, fell back with the incoming tides into the Ouse and inundated the South Level.[74] It seems that the original purpose of Denver sluice – whatever the additional arguments advanced for its subsequent retention – was to block the Hundred Foot waters out of the South Level, and in this sense Vermuyden was the victim of his own blunder. His works were ultimately criticised on other grounds, notably for diverting the land floods into 'four or five streams', in this way dissipating their force, instead of concentrating them into a deeper, embanked channel to produce a more powerful current and scour.[75]

The disadvantages emanating from the existence of several channels cannot be too much emphasised. Under drought conditions each channel contained comparatively little water, with the result that all were in danger of becoming shoal-ridden, choked by weeds, and unable to cope with the unexpected flood. In the past attention has been constantly drawn to the futility of dredging; the sole effective means of keeping waterways open is, of course, by natural scour, hence the argument that if the velocity of the current could be increased the rivers would clear their own channels.

But the sheer magnitude of Vermuyden's work in itself represented a considerable achievement, executed as it was at a time when engineering technology was still in its infancy, and without the advantages of the hindsight possessed by subsequent generations. Also, despite the many difficulties which were to emerge with the passage of time, Vermuyden's works did achieve a number of objectives. He shortened the course of the Great Ouse to the sea by about ten miles, accelerating the passage of the upland waters through the fens. He also halved the flood discharge carried by the old river between Earith and Denver, an advantage which, as we shall see, was considerably eroded by the existence of Denver sluice. Although the Hundred Foot river was in general considered to be too shallow to be of much use during a flood crisis, when tides and rainfall were normal it had sufficient capacity to contain the upland and tidal waters within its banks. For periods of heavier rainfall and high tides another expedient was devised. Great barrier banks were raised along the west side of the Old Bedford river and along the east side of the Hundred Foot, enclosing a strip of land between the two rivers, 18 miles long and approximately 1,000yd wide, comprising about 5,600 acres of grassland. This flood plain or 'washland' served the dual purpose of storing floodwater until the King's Lynn outfall was capable of discharging it, whilst enabling a heavy flood discharge to be carried with a small surface gradient through 20 miles of low-lying fen land. At the same period smaller washlands were established along sections of the Lark, Little Ouse, Wissey and Great Ouse, by the expedient of setting back the flood banks from the river margins, whilst large washlands were eventually formed to the north of Morton's Leam between Peterborough and Guyhirne, and along the river Welland between Peakirk and Cowbit Fen near Spalding.

A number of other works were executed for the speedier discharge of floodwater to the Ouse outfall in the Wash, notably Downham (St John's) Eau. Tong's Drain was cut from Nordelph on Well Creek to the Ouse below Downham Bridge to act as a relief channel when the pressure was too great at Salter's Lode; sluices were constructed at each end of the drain. At the same period Popham's Eau was restored, and the Forty Foot Drain dug, running from Ramsey for the purpose of discharging a proportion of the Middle Level waters into the Old Bedford river at Welches Dam. The fens around Doddington and Chatteris were drained by the Sixteen Foot river. Several other, more minor drains, were made. At this stage Vermuyden seems to have triumphed everywhere, and in March 1652, well in advance of the contractual date, the Bedford Level was officially adjudged to be drained. A thanksgiving service for the successful termination of the work was held in Ely Cathedral.

The financial outlay had been considerable. Some of the adventurers were ruined. William Dugdale asserted, it is uncertain on what authority, that by 1637 the total expenditure had been £100,000, although this seems hardly sufficient.[76] The Earl of Bedford alone had paid out £93,000 from his own resources,[77] and the remaining adventurers most certainly would have expended an amount in excess of £7,000. Sir Miles Sandys of Wilburton was said to have laid out not less than £100,000 on the first drainage works, a suspiciously round figure, however, which was probably somewhat exaggerated.[78] Vermuyden thought that the total outlay up to 1637 had topped £100,000, but gives no indication of the extent to which it was supposed to have exceeded that figure.[79] According to Samuel Wells the original fourteen adventurers and their associates had collectively spent roughly £200,000 during the first stage of draining the Bedford Level, and the weight of the evidence suggests that this may have been a likely approximation of the total cost up to 1637.[80]

But the expenses of draining had not ended here; the second half of the project was, if anything, even more expensive than the first, the undertakers claiming to have spent more than £250,000.[81] This figure is roughly confirmed by the Earl of Bedford's own estimate of 'nearly £300,000'.[82] Therefore it is probably safe to assume that the entire project from its inception in 1630 had incurred a capital expenditure somewhat in the region of £500,000.[83] It was generally supposed that the adventurers had exhausted their estates in the prosecution of the work, 'some to their ruine, but all to very great loss, and in equity ought to have a further recompense and encouragement, the Countrey being the onely gainers'.[84] The profits were not thought 'considerable to the charge and hazard', and Thomas Fuller in 1665 deplored the fact that, 'Many have burnt their fingers in these waters, and instead of draining the fens emptied their own estates.'[85] The difficulties of Sir Miles Sandys were particularly acute and fairly typical: 'I owe divers sums,' he complained. 'I could not pay 100l. now if I had to go to prison. I have had to sell my land to pay my debts.'[86] Even the more affluent fourth Earl of Bedford was obliged to sell some of his estates, the manor of Kingston Russell representing one of the casualties. Miss Gladys Scott Thomson, who was in a unique position to obtain access to the Russell archives, asserted that Francis borrowed money for his various projects, notably the fen venture, partly on mortgage, but chiefly on bonds, from various friends at 8 per cent interest. The amounts borrowed at any particular time ranged from between £1,000 and £2,000. Consequently when his son succeeded to the title there was a debt outstanding of nearly £20,000.[87]

The land even when drained would of course include much that was only partially remunerative. In 1653 the value of some of the reclaimed ground appears to have been inconsiderable, probably due to local drainage difficulties. The Earl of Arundel sent his agent to a meeting of the adventurers for the purpose of informing them of his intention to pay no further drainage taxes, saying that they might dispose of his lands as they thought fit. The lands were finally sold for 3s 9d per acre to William Stephens of the Middle Temple, who might have thought that he was getting a bargain.[88] There is, however, no doubt about the enormously increased value of most of the lands once recovered, assuming that they could be retained in a well-drained condition. Also reclamation on so vast a scale could not fail to have favourable repercussions throughout many sections of the national economy. It may be noted in passing that England moved from being on the bare margin of agrarian self-sufficiency at the end of the fifteenth century to being a small-scale, though regular, exporter of grain by the end of the seventeenth. This may be attributed rather to the increase in the area under cultivation, than to increased productivity per acre at this period.

4

The Foundation of the Bedford Level Corporation

AN EXPERIMENT IN CENTRALISATION

IN 1663 the Bedford Level Corporation was established to administer the drainage of the southern Fenland. This entailed the upkeep of many miles of waterway, as well as about 327 miles of embankment not only for defensive purposes against the floods, but also as towing paths for the convenience of the local navigations. The corporation was also responsible for the repair and administration of several sluices, bridges and causeways, and had the right to enforce the upkeep of all private drains.

On the face of it such a task might well appear to have been no more onerous than might be expected from what, after all, should have been simply a matter of routine administration. Unfortunately, as we shall see, the situation was complicated by many difficulties. Nevertheless no serious doubts were ever entertained about the vital importance of maintaining the drainage works, despite all the problems encountered. Indeed throughout its long history the corporation struggled persistently to provide some semblance of order and prosperity in a region where the frequent total flooding of thousands of acres seemed inevitable, despite all that men might do to prevent it. An understanding of these difficulties is essential to a true appreciation of the achievements of an institution so persistently maligned by its detractors. Although subject to a number of external pressures the corporation was to display a high degree of permanence in both structure and working. It remained the public body almost entirely responsible for maintaining the drained Level until well into the eighteenth

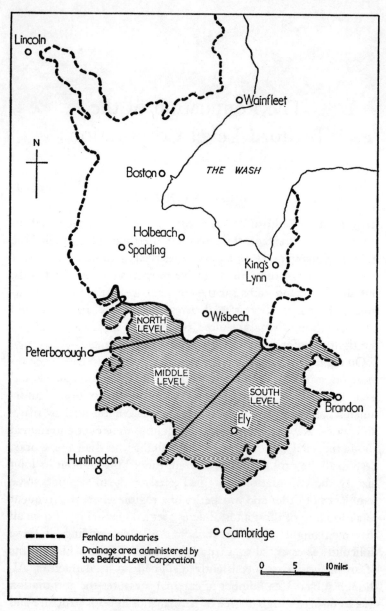

FIGURE 3. The Bedford Level

century, after which its contribution to the Fenland was still considerable.

Two major factors influenced the decision to create an institution of this type. In the first place the unified drainage system now operating in the Bedford Level required a central authority to administer it. The initial work of reclamation had constituted only a part of the overall fen venture. Once reclamation was effected the scarcely less pressing problems of making adequate provision for the future repair, maintenance and administration of the drainage works, and of establishing some form of permanent financial arrangements for acquiring the necessary capital, still awaited solution. Secondly no existing drainage authority could possibly undertake a task so onerous, least of all the Commissioners of Sewers, whose activities were rendered largely ineffective by excessive localism, circumscribed by the relative impermanence of each individual commission, and bogged down by cumbersome modes of procedure and by a general inability on the part of everybody concerned to clarify the scope of their duties. Uncertainties of this nature served to undermine their efficiency. They were at the mercy of 'many obstinate and ill-dispos'd Persons'. To make matters worse there were a 'Variety of Opinions' amongst the commissioners themselves, 'which distract their Resolutions and Judgements'. 'Petitions and Informations' hindered the work, and whilst matters were 'in Dispute', the work was 'deferr'd, Time and Charge lost, and many Parts suffer and undergo much Danger'.[1] This was all very unsatisfactory, and had such a state of affairs persisted nothing lasting could have been achieved. Charles I himself had found from past experience that 'the multitude of Commissioners preferred their little benefit before the general good, and did but perplex and hinder the work'.[2] In fact the sole reason why the commissions had served a useful purpose at all during the Middle Ages was because at that time drainage projects, technically speaking, had been of the most primitive, restricted to certain localities, and carried out through the agency of local effort.

In these circumstances the authors of the General Draining Act of 1663 experienced little difficulty in justifying the creation of the proposed institution. The drainage system of the Bedford

Level, that 'great and noble work ... of much concernment to the whole country' could not be preserved

> without a perpetual constant care, great charge and orderly government, which being represented to the King's most Excellent Majesty ... he hath been graciously pleased to declare more than an ordinary willingness to promote and countenance a work of so publick concernment, and many ways advantageous to this his kingdom.[3]

The obvious need for the corporation, coupled with the warm beams of royal approval shining on the project as an additional, if tenuous, advantage gave every incentive for pressing forward with the work of defining, once and for all, the manner in which the drainage of the southern Fens was to be preserved forever. It was under these favourable auspices, and with scarcely a hint of the intense, disaster-ridden struggle which was to follow, that the Bedford Level Corporation came into being. From the provisions of the 1663 Act 'for settling the Draining of the Great Level of the Fens' it derived not merely its existence, but its powers and responsibilities.

As the corporation was to be vested with powers (especially in the realms of taxation and the confiscation and forcible sale of those lands whose cultivators were in arrear with their drainage taxes) which by the most elementary principles of common law could not be granted by a royal charter, it was essential for recourse to be had to an act of parliament. Charles I, it is true, had incorporated the first adventurers by charter and, with a fine disregard for basic legal principles, had given them just such powers as those mentioned above. But there is no doubt whatsoever that the grant of these powers did not fall within the scope of the royal prerogative, and that Charles I had quite obviously exceeded his by granting them. But Charles had a propensity for committing unconstitutional actions, hence his downfall, and his son in the circumstances can hardly have considered it expedient or wise to imitate his example.

The Bedford Level Corporation included all those adventurers or their descendants, heirs or assigns who had participated actively, that is financially, in draining the southern Fenland.

FOUNDATION OF THE BEDFORD LEVEL CORPORATION

Membership of the corporation entirely depended on the tenure of a part of the 95,000 acres of adventurers' land, of which 83,000 acres were vested directly in the corporate body, the remaining 12,000 acres being owned by the King. A governor, six bailiffs and twenty conservators comprised the board, which carried out the corporation's main active functions. Entitlement to seek election to this élite inner circle depended exclusively on a property qualification, this representing an obvious, if not the only means of selection at a time when the entire social structure of England was based on the wealth and prestige derived from land ownership. The greater landowners' larger stake in the fens was accepted as justification for their control of the administration. Hence the governor and each of the six bailiffs must hold at least 400 acres of adventurers' land; the conservators not less than 200 acres, whilst these functionaries were annually elected at a public meeting by the owners of 100 acres or more of fen.

The position of governor until the mid-nineteenth century was held by the Dukes of Bedford as a sort of hereditary right, and in view of the substantial benefits which the House of Russell conferred on the Bedford Level this can hardly be regarded as surprising or unfair. The board as a whole was drawn predominantly from men who were solely members of the landed gentry. There were few like Samuel Fortrey of Byall Fen who, although a considerable landowner, combined with this a commercial background. With interests extending far beyond the somewhat limited concerns of landownership he was undoubtedly a valued acquisition to the board.[4]

A detailed and orderly administration emerged, in striking contrast to the more haphazard arrangements that had characterised the proceedings of the sewer commissions. A small nucleus of salaried officials was appointed, including a registrar, treasurer, auditor, surveyor, engineer, and area drainage superintendents. Their duties were meticulously defined. Detailed accounts were kept of the work in hand, its progress, and of the weekly expenditure of money on the works. The problems associated with the trustworthiness of employees and the frequent need for a large capital expenditure were sufficient inducements to involve the board in active supervision of the administration. The board exercised a wide range of fiscal and financial powers in connection with levying taxes upon all the 95,000 acres of the adventurers' lands for the maintenance of the Bedford Level, assessing penalties for their late payment, and conducting sales of land whose owners were hopelessly in arrear. It was the board which determined the annual financial estimates; so far as expenditure decisions were concerned its word was law.

The corporation's two chief spheres of responsibility within the confines of the Bedford Level were the maintenance of drainage and navigation. The former was, of course, the most vital, and in this connection the main tasks which the corporation undertook included dredging rivers and drains, repairing banks, causeways, bridges and sluices, as well as such additional mundane, though highly essential, duties as mowing the banks and mole catching. The corporation also had authority to take action against those private landowners who neglected to scour their drains and remove obstructions. Unless they carried out these essential works they were heavily fined.

Even amongst the board members themselves there was some divergence of opinion about the corporation's actual liabilities in the field of drainage, in large measure due to the omission by the General Draining Act to define the exact degree of preservation to be aimed at. Vermuyden, who had been in a good position to ascertain the intentions of the parties concerned, had stated quite clearly that the Earl of Bedford 'did undertake the drayning of the said great and vast level so farre as to make it summer ground', meaning that the land was to be made 'fit for meadow or pasture, or arable' during the summer months only.[5] In the earlier, more uncertain, stages of the venture it had probably been an opinion generally held that the accomplishment of 'summer grounds' was the most that would ever be achieved, and consequently the most that was ever intended. Later the ideal of making the fens 'winter ground' was thought of as a distinct possibility, and was in fact accomplished in some measure. It seems reasonable to assume that the corporation was expected to maintain the Fenland as it found it, ie fit for cultivation all the year round. A more restricted objective would have been illogical, a deliberate renunciation of much that had been gained. Indeed the corporation at most periods does seem to have shouldered the wider liability, at least so far as its attenuated financial resources would allow.

Unlike drainage, the corporation's liabilities in relation to navigation maintenance were defined with considerable precision. Whilst not under a legal obligation to construct works intended exclusively for navigation purposes, the corporation was none the less placed under a definite statutory obligation to preserve navigation in at least its pre-general draining condition; an unpopular proviso in corporation circles, which in practice had a tendency to be consistently overlooked.[6] Although the 95,000 acres of adventurers' land were to be taxed not only for drainage maintenance, but equally for the repair of damage to navigation, the absence of a higher authority to enforce this regulation upon the corporation rendered the latter contingency unlikely. In any event the inevitable rivalry which quickly developed between the drainage and navigation interests was to constitute a fruitful source of trouble in the future.

FINANCIAL WEAKNESSES

The establishment of the Bedford Level Corporation represented the first serious attempt to create a centralised drainage administration in the Fenland. As the experiment ultimately failed, due largely to financial discrepancies, it will be useful to examine these at the outset. During the years following the corporation's establishment the situation in the southern Fens was hardly assisted by its acute financial embarrassments. Shortage of money was to mean that vital works were neglected, which in part helps to account for the eventual collapse of the drainage system in many localities. The corporation inherited a host of financial troubles from the early adventurers, and on this account faced the bleakest of financial prospects. Expenditure on the drainage works between 1631 and 1656 had certainly been somewhere in the region of £500,000, probably more, and it is doubtful whether the freehold tenure of the 95,000 acres was worth anything like that amount.[7] Upkeep of the works was enormously expensive. Any misgivings must have been sharply accentuated by the disastrous winter of 1656, when 'great and successive' floods so damaged the banks that they were said to be 'wasted and impaired'. A loan of several thousand pounds was needed to put them into an adequate state of repair.⁸ Although the general condition of the drainage was, on the whole, good when the corporation took over the reins in 1663, it was estimated in that year alone that an expenditure of £9,500 would be needed to put the Level in perfect working order.⁹

A mass of evidence indicates the financial straits to which the corporation was reduced at this earlier period. The board was incessantly harassed with petitions from workmen and others about its failure to meet the payment of wages and other costs. Lewis Godfrey, the sluice-keeper at Salter's Lode, protested that his salary was two years in arrear, whilst another creditor, Theophilus Turtleby, complained about non-receipt of the money due to him for work undertaken on the corporation's behalf. His own creditors, 'not being soe willing to waite for a pay as hee was' had arrested him and put him to great inconvenience and expense. His petition was endorsed 'nothing done'. We find the ferryman employed by the corporation at Littleport bitterly deploring the fact that his salary was so small that he could not 'live of it to give such Attendance as is necessary'.¹⁰ The corporation was sometimes reduced to the doubtful expedient of using funds that had been allocated to other works, or of borrowing money on the security of the following year's taxes. There were arrears of debts totalling about £4,000 owing to workmen for the year 1672 alone.¹¹ By 1674 a debt of over £22,000 had accumulated, representing more than four times the corporation's gross annual income at this period.¹² The prevailing interest rate of 6 per cent served to augment the deficit, and the financial situation continued to deteriorate.

Although the board theoretically was empowered to tax the 95,000 acres without limitation, its income from this source was doomed to severe curtailment by the need to impose on the adventurers' lands a tax restricted to an amount which their owners could reasonably be expected to bear. In the event of a mass exodus from the lands through penal taxation, the corporation would soon have been left with no income at all. 'The Corporation,' said the board, 'is ready at all tymes to lay out the Taxes they do raise to the best advantage, but such small sumes cannot doe all the Workes that everybody would have done.'[13] In these words lay the germ of a fatal situation. The Bedford Level Corporation was burdened with heavy charges and weakened by low revenues. Its income was both limited in sources and total. The financial provision for the maintenance of the drainage works was so miserably inadequate that soon the corporation's liabilities were perpetually outrunning its assets, and its activities were in effect stifled by the financial constraints inherent in its constitution.

With a cruelly difficult financial inheritance the board must have entertained considerable misgivings. In 1653 the fifth Earl of Bedford had estimated the annual expenditure needed for repairs alone at £10,000.[14] Administrative costs, new works, and repairs rendered needful by unforeseen crises were excluded from this assessment. At this time the corporation's income was mainly derived from taxation, whose annual yield rarely exceeded £7,000, and was usually less. To make matters worse the future income from taxation proved to be subject at times to considerable downward fluctuation, and hence was unreliable. It was an unfortunate circumstance that at times when extra money was needed to repair the works, ie after widespread flooding, the corporation's income was diminished by the need to levy as low a tax as possible from the hard-pressed farmers. It was due to these limitations in its main source of income that the board eventually argued that a restriction should be imposed on the extent of its liabilities, as the corporation could hardly be expected to spend more money than it could raise.[15]

The board, besides being empowered to tax all the 95,000 acres of adventurers' land for the maintenance of the drainage works, could also impose penalties for tax arrears of up to one-third of the amount owing. Because it would have been grossly inequitable to levy the same tax indiscriminately on each acre without regard for widely differing land values, the land was ultimately graded into eleven categories, and taxed according to its alleged productivity. A weakness in this system was that the arrangement involving eleven categories established in 1668 was completely inflexible. There was absolutely no provision made for subsequent adjustments in the event of land improving in some areas or deteriorating in others. As no section of adventurers' land could be taxed without the remainder, the corporation had no scope to alleviate the difficulties of particularly hard-pressed farmers by temporary adjustments in the burden of taxation. As the fens ultimately became alarmingly vulnerable to unforeseen catastrophes, during the course of which literally thousands of acres might be rendered unproductive and farmers lose an entire season's crop overnight, this proved to be a regrettable oversight.

Although there were serious income discrepancies, basic expenditure was of a fairly diverse character, and made heavy demands on financial resources. Expenditure fell into two main categories: first and foremost the cost of maintaining the drainage works, and secondly administrative expenses. These included salaries and a host of miscellaneous items such as the running costs of the Fen Office – the headquarters of the corporation now established in London – travelling and legal expenses, and the entertainment of board members; the latter being an item of somewhat debateable legality, and inevitably encountering criticism from the rank and file taxpayers.

The work of drainage maintenance involved, apart from the costs of building materials and labour, the hire of boats and horses, charges for carriage of materials, often from considerable distances, the purchase, hire and repair of tools, and the expenses of land surveying. Provision also had to be made for emergencies, or what were commonly termed in the account books 'flood bills'. Moreover impecunious landowners made a regular practice of appealing to the corporation for help when the neglect of private drains menaced the safety of entire localities. Where those responsible pleaded a shortage of funds to execute the essential work, the corporation, as conservator of the Level, seems to have considered it its duty to shoulder the burden. Fortunately when mill drainage became essential due to the widespread peat shrinkage and the resulting inability of the interior drains to discharge their waters into the main channels, it was nowhere implied that the corporation was liable to provide the Bedford Level with a comprehensive system of drainage mills, and the matter was left to local endeavour. It was obviously felt that a line had to be drawn somewhere. However whilst the corporation in this way averted an utter financial collapse the southern Fenland, as we shall see, floundered into a quicksand of administrative chaos.

How then was the capital required to maintain the drainage works acquired? Because its ordinary income was insufficient the corporation resorted to the expedient of borrowing large sums of money, usually for specific works, often from individuals whose interests were more or less directly involved. Inevitably the tendency grew of confusing loans with regular income, and of regarding them as indispensable. The glaring disadvantages in this system soon became apparent. Not the least of these was the impossibility – because of fluctuating interest rates – of guaranteeing a continued supply of cheap capital. There was another weakness. The corporation raised capital on bonds, a useful expedient in many ways because these could be repaid at convenient times. Conversely they were callable by the investor at a fixed notice, which meant that the corporation might find itself compelled to repay large portions of the debt at times when it was financially inconvenient, probably through the medium of further loans which might be negotiated at unfavourable interest rates – always assuming that the capital market was favourable to the negotiation of loans at all.

The corporation bondholders were usually very small investors, although a few members of the peerage occasionally lent fairly substantial sums, notably the Dukes of Bedford. The status of the vast majority of the investors, however, is not known, as little documentary evidence, giving information on this interesting point, has survived. They certainly included the Bishop of Ely, a number of clergymen residing in the area, and some Cambridge university dons.[16] Local farmers constituted a dependable source from which loans could be extracted. They, having a direct stake in the fens, were perfectly willing to venture small amounts of capital for the furtherance of works which would be advantageous to them personally. Also corporation bonds were an investment especially favoured by spinsters and widows; a number of these figure in the few extant lists of bondholders. To such investors the question of security would be the overriding consideration, predominating over the question of the size of the return on their capital. This type of investor fell for the most part into that category of rather small savers, who would be prepared to ignore yield up to a point if safety could be guaranteed. Generally speaking they would have a preference for bonds rather than stocks, because although the latter might be expected to pay a higher return their yield was much more irregular, and the risk of total loss greater.

It would be wrong to infer that all corporation bondholders lived locally. London and other parts of England were to some degree represented, although it is probable that many such investors may have had some connection with the fens already, either through direct landownership, or indirectly through relatives.[17] Alternatively they might simply have regarded investment in the fens as a good risk. Corporation bonds would be regarded in the light of a secure investment at this time; in the first place because the structure of the corporation was solidly based on land, a medium which was highly favoured owing to its supposedly superior security over all other forms of investment, and secondly because the prestige enjoyed by the Russells and other well-known landowners on the board, shed an aura of dependability over the proceedings. Charles Cole attributed the comparative ease with which the corporation was able to borrow money to the fact that 'Credit hath been principally supported by the Bedford family', and he was undoubtedly correct in this assumption.[18] The Russells have in fact been termed the Bedford Level Corporation's only real asset.[19]

It was eventually argued that had it not been for the corporation's policy of borrowing heavily on bonds to overcome its shortage of money, the burden of taxation on the corporation landowners would have been much heavier. It is true that the board had no very clear alternative, apart from allowing the drainage works to fall into complete disrepair, which would have been entirely inconsistent with its duty. This does not, however, alter the fact that the practice of unrestrained borrowing eventually proved extremely dangerous. To an income already stretched beyond the limits of solvency was added the interest of the debt, whilst the principal accumulated from year to year, without any immediate prospect of repayment. It was unfortunate that drainage maintenance in the Bedford Level rested on such an unstable financial structure. This created problems which came increasingly to the forefront with the passage of time.

5

The Undertaking in Difficulties

THE SINKING LAND

In 1666 the Fen Office – sited in London in preference to the fens on alleged grounds of easier accessibility for board members of the Bedford Level Corporation – was burnt to the ground in the Great Fire,[1] and most of the documents of the early adventurers destroyed.[2] The more facetious may well have commented in these unfortunate circumstances that the affairs of the corporation were thus bedevilled by the twin destructive elements of fire and water. The superstitious, had they foreseen the quagmire of difficulties into which the corporation was soon to flounder, would doubtless have interpreted the disaster as an omen. Yet almost everything at this period, at least on the surface, and despite an uncomfortable shortage of money, promised well. Financial discrepancies were not yet too pressing and even to the least sanguine the general situation seemed to indicate that the corporation could, in all probability, anticipate a useful, if not very arduous career, reaping the profits from a drainage system which had been largely perfected during the previous three decades, and where the hard work appeared to have been done. In fact the real troubles had not even begun, and widespread disillusionment soon cast its shadow over the enterprise.

But for the present there seemed little cause for alarm. In the Willingham fens great crops of onions, hemp and peas were observed growing for the first time, and travellers remarked on the flax, coleseed, oats and wheat flourishing in many parts of the Level, on ground which had never previously been ploughed.[3] The land, we are told, was so rich after draining that 'weeds grow on the banks, almost as high as a man and horse'.[4] Produce poured out of the Earl of Bedford's Thorney estate in the North Level to his Bedfordshire seat at Woburn. Before the general draining less than one-third of the Thorney estate had been cultivable land, and the improvements which so immeasurably enhanced its productivity seem really to have taken effect after the Restoration. It is significant that the construction of a new granary to house the increasing yield of corn, can be traced to this period. Oats, coleseed and hempseed were being cultivated and as the estate improved cattle breeding began to rival even the corn output.[5] This sudden access of prosperity in the southern Fenland encouraged the Justices of the Isle of Ely to petition the Bedford Level Corporation in 1669 for permission to hold a weekly market at the small Fenland town of March. At this period the region still boasted only two market towns, at Wisbech and Ely, despite the fact that since the general draining the Isle had 'become much more populous than before, and the trade of the said Countrey in Cole-seede, all sorts of graine, hemp, flax, cattell, butter, cheese, and other commodities... greatly increased'.[6] The advantages of a third market to cope with the increasing flow of trade were stressed.

The recent efforts of the land speculators seemed more than fully justified by this – what Thomas Fuller enthusiastically termed – 'deluge and inundation of plenty'. The initial fears of Cambridge, 'more frighted, than since it hath been hurt, now the project is effected', were entirely discredited, at least for the present. Cambridgeshire, as Thomas Fuller pointed out, had not only gained, in material terms, 'more earth' but also 'better air by the draining of the fens'.[7] Any dissentient voices – and there were several – any lingering fears for the future of the enterprise, were swamped amidst the general jubilation. Poems were composed in honour of the event; the famous lines popularly attributed to Samuel Fortrey:

> I sing Floods muzled and the Ocean tam'd
> Luxurious Rivers govern'd and reclam'd...[8]

will be familiar to many.

But despite such premature rejoicings all was not well, and by the closing years of the seventeenth century a dramatic change had occurred. In 1683 Gregorio Leti noted that the countryside around Thorney was 'so subject to inundations, that they are the greatest terror of the inhabitants'.[9] Ten years later, in the month of June, the owners and occupiers of March were complaining that 30,000 acres of their land were under water: 'where wee should be now plowing the fowles of the ayre are swimming'.[10] This was only one of the many similar petitions which the harassed corporation was required to investigate at this time. The records of its meetings are full of complaints about flooded lands, broken banks, blocked drains, and the utter impossibility of navigation. At a Session of Sewers held in 1688 the jury had summed up the position thus: 'that most of the draines, sewers, dikes . . . within the Great Level . . . are grown upp obstructed and very defective for want of ditching and scouring soe as the waters cannot pass', ie to the main drains, and thence out to sea.[11] But flooding, if the main, constituted by no means the sole difficulty. Drought in the fens posed considerable problems during a dry summer, and at this same period the inhabitants of Downham, paradoxically, were complaining that they were 'almost undone by reason of ye Dryness of their grounds which in ye sumer are burnt up for want of water'.[12] A further spate of problems emerged with the passage of time. None of the obvious measures associated with routine drainage administration seemed capable of halting the relentless deterioration of the Bedford Level.

The General Draining Act of 1663 had hinted obliquely at certain difficulties: that some parts of the southern Fens were still flooded, despite the vaunted efficiency of the drainage works; that the drainage of some areas had caused a deterioration in others, and that the maintenance of the Level was likely to result in disputes with the navigation interest and other sections of the local community. In 1664 had come rumblings of yet further difficulties of an even more fundamental character, and these were to frustrate every attempt to administer the Bedford Level in accordance with the aspirations of the authors of the 1663 Act. In that year Colonel William Dodson, assuming the traditional role of the spectre at a far from convivial feast, composed a didactic treatise for the enlightenment of the Bedford Level Corporation.

His ostensible object was to advise the corporation on the best means of managing the drainage works 'at a small charge', so that his treatise partook of the nature of an economic exercise as well as being a technical dissertation. He wished to demonstrate how future floods could be avoided, and the 'vaste expences of yearly repairs' circumvented; from which, as he said, 'great advantage' would accrue to all concerned in the enterprise: to the King, the corporation, and the entire country. Commendably he resolved that his writings should be brief, in so far as brevity was consistent with 'the weightiness of so important an affair'.[13]

His address was admirably designed to perform the functions of an awful warning. The least attentive mind could hardly miss its lessons, and as Dodson, on his own admission, was drawing on a vast reservoir of practical experience accumulated during 'thirty years . . . and more', the corporation in particular would have been ill-advised to disregard his opinions. He had worked with Vermuyden on the 1630 drainage project, and during the Civil War had been appointed Governor of Crowland. In these two capacities he had acquired a considerable first hand knowledge of the problems associated with the region. His warnings of the major difficulties looming ahead were the more disquieting because these, being intrinsically bound up with certain natural peculiarities existing in the locality, would be hard to overcome. The real problem centred round the shrinkage and lowering of the peat surface of the southern Fens, once the water was removed from the peat by draining. This process was accompanied by a corresponding elevation of the river and drain beds above the level of the surrounding lands. The drainage works became gradually more ineffective for, with the main rivers flowing at a higher level than the interior drains, and with the interior drains raised higher than the lands they were supposed to drain, the natural gravitation of water to the sea was increasingly disrupted.[14] It is apparent that Colonel Dodson did not himself completely appreciate the menace implicit in this appalling situation, but he did warn the corporation that 'the bottom of your Dikes grow not up, nor rise as you say'; it was, he stressed, 'your Grounds which shrink'.[15] The solution he suggested, namely to re-excavate the drains when the initial shrinkage has taken place, after which 'your Dikes will hold good for many years', proves beyond any doubt that he misunderstood the continuous nature of the process, hence its causes, and above all that he did not foresee its ultimately catastrophic effects. The process requires some further explanation.

The moisture content of waterlogged peat may be as much as 800 per cent, and when it is drained the immediate effect is a shrinkage of the top layer from which the water has been abstracted. The initial shrinkage in the peat fens after draining was probably more than a foot during the first year. Moreover peat is composed almost entirely of vegetable matter which, when dry, is eaten by bacteria, resulting in further wastage. Subsequent loss from this cause would almost certainly be in the region of at least 1 to 2in in a year. In fact the peat fens wasted at an alarming rate, until the land in many places sank below mean sea level and even further below high flood level. A foremost problem confronting drainage engineers was how to carry the river waters across a constantly shrinking countryside. The Fenland rivers now flowed between artificial flood banks over beds that were considerably higher than the surrounding lands. If in times of flood the banks were breached or overtopped, the water poured down into the low lands, spreading out into huge lakes. Very wide areas could be quickly flooded in this way. Also when the flooding ceased the waters obviously could not flow back into the rivers, but stagnated on the land. In these conditions the safety of the fen lands increasingly depended on the maintenance of the banks hemming in the tidal rivers, and their composition and maintenance became matters of vital importance. It is significant that Colonel Dodson's thinly veiled prophecies of disaster centred to a large extent around this aspect of the problem.

The incessantly lowering peat surface rendered the difficulties of bank maintenance exceptionally complex. Because the mean sea level, which governs the level of rivers, rose as the land fell, the height of the river embankments had to be continually increased, but here engineers encountered another obstacle. The flood banks rested on a foundation of peat and so-called 'buttery clay' – an apt description for the soft, silty clay which overlies much of the Fenland floor beneath the upper coating of silt or

Plate 1 Old and new methods of digging fen drains: *(above)* manual excavation of a drain in the late nineteenth century; *(below)* the Dredging and Construction Company Ltd of King's Lynn excavating a drain in Norfolk Marshland

Plate 2 (above) The Old Bedford River looking north: a major work constructed by the Dutch engineer Cornelius Vermuyden in the southern Fenland; *(left)* the effects of peat shrinkage at Prickwillow after draining. The door shown was originally at ground level

peat. Such a tenuous foundation, incapable of supporting too heavy a weight, placed a definite limit upon the extent to which the banks could be heightened during any one year. Even within the limits imposed the weight of the increasing heights of the flood banks caused the soft, unstable clay beneath them to spread, and the banks to sink still further, creating a vicious circle with remedial work causing even greater instability. And since the peat wasted more quickly on the dry side of the embankments than it did on the river side, the banks settled unevenly, inclining towards the fen, until their outer slopes became dangerously steep. There were other problems. In a peat zone the almost total absence of easily accessible, stiff clay added yet another phantom to the nightmare, as this inevitably resulted in the construction of the majority of the banks from too light a soil. The consequences were obvious and inescapable. The intense pressure to which these 'hollow counterfeit banks, made of so light a composition it will both burn and swim'[16] were subjected at high water, made breaches unavoidable. Colonel Dodson underlined this danger in his address to the Bedford Level Corporation:

> Thus the floods increase in our rivers between the banks, and riseth, and lieth on them at a great height, and as I have said, these moory banks will deceive all that trust in them: it is confessed that the moor earth is tuff so long as it lies wet, but is good no longer then till it is rotten, and that it will be if it lie dry four or five summers, and then it sinks, and becomes a light black mould; and if it chance that a flood lie upon it but three or four days, it soaks in the water and becomes sobbed, and is neither earth nor water, and then it leaves you when you have most need of it, and drowns the fens more, than if there were no banks at all.[17]

It was for these reasons that Vermuyden had stressed the need for a drainage system which avoided a 'multiplicity of banks'. The overriding question was that of the expense involved in their maintenance, a problem which Colonel Dodson had clearly appreciated. It was the vast height at which the flood banks had to be maintained to withstand the spring tides that had prompted him to voice the opinion that 'twenty years hence for want of Earth at a reasonable distance, the Banks will cost more in one

D

year than they now do in four'. He added: 'I wish the charge of those fen lands may not exceed the profit, as some of them have already done . . .'[18]

Suitable earth for bank maintenance was dug wherever it could be found within reasonable distance of the works, often without first resorting to the formality of seeking permission from the owners concerned. Because the Bedford Level Corporation was seemingly no respecter of persons – or simply desperate – over two acres of land belonging to the Earl of Westmorland were cut to pieces to repair breaches in the north bank of Morton's Leam in 1673, and 270 tons of earth were removed from Stanground parish for the same purpose.[19] It was estimated that by the early eighteenth century at least 10,000 loads of earth had been carted from land belonging to Ely Cathedral at Roswell Hill which, although 'lying remote from the River' contained 'strong gault . . . for bankeing'.[20] The corporation was apparently indifferent to transportation difficulties if only suitable material could be obtained from somewhere. Disputes about the removal of earth were very common. The inhabitants of Swaffham Bulbeck, for instance, complained that the corporation had 'dugg up great part of their Comon to amend their Banks whereby their Drove is quite Destroyed'.[21] A long battle was fought against the Swavesey inhabitants, who proved obstructive, 'forceably Detayned' earth, and created so great a disturbance that the local corporation officer Ralph Peirson 'could not soe well proceed in repayring the Banks there'.[22] Agreements with Stanground also proved difficult to effect, primarily on account of the vexed question of compensation for the earth removed.[23]

Meanwhile with the continuing elevation of the river and drain beds above the level of the surrounding land, a substitute for a natural gravity drainage had to be found. In the first instance it became normal practice for an individual farmer, or a small association of farmers, to raise banks round their lands in an effort to exclude the floods, but as time elapsed and the situation deteriorated this remedy proved inadequate. Since a natural flow of water could not be guaranteed it was essential to find some means of lifting the water from drain level to the main rivers. In the desperate search for a solution widespread recourse was had to mill drainage which had already been tested with some success in various parts of the Fens before the general draining of the Bedford Level. The horsemill, an early mode of fen drainage sometimes employed, was gradually superseded by windmills during the last quarter of the seventeenth and the early eighteenth centuries. Windmills alone could provide sufficient power to clear a considerable volume of water from a fairly extensive area at reasonable speed. Thomas Badeslade was convinced that were it not 'for a great number of Landholders throwing the Fen waters over Banks into the Rivers and Drains, by Engines made at their own Expense . . . the whole Body of the Fens would become unprofitable; and Taxes enough could not be raised to maintain the Works, and to pay Salaries'.[24]

The windmills were used to drive scoop-wheels, equipped with paddles set at an angle of about 30 degrees, and designed to rotate in a channel cut through the peat. The windmills themselves, like the scoop-wheels, were built of wood on pile foundations driven through the soft peat into the firmer clay beneath. Those employed in the fens usually had four sails; six was extremely rare. Daniel Defoe described a model with twelve sails, although admitting that he did not see it working.[25] The diameter of a scoop-wheel could be as much as 25ft. As its lift was effective only to about one-fifth of its diameter, this was therefore limited to 4 or at most 5ft. In fact scoop-wheels depending on wind as the motive power worked more efficiently when a lift of no more than 3ft was needed. With the continued peat shrinkage, when lifts of more than 5ft became essential, two or more windmills were used to raise the water in stages.

A Bedford Level Corporation order of 1678 first officially directed attention to the expedient of mill drainage as a remedial measure. The four surveyors employed by the corporation were each directed to buy a mill 'for the better and speedier cleansing and scouring of draynes'.[26] It was this edict which provided the initial impetus for what became the general practice of employing mill drainage in many parts of the fens. From this date may be traced the separation of the Fenland drainage network into two distinct systems: a high level system consisting of the waterways which carried the upland waters through the fens and out to sea, and a series of low level systems, carrying surplus water to the mills for pumping up into the rivers.

Unfortunately the solution of one problem soon gave rise to a host of others. Before long it became apparent that a mill, far from representing an unqualified asset, could constitute a common nuisance by driving water into a main drain which lacked sufficient 'fall' or gradient to remove it quickly enough. Neighbouring lands were flooded, the banks of the drains were damaged, and it was even maintained that mill scoops aggravated the problem of silting by actually lifting dirt up with the water and throwing it into the rivers. For these and other reasons the construction of windmills throughout the Fenland did not proceed without opposition. Petitions against allegedly unauthorised mills showered into the Fen Office. Between 1699 and 1716 more than 120 mills in the Bedford Level were presented at the Sewer Courts as a nuisance, and ordered to be pulled down.[27] It is interesting to note that proposals to drain Norfolk Marshland by two windmills were heavily criticised, not solely on grounds of technical difficulty but also because of the enormous expense. It was estimated that at least thirty-two would be needed, and that the 'prime cost of these Whirligiggs will amount to 14,400l. whereas the prime cost of a natural drain, will not much exceed half the said sum'. P. Bateson continued:

> Amongst our neighbours, consider the engine at Tydd St Giles, which cost 450l., has a vast receptacle for its waters, and but 2,400 acres to drain, and yet cannot do it effectually, the landowners having since erected another for the same purpose. What a wild fancy is it, then, think you, to propose two engines to cope with 40,000 acres.[28]

But windmill drainage, although an artificial and in many ways an unreliable and costly expedient, proved the salvation of the fens, the one crucial factor which saved them from universal reinundation. Windmills quickly became a characteristic feature of the flat fen landscape, and Daniel Defoe was at least one traveller who commented on them with something approaching enthusiasm:

> wonderful engines for throwing up water, and such as are not

seen anywhere else, whereof one in particular threw up, (as they assur'd us) twelve hundred ton of water in half an hour, and goes by windsails, 12 wings on sails to a mill. This I saw the model of but I must own I did not see it perform.[29]

But it was one thing to get the water from the fens into the main drains and rivers, and quite another to get that water out to sea. In this connection two major problems still awaited solution.

The first, and probably most important of these, especially so far as the South Level was concerned, was the lack of capacity in the existing rivers and drains to contain the volume of water pouring into the region from the upland counties during times of heavy rainfall. For this reason Vermuyden had realised how essential it was to exclude the floodwaters in the Wissey, Little Ouse and Lark from the fens.[30] It was with this object that he had proposed his scheme for a cut-off channel to run round the eastern margin of the region to intercept the upper waters in these tributaries and take them to a point near Denver, whence they were to be conveyed seaward by a relief channel. The relief channel was in fact made (although ultimately abandoned) in the form of Downham (or St John's) Eau, which ran from Denver to Stowbridge on the Great Ouse. It was unfortunate that Vermuyden's plan for a cut-off channel was not put into execution at the same time, although the idea was frequently revived and, as will be seen, has been carried out in recent years with considerable success.

Another major problem was, of course, the poor state of the outfalls. Colonel Dodson had urged the point that 'if the out-falls once fail it will be a greater inconvenience than the breaking of a bank'.[31] However it was not until the eighteenth century was well advanced that the full significance of this problem achieved practical recognition. Although great drains such as Morton's Leam and the Old Bedford and Hundred Foot rivers had been cut by the drainers, and the waters from the higher catchment areas channelled into them, the problem of how to get this water to the sea via the outfalls in the Wash had been completely neglected. The river mouths were becoming increasingly obstructed by shelves of sand. Meanwhile 'all our banks and works are in great danger, and the poor Countrey-man in hazard of utter ruine, and the navigation . . . very uncertain and dangerous'.[32]

THE CLASH WITH VESTED INTERESTS

Apart from the peat shrinkage, the difficulties of maintaining the flood banks, the undeniable drawbacks of windmill drainage, the inadequate capacity of the Fenland rivers and the uncertain outfalls, other factors combined to bring the drainage enterprise perilously close to disaster. After the general draining the fens were intersected with an intricate network of drains and waterways many of which, whilst serving a useful purpose on one person's land constituted a nuisance almost everywhere else. Also serious was the inability to define the responsibility for their maintenance. Repairs were often undertaken in a grudging spirit and imperfectly executed. Much has been written about the strong spirit of individualism prevalent among fen dwellers, and their alleged inability to co-operate with their neighbours in a common undertaking has, in the past, had a tendency to become a popular fallacy. Many were inclined to agree with William Elstobb's unflattering verdict that the inhabitants of the fens were a 'hardy, ignorant sort of people, mostly content with such uncomfortable accommodations as nature afforded them, and no way inclined to enter into any great and considerable attempts for improvements'.[33] Actually the rigours of fen life rendered at least a minimum amount of active co-operation essential, for example in relation to the division of responsibility for the upkeep of banks and drains, and also in the development of common and intercommon pasture rights. But there is no doubt that any co-operation which did exist had a tendency to be narrowly local, and an outstanding difficulty confronting drainage authorities was the fenmen's apparently inborn parochialism.

The seemingly irrational fears and prejudices directed by contemporaries towards the drainage works, which found a practical outlet in rioting and the destruction of property, had considerable economic significance. The drainage works were objects to be resisted, and the efforts of the Bedford Level Corporation were from the outset clogged by the necessity of fighting for their existence and of placating opponents. Apart from a handful of large farmers, eager to increase their stock of animals, the seventeenth century fen drainage projects found few native supporters.

The Fenland, as we have seen, consisted predominantly of great commons, extremely lucrative to those who were fortunate enough to hold common rights on any scale, and which represented an integral part of the agrarian economy of the region. Owners of common rights evinced a justifiable alarm at the enclosure of their commons by the drainers. The case of Borough Little Fen near Peterborough is a typical example. This extensive common was depastured by cattle belonging to the inhabitants of Estfield, Newark, Oxney, Allerton and Fletton. There were about 1,000 commoners, all of whom opposed the undertakers.[34]

The General Draining Act of Elizabeth I had decreed that lords of manors, landowners and commoners 'may contract or bargain for part of such commons, wastes and severals aforesaid, with such person and persons which will undertake the draining and keeping dry perpetually'.[35] The establishment of a legal basis upon which such agreements could be formed had represented a considerable step in the direction of providing capital to drain the fens, and the adventurers associated with the Earl of Bedford in the enterprise had in a sense availed themselves of it, with one important omission. In return for draining the southern Fens they had, as we have seen, received 83,000 acres of land to compensate them for the heavy capital expenditure which the work had incurred. For the adventurers to have entered into individual agreements with all the owners concerned would have been a tedious and complex affair, so a certain amount of coercion had proved inevitable. Herein lay the germ of the difficulty. In the first place the independent fen dweller submitted to coercion with an ill grace. Also the 83,000 acres, together with the 12,000 acres allotted to the Crown, were for the most part carved out of the great commons by commissioners who frequently went about the business in a high-handed manner. The adventurers were popularly supposed to have commandeered the most valuable lands, a belief which persisted even up to the close of the eighteenth century, with James Bentham's scathing attack on the Bedford Level Corporation:

> The smallest spots, however scattered or remote, which first showed themselves above the surrounding waters, were eagerly seized upon by these watchful discoverers, and claimed as part of

their allotted reward. By these means they acquired a large and disproportionable share of the higher parts of the Fens, to the no small benefit of themselves and disadvantage to the proprietors of the country.[36]

Although this accusation was not literally true there is no doubt that hundreds of commoners were more or less forcibly deprived of their rights to provide payment for a drainage for which they had not asked, and which they did not particularly want.

The rights of common formed a complex of intermixed and mutual rights, established by so long a usage that change could only be effected by the pressure of unusually strong forces. The commoners, besides being very numerous, were in the face of a mutual enemy frequently highly organised, and always exceptionally tenacious of their rights. There had from the outset been considerable dispute when it came to defining the exact degree of benefit to be derived from a general draining of the fens. The inhabitants gave their own picture of the local economy. Needless to say this varied considerably from accounts circulated by detractors: 'The Undertakers have alwaies vilified the Fens, and have misinformed many Parliament men, that all the Fens is a meer quagmire, and that it is a level hurtfully surrounded, and of little or no value: but those which live in the Fens, and are neighbours to it, know the contrary.'[37] Very many of the inhabitants had insisted that draining was unnecessary, rightly stressing that the winter floods, far from being consistently destructive, produced rich pasture, capable of supporting immense herds of livestock.[38] But the commons not only provided pasturage for livestock. They afforded a livelihood, however irregular, for thousands of poor cottagers, gathering 'reeds, fodder, thacks, turves, flaggs, hassocks, segg, fleggweed for fleggeren, collors, mattweede for churches, chambers, beddes and many other fenn commodytes of greate use both in towne and countreye'.[39] In addition fen drainage had interfered with such traditional occupations as fishing and wildfowling. Those engaged in these pursuits enjoyed a species of hard liberty which they were ill-disposed to relinquish in return for a more conventional mode of existence.

But not only did many of the fen dwellers lose their traditional livelihoods through the draining of the fens; when the 95,000 acres were enclosed they actually forfeited the use of the land. Enclosure was the recognised mode of supplanting common by several, and so entailed the closing of the land concerned against all rights save those of the individual owner. As drainage had involved the infringement of so wide a diversity of existing rights it was foreseeable that in the future discontent would frequently erupt into widespread disorder. Not all had been opposed to the drainage project it is true. The inhabitants of Cottenham, Rampton and Willingham had noted the 'favourableness and profitableness of the work' but even they had emphasised their reluctance to be 'drawn into charge'.[40]

The Bedford Level became the scene of serious disorders. The commoners demolished embankments, damaged sluices, filled in drains, turned cattle into the corn crops and attacked workmen. In 1653 disturbances had been so grave that the Council of State, vaguely alarmed, had ordered 'a troop of horse to go thither to appease the tumult, not holding it fit that people should right themselves in that way'.[41] Nobody really doubted the essential justice of the fenmen's claim, but those owning property in the area deprecated anarchy. Unfortunately old disagreements died hard, and there were several cases similar to that of William Drury in the second half of the seventeenth century. He had purchased 100 acres of adventurers' land, which the commoners of Littleport promptly seized in 1666. Several years later, and even with the corporation's assistance, he was finding it difficult to re-establish ownership.[42] The continuing opposition to the drainage works was an extremely disquieting aspect of the situation; not only because the accompanying violence endangered the works and the personal safety of workmen, but also because it involved an expenditure of money in repairing the damage which could be ill afforded. A typical incident was recorded in 1674 when the inhabitants of Swavesey, hearing that workmen employed by the Bedford Level Corporation were removing earth from the parish to repair the nearby flood banks, threatened to erect a gallows on the bank and hang the workmen. In the ensuing brawl a quantity of corporation property was destroyed or damaged.[43]

An even worse disorder occurred in 1722. About 140 men, working under the supervision of the superintendent of the North

Level, were executing vital improvements to the river Nene outfall. About a thousand of the residents of nearby Wisbech, 'dissolute and disorderly persons', who seem to have been motivated solely by the fear that any reduction in water levels would disrupt their navigation, and encouraged by a number of local lawyers, justices of the peace and commissioners of sewers,

> continued for several hours in Demolishing the ... Works and Burnt and Destroyed great Quantitys of Timber Planks Barrows Stacks of Hay and other Chargeable Materials ... of a very great Value. In Consequence whereof the whole North Level containing about 50,000 acres of land must remain under water all the year.[44]

This unfortunate incident brings us to another source of opposition to the drainage works. The most implacable enemy of drainage was almost certainly the navigation interest. Apart from the inevitable reduction in water levels after draining the existence of drainage sluices created a physical impediment in many Fenland waterways. Denver sluice was a particular cause of dissension, and was frequently damaged by watermen.[45] To that allegedly 'ill formed, and still worse executed project' was attributed the 'Ruin of the Navigation of Lynn, and the deplorable State of the Fens'.[46] So far as navigation was concerned the testimony of Edmond Russell of Thetford, on account of his long experience of the vagaries of the Great Ouse and its tributaries, has particular significance:

> that it is about 60 Years since he used first to go down to *Lyn*, as a Waterman in his Father's Boats; and that he himself hath used the Trade of a Waterman and Merchant for about 45 Years: And that he ... does remember the Building of Denver Sluice, and that before the said Sluice was built, he ... did remember that the Tide did swell as far as *Ebilton-lode*, being within eight miles of the aforesaid Borough of *Thetford*, by reason whereof the Waters did swell so much at the aforesaid Borough, that he, this Deponent, hath had his Barges, as also known other Mens Barges with about ten Chaldron of Coals in them, come up to the *Christopher's* Bridge so called, being a Bridge within the Borough aforesaid. And this Deponent farther saith, That by reason of the building of the said Sluice at *Denver*, it hath so stopped the Tide, that our River is so low with Water, that we cannot now come up to Town with above

two or three Chaldron of Coals at the most, in a Lighter, when the Water is highest by reason of the Floods; and with much less when the Water is low by reason of Draught.[47]

Thomas Badeslade told a similar story, and here the Hermitage sluice at Earith also came under fire:

> And that this Dam or Sluice near *Salter's-lode*, which shut the Tide out of its ancient Receptacles; together with another Dam cross the *Ouse* at the Hermitage near *Erith*, which turned the River from *Erith* down a new shallow Cut, called *Bedford* River, or *Hundred-foot Drain*, to *Salters-lode*, many miles out of his ancient Channel, was really and immediately prejudicial to Navigation, is but too easily proved.[48]

Another bone of contention was that the working of Denver sluice kept the sluice doors shut often for 'many Hours, sometimes Days and Weeks'. During these times the sluice was impassable to boats, which had to be unloaded and 'carried over the Dam'.[49]

It is not surprising to learn that the drainage interest encountered severe opposition from the river towns, and in particular from ports like King's Lynn, whose continuing prosperity relied heavily on the position it occupied as the link between the Fenland navigations and a flourishing coastal and foreign trade. The standard complaints of the navigation authorities centred round the complete disruption of navigation in many places, the increased difficulty in others, and inflated freight costs. The Bedford Level Corporation was harried with petitions and 'cases', and became embroiled in periodical and inevitably expensive litigation. The complaints of the navigation interest furnish evidence of decaying channels and declining trade. According to one Cambridge petition the deterioration of the Great Ouse and Cam threatened the entire loss of navigation.[50] The mayor and corporation of King's Lynn pointed out that the entire river from Lynn to Cambridge was impassable, and in 1696, having gained the unanimous support of Cambridge, Stoke, Brandon, Mildenhall, Thetford and Bury St Edmunds, tried to push a bill through parliament, agitating for nothing less than the complete removal of the drainage sluices.

THE BEDFORD LEVEL IN DECAY

The Bedford Level Corporation was determined to uphold Denver sluice even in the teeth of the widespread opposition. It was considered to represent the cornerstone of the South Level drainage system. The South Level, an exceptionally fertile tract of land when not flooded, could not be put at risk whatever the grievances of the navigation interest might be. The Dean and Chapter of Ely Cathedral, with no navigation interests to speak of, saw in the sluice's retention the one sure safeguard of their agricultural lands or – in the words of their petition to the Bedford Level Corporation – 'the sole Preservation of a vast Quantity of Lands belonging to Ely, and divers other adjacent Towns'.[51] On the other hand the greater majority of the South Level landowners, supported by the landowners of Norfolk Marshland, united with the navigation party in opposing the sluice's continued existence. It was argued that thousands of acres were at stake, with pastures completely 'drowned' and roads impassable.[52]

Denver sluice, whatever its general merits – and these are debateable – seems to have considerably exacerbated the problem of flooding in the South Level at this period. During high tides, and when heavy land floods poured down the Hundred Foot river, the volume of water on the seaward side of the sluice never fell low enough for the sluice doors to remain open for very long periods. It is true that they were opened as 'the Ebb of the Tide gave way' to clear the waters which had accumulated in the South Level rivers, but before this water had time to drain out to sea 'another Flood from Sea came and shut the Sluice Doors'.[53] The water trapped in the Great Ouse, its tributaries and the interconnecting drains rose above bank level, spilling over at any point throughout something like a hundred miles of waterway: 'by which Means the Lands of the South Level became, and have since been much annoyed with Water in Wet Seasons'.[54]

But drainage problems were by no means confined to the South Level, even though they hit that difficult region with particular force. The condition of the Bedford Level as a whole, by the closing years of the seventeenth century, was the reverse of satisfactory. Although the picture was far from being one of completely unrelieved gloom, heavy land floods and high tides, or even an adverse wind direction, were apt to produce crises in many localities, at different times, and without warning. At a later date Samuel Wells stressed this point, observing how 'hazard is inseparable from the nature of fen property'; 'floods and tempests arise . . . whole districts are laid waste' and 'not a vestige remains of the industry of man'.[55] Events at the close of the seventeenth century help to underline the accuracy of Wells' assessment. In 1675 we hear of 'divers breaches in the Bankes and other Ill accidents' throughout the Bedford Level.[56] In 1689 St Catharine's College, Cambridge, donated five shillings 'To a man in ye Isle of Ely ruined by water.'[57] In 1693 a group of fen towns complained 'how much the Waters lye upon them', imploring relief,[58] and during the following year the inhabitants of Ely were 'setting forth what great losses they had sustayned by their lands being so much drowned these last two years'.[59] During the summer of 1696 a 'great Breach of about 10 or 12 pole wyde' was torn in the north bank of the Old Bedford river; 'some endeavours had been used for taking the same, which proved ineffectual'.[60] The Bedford Level Corporation, desperately short of money, found it impossible to meet all its commitments. Matters so far deteriorated that when the sluice-keeper's house at Well Creek collapsed the Surveyor General directed him to rebuild it as best he could, using the old materials, promising however that 'hee should be satisfied when the Corporation had money'.[61] 'Wee are soe hard besett (haveing noe money)', complained the board member John Jenyns in 1697, 'that we know not which way to turn.'[62] During the ensuing year disastrous weather conditions aggravated the situation. In 1698 Celia Fiennes found the fens 'full of water and mudd'.[63] In 1701 John Reynolds, the Duke of Bedford's steward, observed how 'the money allotted this yeare for the Workes of the North Levell is not sufficient to putt the Workes of the said Levell in a defenceable condicion against any ordinary flood that may happen'.[64] The sources paint an equally sorry picture for the first quarter of the eighteenth century, and in 1724, when Daniel Defoe crossed the Gogmagog Hills near Cambridge he saw

Fen country almost all covered with water like a sea: the Michaelmas Rains having been very great that Year, they had sent great floods of Water from the Upland Counties, and these Fenns being as may be properly said, the sink of no less than thirteen Counties ... they are often overflowed.[65]

The situation had not been improved by the sudden collapse of Denver sluice in 1713. A combination of heavy spring tides coming up-river from King's Lynn, and a great volume of floodwater pouring down the Hundred Foot river from the uplands caused the catastrophe. These met at the sluice which, unable to withstand the intense pressure, blew up, the 8ft dam alone remaining intact to constitute a source of future trouble. Until the sluice was rebuilt between 1748 and 1750 under the direction of the eminent Swiss engineer Charles Labelye, the spring tides had free access into the South Level, but the ebb tides had difficulty in returning because the dam obstructed their passage. Also they were overridden by the current of the Hundred Foot river whose bed, it will be remembered, was several feet higher than that of the Great Ouse. Badeslade described how 'the land-floods which descend the high situate *Hundred-foot* in Winter, take their way through the Remains of *Denver Sluice* into the *South* Level, drowning these Lands ... instead of going to their natural outfall to *Sea* by *Lynn*'.[66] In this crisis it was unfortunate that the bed of the Ouse, due to past silting processes, was 4ft higher on the seaward than on the landward side of the sluice, whilst the river-bed was considerably higher at Denver than it was in the vicinity of Ely. In other words the river-bed had a considerable descent from Denver back inland to Cambridge, and 'it was observ'd in *November* and *December*, *Ann*. 1720 that the land-Floods, which so descended the *Bedford*, ran violently up the *Cambridge* River for twenty-one Days together without any Intermission, or any Return to be perceived all that time'.[67] The lands, lamented Badeslade, were flooded 'to such a Depth, that the Sun cannot exhale the Waters, nor dry them up'. He spoke of 'extensive deluge and Depopulation'.[68] Thomas Neale attributed the decay of Manea in the Isle of Ely in part at least to the demolition of Denver sluice. He had:

heard ancient people say, that if Manea heretofore were drowned two feet deep in February by a breach of banks . . . they could plow and sow those lands with oats that same year, but now it is too well known, if it be drowned but one foot deep at that time, it can scarce be got dry all that summer.

He described how 'the vast body of water in every great flood' in its passage to Ely through the wreck of the sluice, flooded between 60,000 to 80,000 acres 'four or five feet deep'.[69] It is not difficult to appreciate how large a number of bankruptcies such total disasters must have left in their wake, when it was not merely a question of poor harvests but of the complete disappearance of crops.

Land values fell sharply in every part of the Bedford Level. For example in 1701 30 acres in Feltwell were sold for 1s: 100 acres in Lakenheath for £2 15s, and 80 acres in Mildenhall for £1.[70] In Haddenham Level, where about 7,000 acres had been perpetually flooded for seven years, land formerly worth £1 an acre had, by 1726, depreciated in value to less than 2s 6d.[71] The mounting difficulties of the fen farmers can be gleaned from a number of circumstances. Many fell into arrears with their drainage taxes and were forcibly deprived of their land. The tax losses sustained by the Bedford Level Corporation escalated from £336 in 1669 to £684 by 1710, £827 in 1712, £877 in 1713, falling to £749 in 1714, but rising again to over £800 by 1717. After this date losses remained consistently high.[72] The year 1728 witnessed the first introduction of the so-called Invested Land Rolls, which comprised a record of corporation land which had been totally abandoned by its cultivators; during the first half of the eighteenth century land entered on these rolls frequently exceeded 13,000 out of a total of 83,000 acres under the corporation's direct ownership.[73] The financial troubles of the Bedford Level Corporation became more spectacular as the century moved on. Its all too evident financial instability, deriving direct emphasis from the appalling condition of many parts of the fens, undoubtedly deterred many would-be investors from risking their money in an undertaking that was becoming so conspicuously hazardous. Meanwhile it was uncomfortably clear that nearly as much or more could still be spent on the drainage as had already been poured into the project's insatiable maw. Confidence, that most precious financial intangible, was ebbing, and it was apparent that some solution would have to be found to meet the growing crisis.

6

The Triumph of Localism

THE NEW DRAINAGE AUTHORITIES

As its financial problems increased not only did it become more difficult for the Bedford Level Corporation to keep the drainage works in good repair; for identical reasons the maintenance of an efficient administration proved impossible. The number of officials employed had to be kept to a minimum, because the corporation's income was too meagre to allow of any great elaboration or subdivision of function. The majority of its employees worked on a part-time basis, utilising moments which could be spared from their other activities, again because the payment of adequate salaries to secure the undivided attention of experts was precluded by a shortage of money. The superintendents responsible for all aspects of drainage administration were for the most part farmers, for whom land surveying and engineering constituted secondary occupations, and whose understanding of the problems involved was at best partial.[1] Many of them lived at an inconvenient distance from the works. This, coupled with the fact that the requirements of farming diverted their attention from giving the required amount of detailed supervision, rendered the arrangements conspicuously inadequate. It was predominantly a question of how long a group of amateurs in this particular field could carry on with a task requiring the specialised knowledge of professionals.

The corporation argued that the employment of men who owned land in the fens ensured that duties were conscientiously performed.[2] This was an admirable theory but did not always work out in practice. Some of the officers were grossly inefficient, and conspicuously tardy in the performance of their duties. The

Surveyor General Roger Jenyns expressed exasperation on more than one occasion: 'I am weary of Writing without I see orders better performed.'³ Hopkins, one of the area drainage superintendents, was 'such a knave and fool he must be turned out'.⁴ On another occasion it was recorded how the sluice-keeper at Floods Ferry had 'lately run away and therby made himself incapable to serve the Corporation'.⁵ Neither was incompetence confined to the lesser employees. John Chicheley, who held the post of Surveyor General between 1717 and 1725 was notoriously indolent. During the severe floods of December 1720 he preferred to remain in London rather than expose himself to the rigours of a Fenland winter, pleading in exoneration of his conduct:

> I agree ... that this would be a proper time for me to have been down with them to have given them the very best assistance I was able could I be spared from hence ... Was the Surveyor Genll to attend all ye Works of ye Banks etc in the Levell during the time of flood who must do all the Business of the office here in Town?⁶

He remained at the Fen Office circulating messages, insisting nevertheless that the plight of his superintendents, struggling to maintain the works in the teeth of appalling difficulties, 'wounds me to the heart'. He exhorted Mr Walsham, more hard-pressed than the rest, to 'keep up your Spirits and Exert yourself'.⁷

There were other weaknesses in the administration. Some of the officers seem to have acquired habits of needless extravagance. Neglect to pay adequate attention to the prices of materials and labour resulted in expenses being incurred which might have been avoided or diminished, and was the subject of incessant resolutions and proddings from the board. In 1712 in particular there were rumblings of discontent about neglect of duty on the part of corporation officers who were responsible for the drainage works, and disquieting rumours began to be circulated about misappropriation of corporate funds. The offending officers were removed and others elected in their stead by an inner junta of the board at a secret meeting in London. The reasons for such secrecy are obscure, unless it was to avert a public scandal. By 1730 the internal affairs of the corporation had fallen into such a state of complete chaos that the personal intervention of the

Duke of Bedford proved essential. He promptly sacked the receiver general, the auditor, the surveyor general and the sluice-keeper at Well Creek, whether for outright dishonesty or general incompetence is not clear.[8]

There were other troubles. Although technical and geographical difficulties, unforeseen in the initial stages of the venture, threatened the entire project more nearly with disaster, lack of money meant in effect that because there were far too many calls on the limited resources available, many important works suffered neglect. The conservators' Proceedings are full of entries concerning essential repairs which had had to be postponed or even abandoned altogether, and give a graphic picture of the struggle to maintain the drained Level. Repeated floods, with their consequent inquiries, complaints and investigations, put the board and corporation employees under considerable pressure, whilst hindering the execution of other vital projects. The range of duties was by no means small. So far as drains and waterways were concerned the first essential was to ensure a free passage for the waters, which involved taking action against those landowners who neglected to scour their drains and remove obstructions. In this connection the cultivation of reed and willow holts, widespread throughout the fens, was subjected to close supervision and strict regulation. The superintendents were required to maintain an unceasing vigilance to prevent abuses of all kinds, but their employment for the most part on a semi-casual basis made this unavoidably difficult. Instances of individual carelessness had unfortunate repercussions. There were innumerable cases similar to that of William Foreman, who 'cutt a hole in the foreland of the 100 foot bank near Oxload to lay his boat in', hence seriously undermining its foundation at that point.[9] The energies of the corporation were dissipated in countless prosecutions. Abuses included the persistent habit of stacking fodder on the flood banks and keeping unacceptable forms of livestock, such as pigs, which rooted up the surface of the embankments.[10] Encroachments were difficult to prevent, and there were even extreme cases of cottage tenants adding to their garden or land by the simple expedient of fencing in large areas of corporation bank.[11] Care was needed in regulating the type of crops grown on the banks. The inhabitants of Manea and Upwell, for example, petitioned the corporation about the practice of growing mustard seed, which made the banks 'spungy, light and loose, and so less Able to withstand ye Force and weight of ye Water'.[12] To make matters worse, in many parts of the fens the river banks represented the regular means of communication between towns and villages. The advantage lay in their elevation above the low-lying lands, as they provided a relatively dry and solid road, of particular advantage during wet seasons.[13] For this reason the banks were used as highways for the passage of livestock, in particular the Hundred Foot bank, over which tramped immense droves of cattle on their way to St Ives market from Norfolk.[14] The corporation quickly discovered that this practice tended to 'Increase and advance' the costs of bank maintenance, whilst through carting the banks were 'very much torne and prejudiced'.[15] The order books and conservators' Proceedings are full of resolutions about the prevention of carting and the passage of drift cattle along the banks. The frequency of the orders demonstrates the extent to which they were habitually disregarded. Moreover the practice was aggravated from about 1732. Attempts on the part of farmers and drovers to evade the tolls levied at the new turnpike at March diverted an ever-increasing flow of traffic along the banks, so that the Turnpike Trustees petitioned the already harassed corporation about loss of business.[16] The towing horses used for local navigations were also responsible for much of the damage caused to the banks. The horses indiscriminately used the tops or the sides. The navigation users thought that the former was preferable: 'it is the fastest and most convenient for them, and the assistance they afford the banks in pressing down and consolidating them, is a sufficient recompense for now and then kicking off a bit of dirt into the river'.[17] However it was estimated that the passage of horses might reduce a bank, originally 8ft wide at the top, by 2 to 3ft within a year: 'the Haling upon the Banks causes them to moulder into the Rivers'.[18]

Such mishaps must have convinced the corporation that it faced real problems, whose solution demanded a capital expenditure considerably beyond its resources, and driving it to seek a means of lightening what promised to be an intolerable burden.

There seemed two possible alternatives: either some way of increasing its revenues – perhaps by seeking wider powers of taxation – would have to be found to pay for the better maintenance of the works and the employment of additional staff, or part of the burden would have to be transferred to other shoulders. It is strange that the first expedient was not adopted in preference to the latter, as the establishment of an increasing number of local drainage bodies ultimately resulted in complete administrative chaos.

From 1726 can be traced the gradual evolution of the private drainage districts, which relieved the corporation of some of its weightier liabilities. In that year the inhabitants of Haddenham Level complained that their lands had been almost continually inundated for seven years, that the Hundred Foot barrier bank was so low that the floodwaters poured over the top, and that the outfalls to the sea were inadequate.[19] In April of the following year a further complaint was lodged, this time about the poor condition of the north bank of the Great Ouse between Stretham and Earith and the defective state of many of the drains in the locality.[20] The Bedford Level Corporation, overwhelmed by a spate of petitions and complaints from landowners in other districts, could do little, and in fact seems to have been fully resigned to the necessity of allowing the Haddenham farmers to drain their lands 'at their own expense'.[21] In 1727 an Act 'for the effectual draining and preserving of Haddenham Level' was passed, apparently without any major objections being raised.[22] The alacrity with which other local communities sought similar acts is indicative of the seriousness of the problems confronting the Fenland at this period.

But the corporation still demonstrated a certain reluctance about surrendering too much of its authority, and was hence slightly inimical to innovations at this time. This is very apparent from the failure in 1728 of private drainage bills introduced by Whittlesey and Waterbeach. Also 1728 was for the corporation an extraordinarily unfortunate year, with its control over the southern Fenland being seriously weakened by events in the North Level. Here the drainage works were so dilapidated that the need to borrow large sums to carry out major repairs was regarded as a matter of urgency. The cost of the proposed works had been assessed at £6,600, and the corporation had no means of raising the money.²³ In the previous year the trustees of Wriothesley, third Duke of Bedford, confronted – in the light of the corporation's difficulties – by the hardly felicitous choice of allowing the drainage of the North Level, and hence of the Thorney estate, to collapse or of expending £3,400 themselves, had chosen the latter course as the lesser of two evils. They now agreed to advance the further sum of £6,600, but only on condition that they retained absolute control of all North Level revenues as security. The corporation, poised on the horns of a dilemma, had no alternative but to agree. This arrangement was to remain effective until the £10,000, plus 4 per cent interest, had been fully repaid out of the corporate funds. As there was absolutely no prospect of this ever being accomplished the corporation's arrangement with the trustees assumed an appearance of permanency. The arrangement had, of course, two aspects, in a sense beneficial to both parties. On the one hand the Duke of Bedford had secured control of the North Level revenues which could now be used exclusively for his own benefit, whilst the corporation was relieved of any future responsibility for the works in the area. But the underlying significance of this arrangement is that we can see in it the first emergence of what Charles Cole termed 'Ideas of separate Interests'.²⁴ He was convinced that from the 1728 negotiations could be traced the ultimate alienation of the North from the Middle and South Levels.

There is no doubt that the growth of separate and conflicting interests within the Bedford Level, which was becoming all too apparent by 1728, owed its inception and continuance to the slow financial disintegration of the Bedford Level Corporation. In 1738 another private drainage act was passed, this time for Redmore, Waterden and Cawdle Fens near Ely.²⁵ In 1741 Waterbeach Level became established as a private drainage district.²⁶ Subsequently the landowners of many more localities applied to parliament for local acts covering their districts, the boundaries of which were meticulously defined. An act, once passed, authorised the establishment of a board of commissioners to be responsible for the internal drainage of the district in question. Subdivision drains were made for draining the lands of each owner by discharging their waters into a main channel. These were cut at the expense of the owners and ran through the entire district, which was then embanked all round with a mound of earth raised to a sufficient height to exclude the floodwaters of other districts. A mill was constructed to pump water from the low-lying district drain up into the nearest main river. The number of mills in each district depended, of course, upon its size and on the gravity of the flood problem. In many cases, where the amount of water to be pumped was beyond the capacity of one mill, a system of 'double lifts' proved essential, with the main mill being fed by smaller mills situated at some distance behind. The entire Bedford Level soon formed a network of small districts, each one pumping its water from the interior drains up into the main arterial channels. The number of drainage mills within the Bedford Level was colossal. Thomas Neale estimated that there were about fifty in Whittlesey parish alone: 'I myself, riding very lately from Ramsey to Holm, about six miles across the Fens, counted forty in my view.'[27]

But apart from the construction of drainage mills the commissioners of each district were authorised to 'make... Cuts, Drains, Damms and Outlets, through the said Fens and Low Grounds'. They played a dominant role in relieving the corporation of numerous liabilities. Hence the commissioners of the Middle Fen District not only undertook to repair lengthy sections of bank along the east side of the Cam and Great Ouse and on the south side of the Lark, but also dredged many of the more important drains, including the Sixteen Foot.[28] Similarly the commissioners of the Burnt Fen District assumed responsibility for the maintenance of the north bank of the river Lark, the south bank of the Little Ouse, and part of the east bank of the Great Ouse.[29]

The area depicted on the map (Fig 4) of Burwell, Swaffham and Bottisham drainage districts amounts to 4,892 acres. If we imagine this detail multiplied many times we shall have some idea of the drainage network which now went to make up the Fenland picture. By the close of the eighteenth century there were more than twenty private districts in the South Level alone. With powers independent of the corporation and of each other they

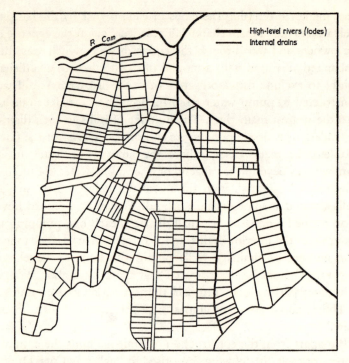

FIGURE 4. Burwell, Swaffham and Bottisham internal drainage districts

each functioned as isolated units, even as rival concerns. The corporation never acquired even the semblance of a hegemony over its discordant neighbours. Local drainage commissioners appointed officers, levied taxes, controlled expenditure, and borrowed money on the security of their revenues. They could punish tax defaulters, as well as offenders caught damaging the works, neglecting drains, or keeping pigs on the banks.[30] It became customary for many private district acts to have what was termed a 'Hog Clause' included in their provisions. The rights of the corporation were in theory preserved, but in practice a significant part of the daily routine administration of the Bedford Level was passing out of its control. This had certain advantages in that it enabled money to be diverted to the maintenance of the barrier banks and other important works, which might otherwise have been frittered away on the upkeep of relatively minor waterways. On the debit side was the total absence of co-operation between the corporation and the drainage districts over matters of mutual concern. Such an anomaly in the administration generated appalling confusion, since no clear policy could be formulated from the mass of unco-ordinated schemes in operation. This situation, which was not remedied until the twentieth century, was a great contributory factor in the failure to carry through comprehensive improvements, and can be held accountable for the poor condition of the drainage in many areas.

Meanwhile the affairs of the corporation had shown little marked improvement. The year 1753 found it, in a mood of dull bewilderment, wilting under the weight of its accumulated liabilities, the debt by this time having mounted to well over £49,000.[31] There was even less money to spend on drainage, though an increasingly strict control was exercised over expenditure. Entries like the following, which appeared in the conservators' Proceedings of 1751, are common:

> The Finances of the Corporation will not admit of any allowance being made for the scouring out of St John's Eau, Fordham and Roxham drains, but the Proprietors are at liberty to scour out any part of them at their own Expense, if they think proper so to do.[32]

The corporation was sufficiently hard pressed to seek drastic economies. Stringent regulations were promulgated to prevent officers from exceeding the annual estimates for their districts, and the board even went to the extreme limit of threatening them with suspension from their duties if they contravened the rules in this connection under any pretext whatsoever.[33]

Nowhere were the difficulties of the corporation more plainly apparent than in the North Level, where events had still further darkened the financial prospect. The debt incurred by this district totalled more than £20,000 by 1751, most of it representing the principal of £10,000 owing to the trustees of the Duke of Bedford, plus accumulative arrears of interest since 1728. This was the more disquieting as the North Level revenues from drainage taxation were usually in the region of £750, sometimes sinking as low as £600, and never exceeding £950, per annum.[34]

It is therefore not surprising that the corporation was compelled to arrive by painful stages at the disagreeable conclusion that not only would the income of the North Level never be adequate to repay the debt owing to the Duke of Bedford, but that it was quite insufficient even to defray the routine expenses of the North Level drainage works. These were in an appalling condition, 'decayed and ruinous'.[35] The Level was 'frequently flooded' and liable to become 'entirely drowned and of little or no value'. In 1753 John Wing, the Duke of Bedford's agent, and others testified that a 'great Part of the ... Level is, at present, overflowed a Foot deep'.[36] In this emergency some remedy had to be sought outside the framework of existing arrangements.

It was proposed by the Duke of Bedford, the Earl of Lincoln, and other landowners whose interests were directly affected, that the North Level, together with lands belonging to the Manor of Crowland in South Holland – also 'frequently flooded' – should unite in one common drainage. This involved making their own future arrangements, quite independent of the corporation, for raising any additional revenue or capital required. It was further suggested that the North Level should be relieved from all future responsibility for corporation debts, and that the North Level drainage taxes, although to be collected by the corporation, should continue to be applied for the exclusive benefit of the Level.

The corporation finally decided to adopt these arrangements. It had in fact little alternative. To ensure that the North Level revenues were spent where the need was greatest, the First North Level Act of 1753 made provision for these to be employed solely for the upkeep of the main works, in particular the north bank of Morton's Leam and other vital banks. An independent body of commissioners was established, equipped with powers to levy extra taxes on all North Level lands and to borrow, at minimal interest rates, sums of money up to a maximum of £14,000.[37]

The impact of this still somewhat limited regional reorganisation on the constitution of the Bedford Level Corporation is open to dispute.[38] Samuel Wells, for many years registrar of the corporation, saw it as 'a pecuniary transaction' rather than as 'an actual severance', whilst admitting that after 1753 the North Level came to be regarded by many corporate members as a 'kind of terra incognita'.[39] Certainly some arrangements continued as before. On the other hand the routine administration of the Level, the management of most of the sluices and drains, and the levy of additional taxes where necessary became the sole responsibility of the North Level commissioners. There seems no doubt that the measures embodied in the North Level Act exerted an erosive effect on the corporation's powers in the region north of Morton's Leam, and a certain waning in its status is indicated.

The eventual severance of the North from the Middle and South Levels, and ultimately of the Middle from the South Level, has been traced back to Vermuyden's original provision which divided the Bedford Level into three units. The corporation's determined adherence to this arrangement[40] was ultimately subjected to strong criticism, even from two such loyal employees as Charles Cole and Samuel Wells.[41] Later writers were if anything even louder in their dissent. Vermuyden was supposed to have 'put asunder that which Nature had joined' so that the interests of the three Levels were 'made to clash to a degree which none but hereditary occupiers can adequately estimate'. It was alleged that the Levels were 'set at variance with one another like a trio of mongrels over a meat biscuit'.[42] It is true that once the three regions were each given a separate identity and a distinguishing title discord and rivalry about such controversial matters as expenditure on the drainage works, income from disputed properties, and representation on the board were probably unavoidable. Even so some form of division was undoubtedly convenient when it came to such administrative details as, for example, the allocation of duties to officers. It remains true, however, that the corporation had in a limited sense signed its own death warrant by adopting Vermuyden's partition of the Bedford Level.

But it was above all unfortunate that the corporation had never been provided with a sufficient income. The arrangement whereby one responsible authority was established to administer the entire Bedford Level was at this period the most satisfactory solution to the problem of maintaining a comprehensive drainage system. The collapse of the administration into a confused mass of separate units, and the triumph of that same localism which had constituted so serious a handicap in the Middle Ages, might have been avoided had the income initially provided been adequate for the maintenance of the drainage works and the full time employment of a professional staff. Hence the fundamental weakness lay, not in the actual system of government established, but in the neglect to furnish that system with adequate resources.

There seems to have been surprisingly little irrational expenditure; on the contrary expenditure was carefully controlled and periodically tightened. Several minor economies were effected, and some ill-conceived ones in such matters as staffing. In 1768 attempts were made to check the soaring 'flood bills', which had become 'enormous'. The costs of ale, bread and cheese supplied to labourers employed in watching and strengthening the banks during high tides and heavy rainfall had become so inflated that it was thought 'impossible for them all to be employed'. In future each labourer was to be given a subsistence allowance of 6d per day or night: 'For it is notorious that many publicans sent in bills last Year for more Ale drank in time of Flood, than they take off their brewer in the course of a year.'[43] Officers were instructed to check that wages were paid only to those who worked and not to the mere idle curious 'coming to see the Floods'. Apparently in the general confusion mistakes were apt to be made. In a further attempt to prevent dissipation of financial resources an investigation was held in 1773 into the costs of materials, and officers were reprimanded for buying such items as nails and tar from 'little Shopkeepers and retailers' as this involved 'large charges'. The board ordered that materials purchased for the future use of the corporation should be obtained at wholesale prices.[44]

But no economy, however stringent, could prevent the debt from soaring to unprecedented levels. The finances of the corporation were in seemingly inextricable confusion, and underwent parliamentary investigation. Its income could not be stretched to meet emergencies and the drainage works in many localities were in an appalling condition. Between 1763 and 1771 there were repeated breaches in the north bank of Morton's Leam. A breach near Peterborough in 1770 measured 120ft wide and 36ft deep; the North Level was 'entirely drowned'.[45] A visitor to the southern Fenland in June 1763 recorded how there were '1,400 cows kept in the parish of Cottenham, which feed on the fens in summer. The water is, in this dry season, up to their bellies'.[46] In 1773 we find Charles Cole complaining that he had been compelled to sell his manor at Haddenham 'it having been drowned these 14 or 15 years and I could get no Rent yet paid the Taxes.'[47] In the same year, when attending the April meeting of the Bedford Level Corporation, he passed through a countryside 'almost overflowed from Cambridge to Ely, and found . . . that nothing could equal the general Distress'.[48] In February of the following year the *Norfolk Chronicle* reported that 'accounts from the fens in the neighbourhood of Ely are very melancholy: they are almost overflowed with water'.[49] Arthur Young gives a graphic account of the Burnt Fen disaster in 1777: 'the bank broke and most of the proprietors ruined'.[50] 'Look which way you will,' mourned James Golborne,

> you will see nothing but misery and desolation; go but half a mile from Ely, and you come to Middle Fen, a tract of sixteen thousand acres, given up and abandoned; there you see the ruins of Windmills, the last efforts of an industrious people.
> If to Ramsey, there you find more than ten thousand Acres occupied by the Waters, and see houses without Inhabitants, and lands incapable of Pasturage or Tillage.[51]

There was no end to the complaints. In 1782 the inhabitants of March were 'in great distress with Water', and addressed anguished appeals to the Bedford Level Corporation for assistance, 'as the season for Plowing is now, and we fear the season will be lost'.[52]

Inevitably the corporation came under heavy fire from its opponents. Its members were accused of being 'too greedy of the profits of their land, and were unwilling to tax it to the full, though its preservation depended thereon'. Poor drainage and indifferent navigation were alike attributed to the corporation's neglect: 'What might have been done, in a regular progression, with a trifling expense, will now cost an enormous sum to effect.'[53] An attempt to justify itself on the grounds of disastrous weather conditions provoked some tart rejoinders. James Bentham observed with his customary felicity:

Now all this is nothing more than saying, that if the adventurers had had no obstacles to contend with ... they would have made a much better bargain than they did ... Could they expect the winter seasons would be constantly kind ... against universal experience to the contrary!⁵⁴

The immediate need was for more money, and to obtain a measure of at least temporary relief the corporation, in 1777, petitioned Parliament for a bill, which was designed to exploit every possible financial resource.⁵⁵ Taxation within the Bedford Level was no longer to be restricted to the 95,000 acres of adventurers' land but was to be extended to all lands. A toll was to be levied on the tonnage of the navigations within the area for a stated period, or until the present difficulties were resolved. The bill elicited a howl of protest from the mercantile and landed interests alike, encountering fierce opposition at every stage. It was feared that the additional revenues would be 'all squandered away in private Jobbs and problematical Projects'.⁵⁶ There were great disturbances at Ely, where a large body of people congregated from all parts of the Fens, 'so that the Shire Hall would not hold them, and they adjourned to Trinity Church ... a general Riot began, and every Body got out of the Church as soon as they could'.⁵⁷ In the teeth of such fierce opposition the corporation abandoned the entire project. The bill proceeded no further than the second reading, after which it fell quietly into oblivion, without any alternative solution having been suggested and without an end of the difficulties being glimpsed.

But it was not all a picture of unrelieved misery and desolation. In good years the farmers raised exceptionally heavy crops from the rich Fenland soils, in fact 'as much wheat or coleseed in one year as would purchase the land on which it grew'.⁵⁸ It was this which heartened local farmers in their incessant battle against the floods.⁵⁹ But the landowner James Bentham realised the great dangers in what he called 'this very inequality of gain'. Farmers relied on its continuance, and organised their affairs on that assumption: 'they have been led on to expect the same advantages every year, which scarcely happen once in ten or twenty'.⁶⁰ In this connection it is not irrelevant to mention the case of the eighteenth-century rector, Thomas Jones, who married a rich

Chelsea heiress, and ruined her within three years by 'adventurous dealing in fen farms'.[61] In 1777 he was imprisoned in the Fleet for debts exceeding £38,000. It was the very unpredictability of fen farming which constituted a significant factor in the bankruptcy of so many individuals. Adverse weather conditions could exercise an appalling effect. What might cause hardship in other parts of England, or even benefit the farmer in some circumstances through increasing food prices, could well represent a catastrophe in an area entirely dependent on a system of artificial drainage. James Bentham attributed the decay of the fens to the want of adequate outfalls, in his view the 'principal occasion of all the mischief the country has suffered'.[62]

DRAINAGE ACTIVITY IN THE NORTHERN FENLAND

North of the Bedford Level lay Norfolk Marshland and also the great fens of south Lincolnshire, some 366,000 acres traversed by the rivers Welland, Glen and Witham. The Lincolnshire Fenland, before its reclamation, was composed of two parts. Of these the larger silt area, consisting of a level tract of alluvial or marsh land, was imperfectly drained and at some periods actually flooded. Interspersed amongst this were the peat fens, always more or less flooded in winter. In all these lands summer grazing was an important occupation.

Whilst great schemes were afoot in the southern Fenland the drainage of Lincolnshire and Norfolk Marshland had remained under the control of Commissioners of Sewers who were firmly entrenched. No serious attempt was made at unifying drainage administration or at evolving a comprehensive system of draining. In Norfolk Marshland the Sewer Courts were engaged in an incessant battle to maintain the banks of the Great Ouse in the teeth of repeated damage caused by the navigation interest and the indifference of local landowners. Apart from this, drainage effort remained localised and sporadic, lacking an overall purpose. This is not to suggest that the region was totally or even partially devoid of enterprises. During the late sixteenth and much of the seventeenth centuries there were many attempts to drain single fens or specific localities. However these schemes were invariably short-lived, successful for a time before being finally wrecked by those local inhabitants whose livelihoods had been placed in jeopardy or totally destroyed. Effort in general was much less consolidated than in the Bedford Level, where the very uniformity of terrain encouraged a unified enterprise. In the northern Fenland the disposition of highlands and coastal salt-marsh and silt carved the region into a number of distinct tracts, whilst encouraging the inauguration of a number of piecemeal enterprises.

As early as 1566 we learn of 'ordinances and decrees established at Sempringham, Co. Lincoln, by the Right Hon. Edward Lord Clynton and others, Commissioners of Sewers, for works in the fens there'.[63] In 1602 discussion was centred around 'the cleansing and repairing drains in the fen ground lying along the river Witham'.[64] Also at this period Thomas Lovell was appointed to drain Deeping Fen, 'a man skilful in like works, wherein he had been beyond the seas much used and employed'.[65] Deeping Fen, a low-lying region between the rivers Glen and Welland, posed considerable problems, and Lovell's efforts here were not attended with spectacular success. The expenses of the undertaking ruined him financially, despite his acquisition of a third part of the drained fen, allotted to him as a reward for his efforts. His works were almost certainly inadequate, and were not assisted by what William Dugdale termed the 'unseasonableness of the times, and riotous letts and disturbances of lewd people, casting down his banks'.[66] At all events Deeping Fen quickly relapsed into its former state. Another attempt to drain it was made during the second quarter of the seventeenth century, this time by a group of adventurers who inevitably included a Dutchman amongst their ranks. This was Sir Philibert Vernatti, that veteran of fen projects, who was at the same time venturing a part of his capital in draining the Bedford Level.[67] In the Lincolnshire Fens, free of the daunting shades of Vermuyden and the Russells, he achieved more personal fame, having a drain and a sluice named after him. The undertaking included, besides the construction of new drains and sluices, the improvement of the Welland outfall and the widening and dredging of the river. In 1637 Deeping Fen was officially adjudged to have been drained, a premature decision as

Plate 3 Two views of the Stretham steam engine; its 37ft-diameter scoop wheel is shown below

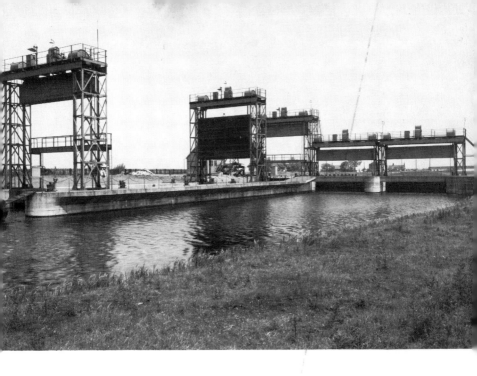

Plate 4 (above) The Dog-in-a-Doublet sluices and lock on the river Nene between Peterborough and Guyhirne; *(below)* bank piling on the river Nene at Wisbech

it turned out, which was reversed by the Wisbech commissioners two years later on the indisputable grounds that the fen was inundated in winter. A tax of 30s per acre was to be levied for further improving the drainage works, but due to the outbreak of the Civil War the project was never completed and Deeping Fen became flooded again.

During this same period the project of Sir Anthony Thomas and a group of adventurers was going forward in the East and West Fens, an extensive tract of land situated between the river Witham and the coast. Operations were commenced in 1631 and the work was completed three years later. The project encountered remarkable success in the first instance despite opposition from 'such Commissioners of Sewers and other persons as they conceive were most backward and refractory in that business'.[68] By 1634 we hear that the fens were 'already so well cleared that there is no doubt they will be forthwith fully drained'.[69] For seven years the adventurers continued in possession of their lands, building houses, sowing corn, and rearing cattle. At the end of that time disaster struck, abruptly terminating the success of the venture. The dispossessed fenmen 'in a riotous manner . . . fell upon the Adventurers, broke the sluices, laid waste their lands, threw down their fences, spoiled their corn, demolished their houses, and forcibly retained possession of the land'.[70] Attempts to drain the Holland Fens lying between the Nene and Welland, and extending northwards towards Boston encountered a similar fate. Subsequently a grant was made to a group of adventurers, giving leave to drain 72,000 acres of the fens between Lincoln and the river Glen. No record of anything being accomplished under this grant has survived.

But despite repeated setbacks efforts continued to be made. Negotiations proceeded for reclaiming individual fens, for example those between Bourne and Kyme (1635) and Peterborough Little Fen (1638). Between 1639 and 1640 the 'embanking and improving' of some of the Sutton marshes had been successful. But generally speaking it was one thing to obtain a grant for the work, quite another to get it done. A crop of difficulties beset every enterprise, resulting in much discussion and negotiation with little tangible being achieved. Even the personal

E

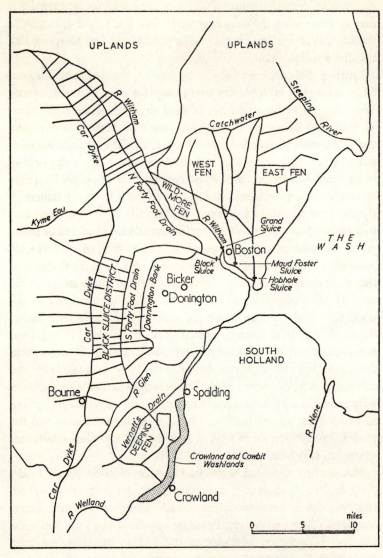

FIGURE 5. The south Lincolnshire Fenland: main drains

intervention of the Crown could not save projects in the Eight Hundred Fen near Boston from disaster. Charles I, to his credit, displayed an equal interest in the Lincolnshire undertaking as in those going forward, with more spectacular success, in the Bedford Level. Indeed he 'signified his resolution to have the whole level of the fens in Co. Lincoln drained'.[71] However his enthusiasm for the project speedily waned, and Sir Robert and Sir William Killigrew took over the enterprise. The South Forty Foot Drain, a major work between Bourne and Boston, was dug. Here we see an important application of the catch-water principle, the purpose of the South Forty Foot being to intercept the waters carried down by numerous small streams from the highlands, and to convey them into the Witham outfall near Boston, without passing through the centre of the fens. Much else was accomplished, land being enclosed and farmsteads established. All went well for a few years until the works were wrecked by the disgruntled fenmen who 'in contempt of all, entered and destroyed the drains and buildings; as also the crops then ready to be reaped, to a very great value'. They succeeded in retaining possession, 'to the great decay and ruin of those costly works, and exceeding discommodity to all that part of the country'.[72]

Vermuyden ascribed the difficulties experienced in the fens around Deeping to the narrow channel of the river Glen, which was unable to cope with the entire body of water pouring through it. The remedy he suggested was to widen the channel by setting back the banks from the river, 'four times so far asunder as now they are'. To drain the fens between the Glen and Morton's Leam he suggested a scheme for a 'cut-off' channel for intercepting the waters of the Glen, Welland and Morton's Leam and carrying them into the Nene and out to sea via Wisbech. He advocated widening the Nene from Guyhirne seawards, and further argued that by concentrating all the waters in a common outfall the channel out to sea would be improved. He estimated that the value of the Deeping and South Holland Fens would increase to £50,000 or £60,000 'if drayned this way'.[73]

But Vermuyden's recommendations were shelved for the time being, and even after the Civil War no major project was undertaken, and still no permanent improvement was achieved. Successes were frequently spectacular but invariably temporary. The Lincolnshire fens as a whole were 'wasted in the late times, and lie overflowed'.[74] Considerable discussion centred around the great East, West and Wildmore Fens; also round the North Holland Fens west of the Witham, formerly drained, however imperfectly, by the Earl of Lindsey. But still no conclusive decision could be reached. The Commissioners of Sewers, despite their glaring inadequacy in a number of respects, assumed full control of those few drainage works which had survived both the depredations of the fenmen and the neglect consequent upon the Civil War period. Nevertheless the Earl of Manchester, apparently undeterred by the persistent failure which had dogged the efforts of his predecessors, headed yet another abortive attempt to drain Deeping Fen. The work, undertaken in 1666, was nowhere near completion by 1671 due to 'the unseasonableness of the weather and other unavoidable accidents'.[75] Even when it was officially completed few landowners could command adequate resources to pay the drainage taxes. These proved disproportionately heavy due to the poor condition of their lands, a circumstance which was attributed to a continuous run of wet seasons and a drainage system still far from attaining even a semblance of efficiency. Conditions throughout the northern Fenland varied at different periods and from place to place, but it is safe to say that, during the century following the turmoil of the Civil War, even the land that had been drained reverted to its former condition and was flooded for large parts of each year. One writer who lived near Kyme Fen described its appalling state during the early part of the eighteenth century. He had

> times out of number ... seen cows loosed out of their hovels and swim across the water with nothing but their faces and horns above the surface, and then take footing at mid-rib-deep, but not one spot of dry land, and then forage till weary and return to their hovels by swimming. No place was more famous for this than Chapel Hill, inaccessible but by boat or riding horse belly-deep, and more in water than mud. I have also known in the whole parish of Dogdyke, not two houses communicable for whole winters round, and sometimes scarcely in summer. Sheep used to be carried to pasture in flat bottomed boats. Clip them in the boat and afterwards fetch them away in the same conveyance.[76]

The road which ran from the uplands on the edge of West Fen to Boston, known as the Nordyke and Hilldyke Causeway, was at times only distinguishable from the surrounding marshes by rows of willows. In places there were swamps which proved quite impassable to strangers in the locality; they were compelled to employ guides walking on stilts to lead them across.

It was not until the eighteenth century was well advanced that the work of draining was resumed. In 1738 an act relating to the drainage of Deeping Fen was passed. Its authors took a gloomy view of the situation, forecasting a large expenditure. The lands had

> for several years last past been and now are so overflowed with waters through the defects of their outfalls to the sea and other causes, that little or no profit can be made of them . . . the said fens can never be made profitable, unless some new methods be taken to recover the same, and which according to a scheme and estimate made thereof will cost about fifteen thousand pounds.[77]

Because the lands were low-lying it was necessary to lift the waters from them up into the drains. By 1763 there were fifty windmills operating in Deeping Fen alone. A few years later improvements were carried out to the Welland itself, including the construction of new sluices, and these measures seem to have effected a marked betterment in the condition of the fen. Nevertheless the large volume of water flowing down from the uplands was still far in excess of what the existing channels could take, and a certain amount of flooding was inevitable. An act passed in 1794 for improving the Welland outfall accomplished virtually nothing, as the proposed works were never completed.[78]

The South Holland Fens fared even worse. Here the coastal embankments were frequently out of repair and the sea broke through on numerous occasions. In 1796 drainage was to some extent assisted by the construction of the South Holland Main Drain, designed to carry part of the Welland waters direct to the sea via the Nene estuary. The North Holland Fens, despite the Earl of Lindsey's efforts in the seventeenth century, had remained unreclaimed. Their condition was appalling. In 1763 22,000 acres had been flooded, and in 1765 an act was passed for improving the lands lying between Bourne and Boston Haven.[79]

A major share of the problems encountered was ascribed to the poor state of the Welland and Witham outfalls. As a result the so-called Black Sluice was erected at the outfall into the Witham estuary of the South Forty Foot Drain, its purpose being to prevent a reflux of fresh or tidal water. As part of the same project several existing drains and sluices were repaired and improved. Individual tracts of land were reclaimed under a series of local acts, being first enclosed and then embanked against the floods.

The Witham Fens, lying to the west and east of the river, were also in a highly unsatisfactory condition, in large measure due to the defective condition of the Witham outfall. Boston Haven penetrated inland more than 20 miles from the sea, and was very winding and shallow, over some sections not more than 18 to 20ft wide. Also the Witham was fed by several large rivers and streams carrying down water from the uplands, and some of these watercourses were actually larger than the winding haven that formed their outfall. Consequently after rain and snow the capacity of the Witham was inadequate to contain the floods. The banks were frequently breached, and the adjacent lands laid under water often to a depth of several feet. This water stagnated, sometimes for three or four months at a stretch; the herbage was completely destroyed, and the land degenerated into an unprofitable waste. In the past several proprietors had endeavoured, at great expense, to protect their lands by the construction of private drains, embankments and mills, but without success. Among the most notable of these local efforts had been that of Earl Fitzwilliam in 1720. He, having applied without result to the Court of Sewers to drain his lands situated on the west side of the river, had resolved to undertake the work himself. He attempted a major project in cutting the North Forty Foot Drain to by-pass the worst bends in the Witham, to intercept some of the upland waters from entering the river, and to carry these in a direct course to the outfall at Boston. A sluice was built at the new drain's junction with the Witham, at Lodowick's Gote near Boston, to exclude the tidal flow. However the undertaking was not wholly crowned with success, due largely to an oversight to repair the river banks, which were in a deplorable condition. The waters overflowed the neighbouring lands, at the same time losing their velocity. Without an adequate current to scour the river-bed siltation increased daily, until the river-bed rose to within 2ft of the top of the banks. In some places the bottom of the river was actually higher than the level of the adjoining lands; being completely dried out it had been converted into grazing and farming land. Great quantities of sea sand were carried into Boston Haven, which was choked up over the entire distance from Boston to the coast. Even barges of 30 tons burthen could not reach the town on the neap tides.

In 1762 an act was passed for draining certain fen lands lying on both sides of the Witham.[80] The region was divided into six districts and the act provided for the management of each district by separate committees consisting of members elected from its parishes. To these were given the powers of levying taxes on the lands likely to profit from the scheme, and the charge of all internal drains together with the management of windmills. Rights of common were obliterated in many places, the lands being divided and allotted to individual owners, each one responsible for embanking his own lands. Many windmills were erected, and the entire region, intersected by a complex network of drains, came to resemble a gigantic chequer board. But many of the works originally envisaged were never carried out.

The Witham was widened and deepened over much of its course, whilst fishing weirs and other obstructions, which had hitherto hindered the free flow of the waters, were removed. The sides of the river were embanked to prevent the waters from pouring over the adjacent lands, whilst its discharge was improved by cleansing and deepening many tributaries and side drains. In October 1766 the centrepiece of the entire undertaking, the Grand sluice, was opened at Boston by the engineer Langley Edwards in the presence of 'a very large concourse of spectators'.[81] The sluice proved a dire disappointment to many who had come to witness the opening ceremony, and to one of the disgruntled visitors may be traced the authorship of the singularly unflattering rhyme:

> Boston, Boston, Boston!
> Thou hast naught to boast on,

> But a Grand Sluice, and a high steeple,
> A proud, conceited, ignorant people,
> And a coast where souls are lost on!

However the works proved of immediate advantage to the drainage of those fens bordering on the Witham. By controlling the tidal influx into the fens the Grand sluice in particular brought some measure of relief, although not enough to render the Witham Fens totally fit for cultivation. It was in fact criticised on exactly the same grounds as Denver sluice, ie that by excluding the tides the outfall was deprived of the 'weight and force of the returning ebbs', which would otherwise have scoured the channel, and facilitated the clearance of the floodwaters out to sea.

To the north the East, West and Wildmore Fens, forming an extensive tract of 40,000 acres, had failed to derive an atom of benefit from the Grand sluice or any of the other works. They remained a vast semi-swamp, with their interiors entirely flooded. The 'deeps' of East Fen were notorious. In 1769 the entire fen was

> in a state of nature, and gives a specimen of the country before the introduction of drainage: it is a vast tract of morass, intermixed with numbers of lakes, from half a mile to two or three miles in circuit, communicating with each other by narrow reedy straits: they are very shallow, none above four or five feet in depth.[82]

Any attempts at improvement remained entirely theoretical. Innumerable schemes were introduced in an atmosphere of intense rivalry which ensured their prompt rejection. The local fenmen opposed all reclamation schemes as a matter of policy, because they interfered with such established occupations as wildfowling, fishing and reed-gathering.

But fish, fowl and reeds were by no means the sole products of the northern Fenland. The newer coastal marshlands were predominantly devoted to arable farming, often producing heavy crops of corn and beans. Much of this land also proved ideal for sheep-rearing. Many localities, particularly the higher grounds further inland, became famous as feeding grounds for livestock; the chief products of these regions were meat, milk, cheese and butter. The silt zone of Lincolnshire, extending into Norfolk Marshland, was exceptionally rich grazing land. Early in the eighteenth century Thomas Cox had estimated the geographical extent of Marshland at about 30,000 acres, 'which turn to more Profit by Grazing than Plowing . . . The soil is so fat that *Tilney-Smeethe* alone is said to feed 30,000 Sheep which would be a great Advantage to the Inhabitants did not the Overflowing of the Sea much lessen it.'[83] In Norfolk Marshland the ravages caused by salt-water floods had continued with undiminished fury. The somewhat ineffectual efforts of the local Sewer Courts had little effect on the situation, even though they were empowered to investigate the responsibility for 'hurts and damages' and could 'tax, assess, charge, distrain and punish' those found guilty. Entries in the Norfolk Court of Sewers Minute Books do actually show them making use of these powers, as for example at a General Session held at King's Lynn in 1754:

> Whereas it was this Day presented by the Jury for the Hundred of Freebridge . . . that four rods and four feet of sea Bank of George Standall, Thomas Banks, and John Waterman lying in the Third Reach in Clenchwharton . . . and within the Jurisdiction of this court against the Great Ouse are very Insufficient for want of a Counter-Shore, [it was] therefore prayed that the said George Standall, Thomas Banks, and John Waterman might be Enjoyned by Order of this Court well and sufficiently to repair the said Counter-Shore by the first day of December next coming, or in Default thereof forfeit and loose to the Use of his Majesty the Sum of Ten Pounds.[84]

But there were so many like cases and so many defaulters that the grossly overloaded administration almost ground to a standstill under their accumulative weight. Nevertheless Norfolk Marshland as a whole was highly prosperous.

So also was much of the south Lincolnshire Fenland. Arthur Young described the grazing lands as 'the glory of Lincolnshire'. Cattle were brought here from other counties to be fattened, and both sheep and cows were exported in immense numbers to feed London's expanding population. We learn that the country between Wisbech and Holbeach in 1790 was 'flat, fertile and famous for breeding horses and cattle'.[85] Until its enclosure in 1801

Deeping Fen remained a vast tract of common land, producing 'exceeding store of grass and hay'.[86] Wool was exported from the Fenland to many parts of England, and in particular to the great weaving counties of Suffolk and Norfolk. But although some areas were eminently suitable for sheep-rearing, on the low-lying damper fens the sheep were extremely susceptible to disease. Hence Arthur Young noted that in 1793 about 40,000 sheep had 'rotted' on the East, West and Wildmore Fens.[87]

But it is extremely difficult to assess the actual condition of the drainage during the closing years of the eighteenth century. Reports from different localities at different periods were widely at variance, although it is apparent that disasters still occurred with disquieting frequency. Whilst one contemporary writer deplored the 'horrible collection of waters' in the Lincolnshire Fens, 'which at present yield us little else than pestilential air, rotten sheep, starved geese, and stunted cattle',[88] Arthur Young was drawing attention to the considerable improvement in the capital value of Deeping Fen 'by draining. Twenty years ago the lands sold for about £3 an acre; some was then let at 7s or 8s an acre; and a great deal was in such a state that nobody would rent it; now it is in general worth 20s an acre and sells at £20 an acre.'[89] Yet in 1800 another writer, William Chapman, sketched the condition of much of the northern Fenland as the reverse of satisfactory:

> Of the last six seasons four have been so wet that most of the new enclosed fens bordering on the Witham were inundated and the crops either lost or materially injured. Many hundred acres of the harvest of 1799 were reaped by men in boats. Of the oats fished up in this way some sold in Boston market at 25s per last, when good oats were selling at ten pounds.[90]

However even Arthur Young admitted that the general condition of the Fenland grew steadily worse during the last three decades or so of the eighteenth century:

> many inundations have taken place, and lately with increasing power and immense mischief. The remedies that have been applied by numberless acts of parliament, obtained with merely local and district views, have been in vain and nugatory, but the burden by taxes immense.[91]

The appalling condition of the outfalls was the traditional scapegoat, thrust to the forefront whenever an explanation was required to account for the deterioration of the Fenland during this period. Discussions regarding the problem proliferated as the century waned to its close.

7

The Great Outfall Controversy

MOVEABLE AS THE WINDE AND SEA

THE estuary of the Wash, as we have seen, receives the waters of the four rivers which drain the fens of Lincolnshire and the Bedford Level. Of these the Great Ouse takes the rainfall from 2,960 square miles of high land and fens, the Nene from 1,132, the Welland from 703 and the Witham from 1,050 square miles. The waters of these four rivers, flowing from an area of 5,845 square miles of country, find their way to the sea through shifting sands which encumber the head of the estuary. The course of the channels is constantly changing, and their position shifting, owing to alterations in the wind or tidal and freshwater currents. The strength of the ebb tide and land waters is thus exhausted in making fresh channels, instead of keeping a deep and rapid course. A foremost problem has been how to train the outfalls to deep water.

From the earliest times all the major difficulties associated with flooding in the fens were attributed to the defective outfalls of the Welland, Witham, Nene and Great Ouse. The river outfalls were, of course, of the utmost importance in the system of fen drainage; an open outfall ensured that floodwater could be discharged out to sea more rapidly. This was especially vital during periods of heavy rainfall or snow. Where an outfall was blocked by sandbanks these held up the floodwaters and prevented them reaching the sea. Farmers relied heavily upon the efficient functioning of the river outfalls for the preservation of their lands, the more so because the system of drainage by windmills was not altogether devoid of serious drawbacks. Among the most conspicuous of these was their inability to pump water from the fields into the rivers when the floods rose above a certain level.

However the clearance of floodwater from the fens was not solely dependent on the condition of the outfalls, important as this was. Another vital factor was the inability of the Fenland rivers to contain within their banks the full volume of floodwater required of them, a circumstance which threw the problems associated with peat shrinkage, the corresponding rise in the mean sea level, and the maintenance of the sinking flood banks into sharper relief.[1] Perhaps a major fault was that outfall difficulties had a tendency to be considered in isolation; that is, entirely divorced from their inherent connection with other equally urgent problems. This has been responsible in many localities for the absence of any really marked progress in draining until fairly recent years.

Outfall problems were no new phenomenon, traceable only as far back as the sixteenth or seventeenth centuries, but on the contrary were of long standing. By the close of the thirteenth century the Wisbech estuary was blocked with silt and sand, carried in and deposited on every tide, and comprised a vast expanse of marshland with a tiny stream of water trickling through the middle of it. The Witham and Welland estuaries were silted to a similar, if rather less spectacular degree. In 1375 the Welland through Spalding was said to be 'so filled with sand at every tide that it could not be cleaned'.[2] During floods the flow of water out to sea was much impeded. The Great Ouse was, if possible, in an even worse condition.

Silting in the outfalls may be attributed to (1) the very slight gradient of the river-beds, (2) the inadequacy of the resulting slow-moving currents as scouring agents, (3) unusually strong tidal action in the Wash, against which the abnormally weak action of the freshwater currents could not compete, and (4) the presence of an exceptionally long ebb-tide with scarcely any momentum. The above points require a little additional explanation.

The sea-bed of the Wash consisted of silt and sand so extremely loose as to be 'moveable as the winde and sea forces them'.[3] Vast quantities of this sand were torn up and carried into the rivers by the force and impetus of the incoming tide, but could not be carried away again because the long ebb was too weak to clear the channel. The weak ebb also had the effect of damming back the land waters in their passage to the sea. Such conditions favoured the deposition and accumulation of silt. Sir William Dugdale had noted the difficulties associated with the Fenland river estuaries:

> Whosoever hath observed the constant tides which flow up the river of Ouse, at Lynne, will find the water always very thick and muddy there; because the sea, bearing a larger breadth northwards from thence, worketh with so much distemper: It is no wonder, therefore, that a great proportion of silt doth daily settle in the mouth of that ostiary, and likewise in the other, viz. of Wisbeche, Spalding, and Boston.[4]

It was essential to find a means of increasing the velocity of the freshwater currents and of shortening the long, slow ebb of the tide for the purpose of providing a sufficient current to dredge the outfall channels. Dugdale advocated as a remedy 'some artificial helps to quicken the current upon its evacuation at every ebb . . .'[5]

The wretched state of the Fenland river outfalls provoked endless controversy during the eighteenth century, but the obstacles in the way of finding a material solution were immense. There was an acute conflict of divergent interests. Delays occurred whilst engineers and landowners debated the merits or demerits of rival schemes. Even when a plan was finally agreed upon there still remained the problem of raising money for the huge capital expenditure required. The invariably long drawn out parliamentary proceedings involved in obtaining an act of parliament – essential when any large-scale work was envisaged – caused further delays. Meanwhile silting in the outfalls not only aggravated flooding inland, but gave rise to complaints from traders that the rivers and harbours were becoming too shallow for ships. Henry Ashley, a proprietor of the Great Ouse Navigation in Huntingdonshire and Bedfordshire, like the rest of his contemporaries, betrayed a complete ignorance of the root cause of the trouble. He acknowledged that silting caused many grievances, but observed that 'the Cause of this Evil, and the proper Remedies to it, are the subject of much variety of opinion'.[6]

Outfall problems dominated every discussion. The construction of the great sluice over the Ouse at Denver and of the Grand sluice across the Witham at Boston, by stopping the tides and penning back the land waters, thrust into prominence the entire question of the erection of drainage sluices across tidal rivers. Both Colonel Armstrong and Thomas Badeslade condemned the construction of the sluices and recommended a return to the principle of a free tidal influx, on the now familiar grounds that the ebb-tides increased the ability of the freshwater current to dredge the channel.[7] They campaigned specifically for the removal of Denver sluice – or what remained of the troublesome 1713 wreck. Badeslade argued at considerable length that before the construction of Denver sluice the great quantities of seawater ebbing out of the Ouse and its tributaries, combined with the freshwaters twice every 24 hours, had acted as a scour on the channel of the river below Denver, whose beneficial effects had extended 10 miles to seaward. According to Badeslade it was a direct consequence of the loss of this scour that silting began in the channel between Denver and Lynn Haven.[8] But whatever the arguments for and against Denver sluice there can be no doubt that the process of silting from the latter half of the seventeenth century onwards became so severe that the bottom of the Ouse, originally 14ft below the level of the adjacent lands had, by 1725, become in several places 'as high as the Soil of the Fens'.[9] Naturally contemporary engineers and others directly affected – as for example navigators and farmers – were acutely disturbed by this horrifying phenomenon.

Badeslade was convinced that it was not simply the check which the tides received at Denver, but also their diversion out of the Great Ouse into the Hundred Foot river, which lay at the root of the trouble. The Hundred Foot, being narrower and shallower than the old river, could absorb only a comparatively limited flow of water, which caused a stagnation of the remainder against the sluice 'at least an Hour'. The tides, 'finding a Resistance there ... make a Stand until the Flood be almost half run; by which means the Silt and Sand which the Tides bring up in great abundance, have time given them to fall and settle'.[10] In this way vast quantities of marine silt were deposited in the river below the sluice which, it was asserted, the diminished ebb could not clear away. Badeslade described how he found the river-bed at Lynn so badly silted that 'People frequently walk over, where anciently Ships used to ride afloat at Low-water.'[11]

The Grand sluice at Boston provoked intense criticism for similar reasons. The tidal stream, arrested in its progress by the sluice, stagnated; the silt and mud brought up and held in suspension whilst the water was in motion, sunk directly stagnation took place, forming a deposit on the bed of the Haven. In dry seasons the sluice doors were invariably blocked with silt, which occasionally accumulated to a depth of 10ft. When the doors were very badly silted – as for example during the 1799 summer – the water failed to drain away when the heavy rains came, and vast acreages were flooded. John Rennie advocated the removal of the Grand sluice, comparing its adverse effects on the outfall with those commonly associated with the sluice at Denver: 'which by stopping the flow of the tide up the Ouse damaged Lynn Harbour'.[12]

However before the close of the eighteenth century outfall disputes had, partially at least, taken another direction. In 1720 Charles Kinderley had called attention, not so much to the problems associated with sluices on tidal rivers, but rather to the tortuously winding, wide and shallow outfall channels of all the major Fenland rivers.[13] The great bend of the Ouse above King's Lynn, describing almost three parts of a circle, was especially deplored because, by impeding the free flow of the current, it encouraged siltation. To overcome the difficulty Kinderley had suggested a straight cut from Eau Brink near Wiggenhall St Germans to the upper end of Lynn harbour, an idea which, in 1751, was revived by his son Nathaniel. Its ostensible purpose was to eliminate the 6 mile detour, improving both the gradient and scour of the river. It was hoped that the resulting increased velocity would enable more water to be run out of the fens at greater speed.[14] However none of the arguments in favour of the scheme produced any immediate action.

The state of the Nene below Wisbech was also deplorable. In 1745 Labelye found it 'greatly obstructed with many loose sands, frequently shifting by the various actions of the winds and tides'.[15] During the short space of time between June 1721 and June 1723 the channel had moved a mile towards the east.[16] Even a gale of

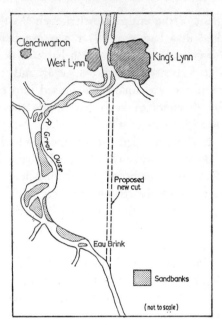

FIGURE 6. The proposed Eau Brink Cut, after N. Kinderley (1751)

wind was sufficient to cause considerable alteration in its course; wrecks were frequent. This state of affairs rendered the upkeep of the North Level drainage works virtually impossible, due to the difficulty of running water out of the fens with sufficient speed to prevent breaches in the banks. Charles Kinderley had suggested that embankments be made to confine the outfall to one comparatively narrow channel through the sands as far as Peter's Point, 7 miles below Wisbech. He hoped that by these means a fall of something over 5ft would be obtained. His suggestions were adopted by the Bedford Level Corporation, which entered into an agreement with the town of Wisbech for the execution of the project. The partnership proved an unmitigated disaster. The work started, but before its completion the Wisbech authorities, fearful for their harbour and the loss of its navigation through a diminished tidal inflow, took steps in the Chancery Court to halt the undertaking. The whole unfortunate episode aroused violent passions; ill-feeling ran high and considerable litigation ensued, all to no avail. The work was suspended for fifty years, delaying the improvement of the entire North Level: 'In the meantime, Wisbech exulted in a bad river.'[17] It was not before alarming breaches had occurred along the north bank of the river Nene, entailing serious expenses in 1763-4, 1767 and 1770 that the Wisbech Corporation was finally galvanised into taking action. Confronted by disasters of such magnitude the fever of the opposition abated, and in 1773 the Tydd and Newton Drainage Act was passed. This provided for the opening and extension of the long-abandoned work. The finished channel was called 'Kinderley's Cut' as a memorial to its principal advocates. It lowered the water of the North Level by 5ft, whilst considerably improving navigation from the sea up to Wisbech. But improvement was short-lived, and the state of the river Nene once again became a subject of general complaint: 'so much so,' wrote Samuel Wells, 'that a respectable alderman of Lynn facetiously observed, that he regularly attended the river Nene meetings, until he saw on his way thither, persons making hay in the bed of the river; after which, he thought such attendance perfectly unnecessary'.[18]

The Bedford Level Corporation has sometimes been pilloried for its attitude to the outfall question, and in fact it may seem surprising that nothing concrete was achieved in the way of improvement until the early nineteenth century.[19] In justice to the corporation it should be borne in mind that its attempts to remedy the Nene outfall and the consequent enforced abandonment of the project through misplaced caution or inertia on the part of the Wisbech authorities, had constituted an obvious deterrent towards any further attempts at improvement. A considerable capital had been dissipated and a continuing shortage of money acted as an added disincentive towards undertaking a really major project. Also the corporation had been buffeted by a long chain of disasters, which by degrees had conditioned its members into a far from positive attitude towards their responsibilities. Whilst accepting liability to maintain the drainage works according to the terms of the 1663 contract, any suggestion that they ought to concern themselves with remedying the all too obvious defects in the existing system was repudiated. Nevertheless the corporation lent its support, after initial vacillation, to the idea of a straight cut from Eau Brink to King's Lynn on the Great Ouse. It was hoped that by confining a wide, shallow waterway into a comparatively narrow channel the velocity of the current would be increased and hence its scouring action. Twenty years were consumed in discussing plans for the proposed work. In 1795 the first Eau Brink Act was passed.[20]

OUTFALL PROJECTS

In 1664 Colonel William Dodson had stressed the need for efficient river outfalls: 'if we cannot be master there, all other endeavours signifie nothing'.[21] By the beginning of the nineteenth century outfall improvements were still regarded as a matter of supreme urgency. It was by then all too apparent that the drainage efforts of the seventeenth and eighteenth centuries had encountered only partial success. In 1793 the state of the Huntingdonshire Fens, comprising roughly 44,000 acres, was described as 'disgraceful'. They were 'constantly either covered with water or at least in too wet a state for cultivation'.[22] Very considerable portions of the fen districts were occupied by meres, 'awful reservoirs of stagnated water, which poisons the air for many miles around, and sickens and frequently destroys many of the inhabitants, especially such as are not natives'.[23] In Cambridgeshire in 1794 there were 200,000 acres of waste and unimproved fen, compared with 50,000 acres which had undergone some form of reclamation. Charles Vancouver walked over every parish in the region in order to obtain reliable information. Except on foot he could not penetrate into the recesses of the district. The roads were impassable, and almost everywhere we hear of the 'deplorable condition of the drainage' and the 'miserable state of cultivation', which prevailed on the open field lands.[24] In Lincolnshire the East, West and Wildmore Fens were 'under better regulations than any others in the fen country', but even these were 'extremely wet and unprofitable'.[25] The drainage works still encountered isolated pockets of resistance: hence 'Any attempt in contemplation of the better drainage' of Burwell Fen on the Suffolk border, 'constantly inundated', was 'considered as hostile to the true interests of these deluded people'.[26] Arthur Young was emphatic that the fens were 'in a moment of balancing their fate; should a great flood come within two or three years, for want of an improved outfall, the whole country, fertile as it naturally is, will be abandoned'.[27] As if to lend emphasis to his prophecy the spring floods of 1808 caused damage 'to the amount of at least *One Million*'.[28] As late as 1827 many people were still 'fearful of entering the fens of Cambridgeshire lest the Marsh Miasma should shorten their lives'.[29]

As the discharge of floodwater from the fens was so extremely unsatisfactory it was popularly supposed that the appalling state of the outfalls in the Wash represented the hard core of the difficulty. It was felt that if this problem could be solved all would be well. Unfortunately delays in executing the improvements were unavoidable for a number of reasons, of which the most conspicuous were shortage of capital coupled with frequently high interest rates. The Bedford Level Corporation, still the main drainage authority in the southern Fenland – howbeit with diminished powers – continued to be crippled by financial difficulties which rendered it incapable of meeting even its existing obligations, without the added burden of fresh projects. The smaller drainage authorities were in a similar plight. Charles Cole attributed the corporation's troubles to 'the Decrease in the Value of Money' and the 'Increase of the Value of Labour and Materials necessary for carrying on and supporting their Works'.[30] What he was implying in effect was that in an era of rising costs the corporation could not rely on a steadily rising revenue to at least maintain the balance. Wage inflation – always the enemy of large-scale undertakings – constituted a factor of at least mild significance in the eighteenth century Fenland. Here, even when conditions were normal, wages, especially for labourers employed on bank work, were rather above the national average, including even London where levels generally speaking were higher than elsewhere.[31] This may have been due to the demand in the fens for more meticulous workmen (bank work was somewhat exacting), to the greater irregularity of employment (most of the work, apart from emergencies, was completed during the summer months), and to competition at haymaking, harvest time etc between the various drainage bodies and local farmers for the services of labourers.[32] Evidence for the exact percentage of inflation to which corporation costs were subjected is rather too sparse to be conclusive, but there is no doubt that some difficulty was being experienced in this field, otherwise Cole would hardly have made a point of mentioning it.

Rising interest rates, especially during the Napoleonic Wars, constituted another setback to the undertaking of large projects. During the first phase of the conflict in particular, construction work throughout England as a whole was inevitably curtailed by the national shortage of capital; men hoarded their money and there was a run on the banks. To carry on the war the government resorted to its customary practice of raising loans from the public by guaranteeing high capital returns on its stock. There was a general increase in the cost of borrowing money, yet despite higher interest rates money was unprocurable. There was an absolute dearth of uncommitted capital in London and in 1795 the registrar of the Bedford Level Corporation exhorted the engineer James Golborne to use every means in his power to obtain funds locally in the fens. He was able to raise £600, although with extreme difficulty. By 1799 the situation had deteriorated still further, and again the registrar urged Golborne to borrow money locally. The fact that in war time money had a tendency to flow out of the provinces to the capital, and was deflected from private to public use, probably accounts for why James Golborne's desperate search for a loan was no more successful in the fens than that of the registrar had been in London.[33]

Meanwhile in many instances money wages throughout the Fenland approximately doubled, influenced by the national shortage of manpower due to the expansion of employment in the armed forces and industry.[34] However, this situation changed completely after the war. Then the slump in food prices throughout England, coupled with the slackened demands of industry, resulted in a widespread shortage of work amongst labourers, whilst men demobilised from the armed forces drifted home, only to swell the ranks of the unemployed. The abundance of manpower correspondingly cheapened the labour market, whilst after 1815 interest rates fell back to their pre-war level. It is significant that a real boom in drainage construction took place during this period, deriving an impetus from the post-war deflation, and in this way demonstrating its sensitivity to national economic conditions. Nevertheless in some localities these benefits were offset in some degree by the acute difficulties – through falling agricultural prices – of many farmers, making it impossible to raise large sums of money immediately. The situation was in fact so bad in the Wisbech area that in 1822 the Wisbech Corporation urged that proposed improvements between the Nene outfall and Peterborough be postponed at 'this period of unexampled Distress as tending materially to encrease the Burthens of the landed Interest already so heavily oppressed'.[35]

Of the drainage improvements which can be traced to the post-war years those executed to the fen river outfalls from 1817 onwards had considerable significance, however temporary or local. Various remedies were tried, involving cuts, training walls and harbour improvements near King's Lynn, Wisbech, Spalding and Boston, with the aim of concentrating the discharge from the rivers into narrow, defined channels so that, instead of dissipating its energy over a large estuary, the increased velocity would tend to be self-cleansing and maintain an open outfall. It was hoped that deeper, confined channels would accelerate the passage of the land waters out to sea, counteracting any tendency for a long, slow ebb to retard their clearance before the next flood-tide. Prominent amongst these projects were the improvements carried out to the Great Ouse and Nene outfalls. The Bedford Level Corporation did not itself undertake these works as its financial resources were quite insufficient to meet the necessary capital expenditure. It did, however, take up the forefront position in the campaign to obtain parliamentary authority, particularly for the construction of the Eau Brink Cut in the Great Ouse tideway. Confronted by the prospect of the considerable advantages, financial as well as technical, to be gained, it left no stone unturned to ensure that the Eau Brink Bill became law, and in the intensely febrile atmosphere which the bill provoked it inevitably bore the full brunt of the strong opposition which emanated from many quarters, and with particularly virulent force from the navigation interest.

Even though the situation encouraged the circulation of every form of voluminous mis-statement, it should have been obvious to all that the corporation lands on their own account could not sustain the high level of taxation essential to capitalise the undertaking. The misrepresentations circulated by James Bentham[36] and others, which were as wild as they were malevolent, and the resolution passed by the Eau Brink Navigation Commissioners that the corporation should draw on its 'vast Funds' to complete the works 'unjustly imposed on others',[37] were a long way from meeting the true facts of the case. Really such comments constituted part of a deliberate campaign waged by the owners of non-corporation land and the navigation interest to evade their share of the financial responsibility for the proposed works.

Despite the opposition many individuals pinned great hopes on the successful completion of the new cut. The Earl of Hardwicke considered the project

> likely to prove in its consequences the most effectual plan that has been suggested for the improvement of the Fens since their original drainage in the last century by the Earl of Bedford. It is an object of great importance, in a national view, to bring into a more certain state of cultivation a considerable tract of country, the produce of which is comparatively small, and to render fruitful other districts that now produce neither corn nor herbage, and are incapable of any cultivation at all.[38]

Even lesser individuals, as 'Talbot, a poor man of Downham', were hopeful of the outcome. Talbot had

> built himself a hut in this fen ... At last the floods increased so as to drive him away, and now he lives in the town of Downham. The fen was too wet to let him make a garden; but if the eau-brink cut was made, and he had a house there, he would, he says, soon have a garden, and a little farm too, if they would let him.[39]

After long and bitter controversy the cut was finally completed in 1821 by the contractors Joliffe & Banks, although on the advice of Thomas Telford its dimensions were subsequently enlarged by a third. The immediate effects seem to have been extremely beneficial, and Telford expressed himself completely satisfied with the results of the new work:

The effect of the new cut, after this enlargement, has exceeded expectation. During the first winter after it was opened, the river-channel from Denver Sluice to Lynn was scoured and deepened five feet, on an average; Between Lynn and Denver Sluice, the whole bed of the river Ouse, including the Eau Brink Cut . . . has since gradually deepened itself nearly fifteen feet, on an average, so that the outfall sluices of the drains on each side of the river, and the beds of the drains may now be lowered to a corresponding extent, and the expense and uncertainty of windmills may be in a great measure avoided. Advantage, however, has not been taken of the improved means of drainage afforded by the Eau-Brink Cut in the interior of the Middle and South Levels, so that there are nearly as many windmills as ever, but their efficiency is increased by the more rapid discharge of the waters resulting from the improved outfall.[40]

It was the success of the Eau Brink Cut which seems to have given a decisive impetus to the execution of similar works on the river Nene. In August 1821 it was resolved to make an outfall cut from Gunthorpe sluice to Crabhole, 'this new cut being the foundation of all the other improvements, and combining in itself the most important benefits to drainage and navigation'.[41] As in the case of the Eau Brink Cut the money was to be raised by the imposition of an acre tax on all the lands most likely to benefit from the project, as well as from a tax on navigation. It was the 'Continued Depression in the prices of all kinds of Agricultural Produce and the increasing Distress under which the Occupiers of Land are now labouring' which delayed the start of the work for some years.[42] In July 1827, as soon as the economic situation had improved, the enterprise commenced. The work was undertaken by Joliffe & Banks, still flushed with triumph from their recent success at Eau Brink. The Nene Outfall Cut was opened in 1830. As an essential part of the scheme the Nene above Kinderley's Cut was straightened in alignment by the Woodhouse Marsh Cut, completed in 1832 and sometimes called 'Paupers' Cut' because it was constructed by labourers thrown on the poor rate.[43] Once again Thomas Telford was pleased with the results of the venture. At Wisbech the bed of the Nene was lowered by approximately 10ft by the increased scouring action of the current. From the extra fall gained in the river the neighbouring silt

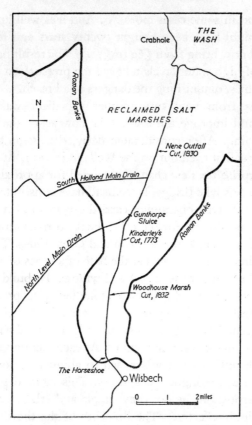

FIGURE 7. The river Nene outfall

lands derived a natural drainage without having recourse to pumping engines of any sort. The North Level benefited considerably from the improved outfall, a circumstance of which the commissioners for the Level were quick to take advantage. They constructed the North Level Main Drain between 1831 and 1834. This was dug from Clough's Cross to Tydd Gote, discharging its waters into the Nene outfall, and replacing the tortuous route of the old Shire Drain, besides being 8ft deeper and having a six times greater capacity. The Nene outfall works exerted an immediately beneficial effect. It was stated in evidence before a committee of the House of Lords in 1848 by Tycho Wing 'that the value of land in some parts of the North Level had increased 100 per cent, and in some cases more ... And it is well known that land that might have been bought twenty years ago for £5 per acre, would now bring from £60 to £70.'[44] The resulting speedier reduction of high water levels relieved the pressure on the banks at critical times, diminishing the dangers of a breach.

But apart from new cuts another expedient was used to straighten and improve the lower tidal courses of the rivers by fascine training. After considerable delay, discussion and argument this was first tried out on the Welland in 1837. At this stage of the enterprise the new channel extended for approximately 1½ miles below Fosdyke Bridge. It seems to have constituted the first instance of this type of training carried out in England, but the expedient was adopted for the other Fenland river estuaries at a later date, for example the Witham and Great Ouse. The design of the training walls consisted at the base of a series of mattresses constructed of reed, brushwood and willow. To build the walls thorn faggots, protected by rubble stone facing to prevent their 'being washed up by heavy freshets or torn from their place by ice', were used.[45] The faggots were initially weighted with clay or sods, and laid in the water in sections. As each section sank others were added, until a bank was raised to about half-tide level, ie just covered at the highest neap-tides. This method proved for practical purposes to be not only simple and relatively inexpensive, but highly effective: 'The branches of the thorns interlace one with another, and the silt brought up by the tides rapidly deposits amongst and at the back of this fascine work, and thus a solid embankment is formed, of sufficient strength and tenacity to withstand the strongest tidal current.'[46]

Outfall works were also being executed on the Witham. Schemes proliferated, with effort being concentrated on the channel below the Grand sluice, notoriously defective. In 1812 an act had been passed for the improvement of Boston harbour, which provided for the dredging of the estuary between the Maud Foster sluice and the Grand sluice.[47] Twelve years later Sir John Rennie lent his support to a project for a seaward cut from the Maud Foster sluice via Hobhole sluice to Clayhole. By an act of 1827 the meandering course of the river was shortened by a straight cut 800yd long.[48] In 1841 attempts were made to train the channel by fascine work, although the project was confined by the usual shortage of money. The works generated some improvement although the outfall still remained unsatisfactory in a number of respects.

Meanwhile in the interior of the Fenland the condition of drainage was still far from perfect, despite the concentrated effort and many improvements of recent years. This was particularly so in the Middle Level, which was networked by a complex system of drains, for the most part running parallel to each other and to the outfall. The problem of discharging surplus water was acute. The outfall into the Great Ouse via Well Creek and Tong's Drain had proved to be completely inadequate. In 1810 the Middle Level had obtained an act to improve internal works, but despite an expenditure of £80,000 little progress towards an improved drainage had been made.[49] 'And I am not surprised at it,' commented F. A. Ruston, a Chatteris solicitor:

> for when I stood the other day and looked at the two little openings from Well Creek into the Tong's Drain, through which nearly the whole of the Middle Level waters had to pass, I felt amazed that the owners of Middle Level land could, even for a short time, have rested contented with such a miserable apology for drainage.[50]

Against a background of seething discontent and the flooding of almost the entire Middle Level in the winter of 1841–2, various schemes had been brought forward, but even in this crisis no clear policy could be formulated. The various rival groups were 'swallowed up by one another, and nothing seemed likely to be done'.[51] Finally a plan submitted by the engineer James Walker had been adopted. Under the provisions of an act of 1844 he had cut the Middle Level Drain, about 12 miles long and 50ft wide at the base, with sloping sides and confined by strong banks.[52] Designed to lower the water level by 6ft, it ran from the north end of the Sixteen Foot river, through Norfolk Marshland to the Eau Brink Cut near Wiggenhall St Germans. Near the point of entry into the Great Ouse the Middle Level sluice had been built. This consisted of a bridge with three arches, each with a 20ft span, resting on piers and flanked on both sides with walls to support the adjacent banks. Each of the arches enclosed a pair of great oak doors, which constituted self-acting sluices, allowing the waters to pass outwards, whilst preventing tidal water from entering the drain. The cost of the scheme was about £650,000, the money being raised by dint of a heavy acreage tax on the lands benefiting from the project; also the Bedford Level Corporation made an annual contribution in return for being relieved of liability for the future maintenance of Tong's Drain. The scheme had represented a considerable improvement on the previous arrangements, as the Middle Level waters were now discharged into the Ouse 9 miles nearer the sea, thereby reducing the volume of water requiring outlet by Well Creek and Tong's Drain. Having secured this improved outfall Walker had next attempted to adapt the internal works of the Level to the new cut, increasing the dimensions and depths of several existing drains where this proved necessary. The works were enormously expensive, and hence a considerable burden on the Middle Level farmers. The £200,000 outlay initially authorised by the 1844 Act was quickly swallowed up, and by an act of 1848 a further sum of £250,000 had been raised on the security of an additional acre tax.[53] For some years there was a marked improvement in the condition of the Level, but eventually disaster struck. In May 1862, due to excess water pressure, the Middle Level sluice collapsed, admitting the tidal waters of the Great Ouse, and causing extensive flooding in Norfolk Marshland. Fortunately many of the farmers had sufficient warning to enable them to remove much of their livestock to a place of safety:

> But the homesteads, crops, implements, and those goods which were not easily removeable were soon covered with water to a depth of several feet, causing great destruction of property in a district of much fertility, rich with the promise of valuable crops. The Wisbech and Lynn railway line was under water, the trains being sent via Ely, while the telegraph poles were carried away and the adjacent country was like an inland sea.[54]

A dam and siphons erected to re-drain the area never proved a wholly satisfactory expedient, making the construction of a new sluice in 1880 essential.

Apart from this there were still problems in all the river

estuaries. The difficulties encountered in the Witham were typical of all Fenland outfalls. The estuary was

> shallow and full of shifting sands, which are gradually but surely extending and gaining on the sea. The great quantities of mud held in suspension by the waters discharged from the rivers in time of flood mixes with the silt washed up by the tides; the two opposing currents meeting, stagnation takes place and a deposit is left, which the backwaters are not strong enough entirely to remove.[55]

In 1882 we find the engineer W. H. Wheeler complaining that the river Nene was 'in a most unsatisfactory condition' and the outfall 'encumbered with sand'.[56] The state of the Welland was equally deplorable. Here the fascine walls were too short to be of much use. The river discharged 'into a sand bed 4 miles distant from deep water; in fact, it may be said that when the water leaves the fascine work it no longer has any defined channel, but meanders over the sands, continually shifting its course'.[57]

Although much had been achieved, with a correspondingly spectacular advance in the overall prosperity of the region during the first half of the nineteenth century, the real difficulty of providing a sufficiently rapid discharge of floodwater to alleviate the pressure on the flood banks remained largely unsolved. No amount of work on the outfalls could alter the fact that the rivers inland, almost without exception, represented a potential danger to the lands they were supposed to drain. Although outfall improvements, by accelerating the flood discharge out to sea, were of fundamental importance, if carried out in isolation they could only produce temporary or partial benefit in reducing water levels inland. Some means of lowering the surface-gradient of the river waters during floods had to be found. This vital problem was bequeathed to the twentieth century.

8

The Turning-point

THE POWER OF STEAM

WITH the improvement of drainage and the continued sinking of the land satisfactory gravity drainage from field to drain and from drain to river proved impossible. As we have seen windmill pumps had been introduced to lift field water into the drains, although this expedient ultimately proved inadequate and unreliable. Windmills had not sufficient power. Even the system of double-lifts in no sense represented a permanent solution. Because windmills were not able to guarantee a satisfactory drainage their gradual substitution by steam-engines was inevitable, constituting a technical innovation of considerable significance. Although other improvements played their part, the steam-engine was undoubtedly the most vital single factor that converted the desolation described by Arthur Young in 1805 into the rich arable and pasture lands for which the fens became famous.[1]

Windmill drainage was attended by so many disadvantages that it is surprising that the changeover to steam did not take place earlier than it did. Although Rennie had recommended the use of Watt's steam-engine to pump the water from Bottisham and Soham Fens as early as 1789, the innate conservatism of the fen-men made them cleave to their unsatisfactory windmills for almost another thirty years. They were extremely reluctant to apply the new ideas. There was considerable prejudice against the use of steam, coupled with a general unwillingness to scrap existing arrangements, however imperfect, in favour of untried expedients involving the investment of large sums of money. But the weaknesses associated with windmill drainage ultimately convinced most people that a change was desirable.

Windmills possessed a considerable drawback in that they frequently flooded the lands they were supposed to drain, or lands adjacent. Thomas Neale had attributed the appalling condition of Manea, situated in the Middle Level, partly to the fact that 'A great number of these mills throw their waters directly upon Manea.' He complained that rents in the parish had depreciated so much that 'the whole lordship, taken together, is reduced, I believe, to one half the rent it was let at thirty-five years ago . . . great part of it being wild and waste, and in as bad condition as it was at the general draining'.[2] Windmills besides were vulnerable to changing weather conditions. Lack of wind rendered them completely inoperative, often during periods of heavy rainfall when they were most needed. This was a frequently reiterated complaint: 'we have but too much reason to fear the mills will not be commanded when we stand in need of them'.[3] John Rennie emphasised that windmill drainage was 'very imperfect and expensive . . . especially when wet weather is succeeded by calm weather, the mills cannot work, and therefore the water lies on the surface of the Fens, and does incalculable injury'.[4] A considerable wind velocity was necessary before the mills could work effectively. It sometimes happened that windmills remained idle through lack of wind for as long as two months at a stretch. William Swansborough, an engineer with wide experience of Fenland drainage problems, estimated that the windmills worked an average of one day in five.[5] Almost as serious a disability was that when water-levels rose too high the mills could not pump; the windmill could lift water only about 5ft. For these and other reasons John Rennie thought that 'a Windmill drainage is the most imperfect of all modes and in many cases the adoption of such a mode may be said to be a useless waste of money'.[6]

Steam-engines were not handicapped by any of these disabilities. They could work at any time, unhampered even by periods of relatively hard frost because they usually had sufficient power to break the ice. Conversely windmills were equally incapacitated by frost and thaw; during a frost they were frozen solid and when the thaw came, and with it the floods, water-levels in the channels rose too high for the windmills to work against them. The great advantage of steam-engines lay in their ability to clear the drains during frost, so that when snow and ice melted on the land, the level of water in the drains was low enough to take excess water. Also steam-engines were labour-saving. A large engine, manned by an engineer and a stoker, could do the work of many windmills.

Many engineers, among them John Smeaton, had predicted that steam would one day drain the fens, and even before the year 1800 the possibilities of employing steam-engines seem to have been seriously entertained. In 1789 the commissioners of the Middle Fen District near Ely demonstrated their interest, even to the point of authorising one of their members, Robert Wild, to obtain estimates of the likely cost of an engine. Nothing materialised from his inquiries at this time; nevertheless the interest of the Middle Fen commissioners gave an indication of future developments. Most contemporary writers were unanimous in their approval of steam. In 1794 Thomas Stone wrote:

> Wherever engines are necessary to facilitate a drainage, I recommend the steam-engine, to accompany the wind-engines in a considerable work; because it too frequently happens, that a calm succeeds an abundant fall of rain, for a considerable length of time.[7]

Arthur Young in 1805 noted that

> the application of steam-engines to the drainage of the fens, instead of windmills, is a desideratum that has often been mentioned, but not yet executed: When it is considered that the windmills have been known to remain idle for two months together, and at seasons when their work is most wanted, it must be evident that the power of steam could nowhere be employed with greater efficacy or profit.[8]

In 1811 Richard Parkinson ventured to 'observe, that water engines in this and many other places would be much better worked with steam, than wind'.[9] However several writers, like Thomas Stone, did not immediately envisage the exclusive employment of steam-engines throughout the fens as a whole, but rather saw them as useful supplements to the existing windmills. In the initial stages steam-engines were often built with this end in view. Many early suggestions were for small engines to work in

Plate 5 The 1947 floods: *(above)* inundated farmland in Haddenham Fen; *(below)* pumps which helped to save the fens from disaster: the interior of the Tydd pumping station, showing four sets of engines

Plate 6 (above) The River Welland Major Improvement Scheme: the Spalding Coronation Channel. The confined course of the river through the town centre is clearly visible in the background; *(below)* The Great Ouse Flood Protection Scheme: view taken on the completion of the Tail sluice

conjunction with windmills, or even for engines coupled to windmills to work the scoop-wheel when there was no wind. They also helped the windmills during a period of calm by pumping deep water out of the drains; when the wind finally blew water-levels were reduced to a height which the mills could effectively handle.

The decision to erect a steam-engine rested with the commissioners of each local drainage authority. There was no general or uniform policy throughout the fens, every district making its own arrangements. Each engine had to be adapted to local conditions. In some localities there were legal difficulties to surmount. It would appear that the first steam-engine for drainage purposes was built at Sutton St Edmund near Wisbech.[10] This seems to have been in full working operation by about 1817. Although its life span may have been comparatively short – it no longer served a useful purpose after the completion of the North Level Main Drain in 1834 – it was the forerunner of many others, some of which were in use for almost a century before their ultimate replacement by diesel engines. The annual operating cost of the Sutton engine was about £200. According to Tycho Wing, the Duke of Bedford's agent in the North Level, it had 'only a twelve horse power . . . and drains upwards of 4,000 acres'.[11]

After Sutton St Edmund others quickly followed. For a span of 150 years or so the windmill had played a vital, if inadequate, role in the economy of the region. The success of the steam-engine sealed its fate. Everywhere windmills disappeared before the rapid advance of steam. In 1820 a 30hp engine (increased to 80hp in 1843) was installed along the Ten Mile Bank of the river Ouse, approximately 3 miles south of Denver sluice. In the same year a 30hp engine was built at Borough Fen in the North Level. However like the engine at Sutton St Edmund this became redundant on the completion of the North Level Main Drain, which effectively substituted the need for a mechanical drainage with a natural gravity one. Also in 1820 the Swaffham and Bottisham drainage commissioners consulted John Rennie about the possibilities of a steam-engine for their district. Some delay was experienced, pending the result of an argument about whether the customary scoop-wheel or a pump should be employed.

Rennie's preference was for a pump, although he was the last man to ignore the ingrained prejudices and possible limitations of the fenmen at this time:

> I think it is not very probable that they would keep it in order and as the scoop wheel is quite familiar to fen men — I believe it will be best on the whole to adopt the scoop wheel.[12]

In 1821 a 24hp engine was finally installed.

By 1825 Deeping Fen (25,000 acres) was being drained by two steam-engines, one of 60hp the other of 80hp. March West Fen was drained by a 40hp engine, completed in 1826. In 1829 an 80hp condensing beam-engine with a steam pressure of 15lb per square inch was installed on the Hundred Foot Bank to assist the Ten Mile Bank engine in draining the Littleport and Downham district. Two years later the 60hp Stretham engine was completed to drain the 5,600 acres of Waterbeach Level, situated between Cambridge and Ely. From 1832 onwards the switch from wind to steam was greatly accelerated. Before that year the tax on sea-borne coal – increased to high levels during the French Wars – had inflated the price of sea coal in England by about 25 per cent. The repeal of the tax may in some part account for the rapid increase in the number of steam-engines throughout the Fenland after 1832, deriving an impetus no doubt from the falling price of coal, which effectively reduced overhead running costs. In 1832 Middle Fen near Ely (about 7,000 acres), Waldersea District against the east bank of the river Nene (about 6,500 acres), and Pinchbeck in Spalding Marsh (over 4,000 acres) were all being drained by steam-engines.

It is significant how great a number of windmills one steam-engine could replace. Stretham engine superseded four windmills, a comparatively modest number when compared with some. The achievement at Littleport Fen was more spectacular. The civil engineer, Joseph Glynn, an early pioneer in the use of steam throughout the region, commented:

> Before steam power was used, there were seventy-five windmills in this district; and often has the Fen farmer, in despair, watched their motionless arms, and earnestly hoped a breeze might spring

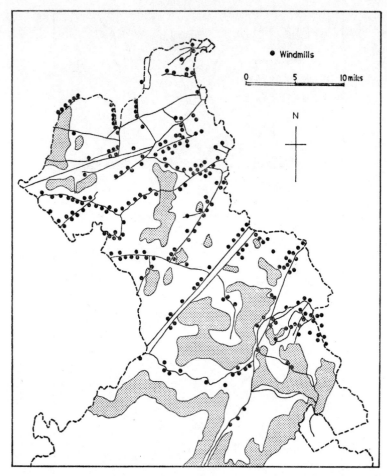

FIGURE 8. The Bedford Level: windmills, from 'Map of the County of Cambridge, and Isle of Ely', surveyed by R. G. Baker (1821)

up to catch their sails, whilst his fair fields gradually disappeared below the rising waters, and the district assumed the appearance of an immense lake.'[13]

In 1848 J. A. Clarke remarked on the subsequent improvement: 'Littleport Fen . . . was formerly badly drained by 75 windmills but there are now two 80hp engines, one of which raises about 40,000 gallons per minute.'[14] In the Waldersea District, before the

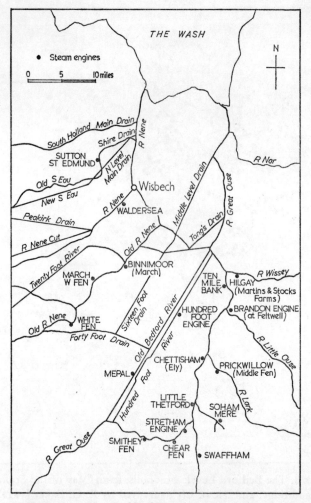

FIGURE 9. The Bedford Level: steam-engine sites

advent of steam, the existence of a colossal number of windmills, which included many private ones erected by farmers to pump the water from their lands, could not save the region from frequent inundation: 'previous to the erection of the powerful steam engine... at certain periods of the year, boats went over the land, which was the habitation of wildfowl'.[15] According to J. A. Clarke the total of windmills in the Fenland as a whole had once exceeded 700; by 1852 their number was reduced to about 220. He estimated that seventeen steam-engines were employed in the Lincolnshire Fens, ranging from 10 to 80hp, and forty-three in the southern Fenland:

> They lift water from 6 to 16 or even 20 feet; and the area of land which they drain may be computed at not less than 222,000 acres. This rapid application of an unfailing though costly power to the performance of duties hitherto entrusted to the changeful and often disastrous caprices of the wind, is a striking example of agricultural progress.[16]

The quantities of water discharged in each individual case were impressive. For example the engine draining March West Fen raised 70 tons per minute, and the Waldersea engine 63 tons. The latter 'appears to have done its work well', wrote S. Jonas in 1846, 'for immediately after the erection . . . the lands were laid dry and splendid crops of corn grown the first year. I went over this land just after a flood, and the lands were as dry as any in the country.'[17] It was the same story at Spalding Marsh. Until the Pinchbeck engine was built in 1832 the land was 'very wet . . . and great numbers of sheep caught the rot; it is now a beautiful district of good rich land, of clay and silt containing between 4,000 and 5,000 acres'.[18] This engine was a 20nhp low-pressure condensing beam engine, driving a scoop-wheel of 24ft diameter and 2ft 2in wide, the scoops being 5ft long. The wheel made seven revolutions to twenty-eight of the engine, and worked against an average head of 5 to 6ft, rising to 8ft in floods. An unusual feature of the Hundred Foot engine in the Littleport and Downham District was that its scoop-wheel could be worked at two different speeds according to conditions in the tidal Hundred Foot river. At high tide this was adjusted to discharge 21,980 gallons of water, and 32,880 gallons at low tide.[19]

The increased power that steam provided enabled somewhat larger scoop-wheels to be used than the 25ft which had been the maximum practical diameter for those driven by wind. 'The Scoop Wheel as now used,' wrote W. H. Wheeler in the 1860s,

> resembles a breast water wheel with reverse action. In its simplest form it consists of an axle, upon which are fastened discs, to which

are attached radial arms, terminating in a rim, upon which are fastened arms with boards, called scoops, floats or paddles. The wheel revolves in a trough, connected with the drain on one side and the river or place of discharge on the other. The scoops lift the water from the lower to the upper side, the waterway on the river or outlet side being provided with a self-acting door which closes when the wheel stops. These wheels vary in size, up to 50ft in diameter. The largest in this district are those at Podehole, for the drainage of Deeping Fen, which are 31ft in diameter.[20]

Scoop-wheels did vary somewhat in size. The engine at March West Fen drove a 28ft diameter scoop-wheel, whilst the scoop-wheel of the Stretham engine originally had a diameter of 29ft. As the continued peat-shrinkage made this inadequate it was subsequently increased to 33ft in 1848 and to 37ft by 1896. The last wheel, which was equipped with forty-eight paddles each 2ft 6in wide, was able to lift 30 tons of water on each revolution. With a normal work-rate of 4rpm it could therefore raise 30,000 gallons, ie 120 tons, of water per minute. The largest scoop-wheel in the fens, which was fitted to the Hundred Foot engine in 1881, had a diameter of 50ft with sixty paddles, and weighed 75 tons. This superseded a scoop-wheel of about 41ft.

In the earlier days of steam drainage scoop-wheels were almost universally employed throughout the fens, the most notable exception being the Waldersea engine. This worked a bucket-pump, designed to cope more effectively with conditions in the tidal river Nene. Although windmills sometimes drove this type of pump, for draining a small area it was not in general popular for the simple reason that the valves and working parts were liable to become clogged with weeds and mud. Scoop-wheels possessed many advantages, and were in fact preferred throughout the fens. They were simple to operate and easily repaired. They could pump out a phenomenal amount of water per revolution when the drains were full, and so lowered the water-level for the first few inches very quickly. They inspired enormous confidence:

> To the minds of those living by the side of the rivers and drains of low flat countries and accustomed to the slow practises of an agricultural life, there is a sense of power and solidity about a massive beam engine, with its slowly revolving fly wheel and

heavy beam, rising and falling, driving a ponderous water-wheel, lifting a large mass of water.²¹

But scoop-wheels, despite the great services which they rendered to the fens, were not completely devoid of drawbacks. They were exceptionally heavy and cumbersome. A wheel with a diameter of 30ft weighed between 30 and 40 tons, hence requiring very heavy foundations and expensive masonry for the wheel race. The slow-speed engines essential for driving the wheels were themselves exceptionally ponderous, and also needed weighty foundations and a large area of buildings. Scoop-wheels were

> very wasteful of power, and badly adapted to meet the alterations in the level of the water due to the falling of the level on the inside, as the water is pumped out of the drains, or on the outside, due to the rise and fall of the tide; or of flood waters in non-tidal rivers.²²

Gradually pumps were brought into wider use, the most notable being the Appold centrifugal pump. This had been an object of intense wonder at the Great Exhibition, where it was first demonstrated. Many people, among them J. A. Clarke, were fully aware of the relevance of its application to fen problems: 'its light disc running rapidly with but little friction will most probably supplant the scoop-wheel, which slowly revolves with many tons weight upon its axle'.²³ The pump's performance at Whittlesey Mere assured its future.

Whittlesey Mere in Huntingdonshire, at this period about 1,000 to 1,500 acres in extent, was the largest of the remaining, and now rapidly diminishing, Fenland meres. As the shallowing became more apparent a group of local landowners, in conjunction with the Middle Level commissioners, financed a scheme to drain it. Although the Mere had constituted something of a local amenity, being widely used for fishing, boating and, in winter, skating, there seems to have been little or no opposition to its draining. The presence in the locality of so large a concentration of water, threatening a severe flood in the event of a bank breaking, was felt to be a potential danger, which explains why all the neighbouring inhabitants were unanimously in favour of the project. The Mere was finally drained, after initial setbacks, by an

Easton and Amos horizontal-spindle Appold centrifugal pump, with a revolving fan, driven by a 25hp double cylinder beam-engine, capable of drawing the waters out of the Mere at the rate of 1,500 to 1,600 gallons a minute, against a 6 to 7½ft lift. The water was discharged out to sea via Bevill's Leam, the Middle Level Drain, and the Great Ouse. The episode marked not merely the end of one epoch but the beginning of a new one.

Once started work on the Mere had progressed rapidly and 'the wind, which, in the autumn of 1851 was curling the blue water of the lake, in the autumn of 1853 was blowing in the same place over fields of yellow corn'.[24] The annual value of the Mere, which had been £1,160 before draining, was now £12,350.[25] After this spectacular success centrifugal pumps became increasingly popular and their use gradually spread. A great advantage of centrifugal pumps over scoop-wheels was their ability to adapt themselves much more rapidly to varying lifts, whilst they automatically adjusted the work thrown on the engine as the lift varied. Also more modern engines with faster revolutions could drive the pump, replacing the heavy, slow-speed engines essential for driving the scoop-wheels. Nevertheless it was universally agreed that the centrifugal pump lacked the psychological advantages of its rival. It could hardly be expected, in the initial stages at least, to inspire the same confidence as the massive scoop-wheel, 'in place of which the small parts of a centrifugal pump, with its rapid movements, seem but a poor substitute'.[26] Even though the pump – which, being smaller did not require such heavy foundations or such a large building to house it – was cheaper to install, the idea still persisted that scoop-wheels were equally as efficient 'and are preferable on account of their being . . . simpler to manage and less liable to wear and tear'.[27] Even so the advantages of the pump were too obvious to be ignored. In 1867 centrifugal pumps were being used to drain the East, West and Wildmore Fens of Lincolnshire. Yet another Fenland drainage milestone had been passed.

FROM CHAOS DREAR

Apart from, or in spite of, isolated disasters, most parts of the Fenland achieved a more stable economy during the first half of the nineteenth century. In addition to the introduction of steam pumping there were other factors which, although individually less spectacular innovations, contributed none the less to the increasing prosperity of the region. During the first three or four decades of the century, in particular, a number of improvements were carried out in the interior of the Fenland, involving banks, channels and sluices.

In Lincolnshire the elder John Rennie was reaffirming his profound belief in the system of catchwater drains, first advocated by Vermuyden in 1638. Rennie traced the causes of flooding to the great quantity of water which entered the fens from the highlands, and considered it essential for the water descending from a higher level to be prevented from mixing with the local fen water and overriding it, whilst causing it to stagnate 'at points the most difficult to relieve'. For this purpose he recommended that the Cardyke should be dredged and brought back into use as a catchwater or receiving drain to intercept the floodwaters flowing down from the uplands. These waters were to be channelled into the North Forty Foot Drain, and so discharged out to sea. By this means the adjacent fens would be greatly improved. These recommendations, although not carried out in the Black sluice district, to which they specifically applied, achieved more practical success in the East, West and Wildmore Fens. In 1800 Rennie submitted two reports on the possibilities of draining these fens, which failed, however, to gain unanimous acceptance.[28] But despite great opposition, particularly from the commoners who dreaded the loss of their traditional livelihoods, an act was passed in 1801 and work commenced.[29]

Rennie divided the upland from the lowland waters and conveyed them separately through the fens in question. An extensive main drain was cut through the West and Wildmore Fens to the Maud Foster sluice on the river Witham. This drain measured from 18 to 30ft wide, and was dug so that it achieved a fall of 6in to a mile. The sluice itself was improved with lifting gates, one set pointing towards the Witham in order to keep out the tides and river floods, the other set to landward, to prevent the water from draining too low in summer, thereby disrupting navigation and the irrigation of the land. The waters of the East Fen were carried

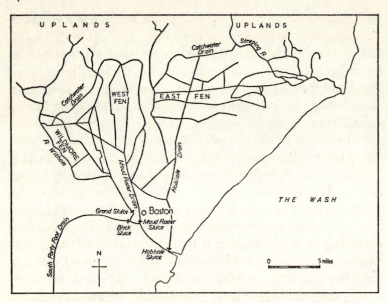

FIGURE 10. The Wildmore, West and East Fens: main drains

out to sea by the new Hobhole Drain, a straight cut dug about 40ft wide, and with a fall of 4in to a mile towards the sluice at Hobhole. This drain in particular was an immense work, defended by great banks to prevent its waters flooding the surrounding fields. Both of these cuts ran through the centre of the districts they were designed to drain. A network of smaller channels, together with catchwater drains carried round the base of the highlands skirting all three fens, were constructed to feed the upland waters into them, without otherwise being allowed to mix with the fen drainage at all.

Shortage of money delayed the work and it encountered some opposition. One Lincolnshire landowner remarked:

> Our fine drainage works begin now to show themselves, and in the end will do great credit to Mr Rennie, the engineer, as being the most complete drainage that ever was made in Lincolnshire, and perhaps in England... notwithstanding the excellency of Mr Rennie's plan, we have a party of uninformed people, headed by a little parson and a magistrate, who keep publishing letters in the newspapers to stop the work, and have actually petitioned Sir

Joseph Banks, the lord of the manor, against it; but he answered them with a refusal in a most excellent way.[30]

Sir Joseph Banks' support for the project turned out to be more than fully justified. By the drainage of Wildmore and West Fens 40,000 acres of valuable land were completely reclaimed, and within a few years were yielding heavy grain crops. From East Fen two to three crops of oats were ultimately harvested in rapid succession. The cost of the works had amounted to about £580,000, against which had to be set the value of the lands reclaimed. The increased net value of the drained lands was estimated at £81,000 per annum.[31] It was unfortunate that, due to the very rapid peat shrinkage following this otherwise successful project, recourse ultimately was had to steam-engines. In 1867, as we have seen, centrifugal pumps were being used to assist in the drainage of the locality.

Meanwhile in the southern Fenland the Bedford Level Corporation, having screwed up the rents of its properties whilst inaugurating cut-backs in expenditure by dint of stringent economies, was at last able to adopt, for possibly the first time in its history, some form of planned strategy. Its attainment of greater financial stability at this period made the undertaking of a comparatively ambitious construction programme possible. In 1809 the corporation spent more than £9,000 on the drainage works still under its care, which included £3,600 expended on improving the north barrier bank of the Old Bedford river and £2,505 on the south bank of the Hundred Foot.[32] Between 1821 and 1832 all the major sluices under its control were either extensively repaired or completely rebuilt: Denver in 1821, Stanground in 1825, and the Hermitage in 1826. In the same year a new sluice was erected at Salter's Lode, incurring an expenditure of £7,000, whilst in 1828 the Old Bedford sluice was rebuilt.[33] Finally Denver sluice was completely reconstructed in 1832 from a design of Sir John Rennie.

A project at Welmore Lake, at the northern extremity of the washlands lying between the Old Bedford and Hundred Foot rivers, was of especial significance. Here, between 1825 and 1826, expenditure on works, which included the construction of a sluice, dam and tunnels, topped £5,000.[34] The new works replaced wholly inadequate arrangements. In 1756 a dam had been built at Welmore Lake for the purpose of excluding the tidal inflow along the Hundred Foot river from the washlands. This had proved an extremely unsatisfactory and cumbersome expedient. Samuel Wells outlined the reasons why in a letter to the Duke of Bedford. During floods the major part of the upland waters of the Great Ouse passed down the washlands, confined by the Old Bedford and Hundred Foot barrier banks. At these times a space had to be opened in the centre of the dam to facilitate the clearance of these waters out of the washlands. But once the floods had subsided the dam had to be rebuilt, at considerable expense to the Bedford Level Corporation: 'Your Grace will, I think, smile at such a system of drainage.'[35] It was to end this anomaly that the corporation constructed Welmore Lake sluice, which enabled floodwater to be discharged out of the washlands with comparative ease. Even so the work did not escape criticism. J. H. H. Moxon unflatteringly compared the 'endeavour to drain the Welney Wash quickly by means of this paltry hole' to much the same thing as trying to 'empty the great butt of Heidelberg by

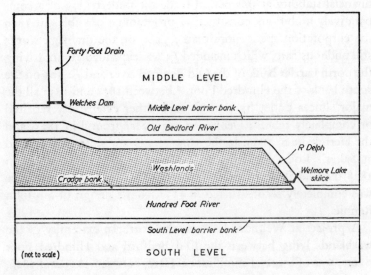

FIGURE 11. Welmore Lake sluice, the cradge and barrier banks

making a hole in the bottom of it with a packing needle, while two people on the top are assiduously pouring water into it with buckets'.[36] Nevertheless a vast improvement had been effected. There were many others. Between 1825 and 1838 the Bedford Level Corporation undertook additional repairs to the Hundred Foot banks. The Hundred Foot channel was widened and dredged. Of the capital required to finance these various projects more than £20,000 was borrowed from private individuals through the medium of bonds, £7,252 was obtained from voluntary subscriptions, from individuals or private drainage districts benefiting directly from the works, and the remainder was allocated out of the ordinary revenues of the corporation.[37]

But the Bedford Level Corporation was by no means the sole active drainage authority in the southern Fenland at this time. In 1824, for the purpose of improving the discharge of the Ouse floodwaters into the washlands, the Hundred Foot Wash commissioners built the Seven Holes sluice at Earith, replacing the existing Nine Holes sluice. Between 1827 and 1830 the South Level commissioners straightened the Ouse by a cut running from a little below Ely to Sand Hill End near Littleport bridge, a scheme which had been discussed at intervals for more than two hundred years, but never accomplished. This measure effectively eliminated the great bend in the existing waterway flowing into Burnt Fen, thus increasing the velocity, and hence the scouring action, of the current. In conjunction with this project a massive dredging operation was carried out in the Great Ouse and some of its tributaries, notably the Cam from Clayhithe to its junction with the Great Ouse and the Lark up to Swale's Reach. The undertaking also included within its scope many of the drains flowing into these rivers. A further dredging operation involved the Old West river between its junction with the Cam and the Hermitage sluice. It was becoming heavily silted, and constituted a serious menace to the drainage of the locality. This work was undertaken between 1836 and 1838 by the Eau Brink commissioners.

Other developments improved the condition of drainage throughout the Fenland at this period. A method of strengthening the banks, then widely adopted, was the system called 'puddling'.

This entailed opening the bank to a depth of several feet and inserting strong gault or clay:

> and to make the clay resist water, a man in boots always treads the clay as the gutter is filled up. As the fen moor lies on a clay the whole expense of this cheap, improved and durable mode of water-proof banking, costs in the fens only sixpence per yard.[38]

As this method came into more general use seepage through the banks, which had hitherto posed a perennial problem, gradually diminished, thereby reducing the volume of water which needed to be pumped from the lands.[39]

There is no doubt that improved drainage immeasurably increased the prosperity of the region. The report of William Bower in 1814 underlines the very altered condition of the East, West and Wildmore Fens after John Rennie's catchwater project had been completed: 'It is satisfactory to state that every wished-for object in the drainage of the whole of the fens and of the lowlands adjoining is effectually obtained, and the lowest land brought into a state of cultivation.'[40] That this improvement was sustained is apparent from the comments of another writer almost half a century later:

> The rapid waters of the upland becks are intercepted by catchwater drains surrounding the district, whilst the sluggish fen-water seeks the outfall through canals upon a lower level. The fields are now divided by neat whitethorn hedges, and the surface, both of clay, silty loam, and peat earth, is under a high state of cultivation.[41]

Nothing could exceed the enthusiasm of William Cobbett, travelling through the Fenland during the spring of 1830. He was very impressed by what he saw.[42] The country between Ely and Cambridge was one of 'corn and pasture, of fat sheep and fat oxen'. In the Lincolnshire Fens there were 'more good things than man could have the conscience to *ask* of God'. All the way to Boston there was 'endless grass and endless fat sheep: not a stone, not a weed'. By 1847 S. Jonas was referring to the Cambridgeshire Fens as the 'most productive and most valuable land in this country'.[43] Although no absolute mastery of drainage problems had yet been achieved, and whilst allowing that there was still much scope for improvements, the Fenland was, on the whole, a 'fruitful and salubrious country' of rich soils, lush pastures, fat livestock, and abundant, luxuriant crops.[44]

Farming improvements went hand in hand with improved communications. After the opening of the Eau Brink Cut navigation on the lower reaches of the Great Ouse became correspondingly easier, with tonnage figures demonstrating a steady increase.[45] The effects of the Nene Outfall and Woodhouse Marsh Cuts, dug between 1830 and 1832, were also decisive. Vessels were no longer stranded on the sandbanks a few miles below Wisbech. By mid-century, 'Instead of the uncertainty of former times, a vessel can now sail with the utmost regularity, and may safely calculate on the passage from Wisbech to the sea offering no obstruction to her voyage.'[46] It is significant that the port's tonnage figures climbed from 55,040 in 1829 to 108,000 by 1836, reaching over 167,000 in 1847.[47] Works carried out to the Witham outfall had a similar effect; vessels of 300 tons could now penetrate up to Boston.[48] Improved communications undoubtedly gave an impetus to agricultural expansion. Before the advent of the railways there were few areas with better transport facilities. A network of navigable waterways intersected the Fenland whilst other regions were still largely dependent on the packhorse and execrable roads. In this sense the navigations were of the greatest economic value, giving 'aid to agriculture, and spirit to trade; and tend to lessen the number of horses which are the greatest devourers of the produce of the earth'.[49]

But this was only echoing the opinions of an earlier writer, who had pointed out that a waterman could carry as much merchandise with one horse 'as the Carters do with 40'.[50] Land carriage had long been considered a precarious occupation, incompatible with the best forms of husbandry. The appalling condition of the midland roads, where the heavy clays for long defeated even the most primitive attempts at road mending, lent strength to this opinion. Produce could be shipped via the Fenland navigations to such towns as Peterborough, Spalding, Stamford, Bedford, Cambridge, Newmarket, Wisbech and London, and even as far afield as Yorkshire and Lancashire. Cattle and sheep were sent to Rotherham by water from the Lincolnshire

Fens: 'By this means they can be conveyed very commodiously and saving the loss of 3s a-head by driving.'[51]

With the coming of the railways and the decline of navigation there was no loss of hard-won prosperity. The obvious technical superiority of the railways in speed and relative cheapness soon became increasingly apparent to all. Even those farmers who had feared railway expansion quickly discovered that they could get their supplies more cheaply, as well as gaining access to the best markets for their livestock and produce. The increase in the number of railway lines throughout the fens, by extending markets and reducing transport costs, also increased the letting value of farm land, the actual extent of the increase depending, of course, on the proximity to a station. But of equally decisive importance to the Fenland at this time was that technical improvements and expanding communications had been paralleled by more effective soil utilisation. The improvement in general agricultural practice was one of the great factors which contributed to the steadily increasing prosperity of the Fenland during the first half of the nineteenth century.

9

The Post-drainage Economy of the Fenland

THE BEDFORD LEVEL: PATTERNS OF AGRICULTURE

AFTER the deceptively successful termination of Vermuyden's project, the 300,000 or so acres which comprised the southern Fenland were placed under the direct or indirect control of the Bedford Level Corporation. Of these, 83,000 acres of so-called 'adventurers' land' were directly vested in the corporate body, although their individual tenure was freehold.[1] Their owners could convey, lease or devise the lands without restriction or interference from the board, apart from the obligation to register all ownership changes at the Fen Office, a measure designed predominantly to clarify the identity of the tax payers. The 83,000 acres of corporation land were divided into twenty lots or shares, each lot containing land, not in a single consolidated block, but dispersed in various parts of the Level, and rated for taxation purposes on the assumption of eleven differing values.[2] Of the 12,000 acres allotted to the Crown, the King granted 2,000 to the Earl of Portland, and after 1692 the remaining 10,000 acres also passed out of the royal control. They were granted to Arthur, Earl of Torrington, 'in consideration of his good and faithfull services, and in support of his dignity of Earl'.[3] A clause in the Tax Act of 1667 permitted the King's share to be taxed by the corporation, and changes in ownership exercised no effect on this provision.[4] The remaining lands within the Bedford Level, the so-called 'free lands', were completely outside the corporation's jurisdiction so far as fiscal arrangements and general management were concerned, but the board could intervene where channels, banks or other drainage works were being systematically neglected. The board could also construct drainage works in any part of the Level, whether on free or adventure land, and seems to have had authority to requisition essential materials.[5]

The process of enclosing the adventurers' lands first began in 1637–8 and was completed by about the mid-seventeenth century. These enclosures formed part of a national and continuous enclosure movement which, commencing in England in the sixteenth century, continued steadily throughout the seventeenth, eighteenth and nineteenth centuries. So obvious were the advantages that the General Draining Act of 1663 had permitted the enclosure even of non-corporation land.[6] This had proceeded to such an extent – large parts of the commons and wastes being cut 'into small pieces' – that by 1684 the practice was considered 'very prejudicial'. The enclosures were effected haphazardly, without any uniform plan, and seem to have been productive of confusion and inconvenience. It was alleged that much ground was wasted in division dykes; that there were disputes between parties, and that the practice entailed 'great diminution of stock and decay of houses', because many persons were 'selling their shares of common from the house it belongs unto, to a greater impoverishment and increase of the poor'.[7] The Enclosure Prevention Act of 1684 repealed the right to make any further enclosures in the Bedford Level, although confirming those already made.[8] The continuing predominance of commons following the passage of this statute indicates that the open field system was never widely distributed in the locality. In fact, with the exception of a few parishes in the neighbourhood of Ely, the fen lands as a whole at no time constituted a part of the common field system. Further proof of this is furnished by the enclosure awards of the eighteenth and nineteenth centuries relating to fen parishes, which show the total acreage of open field arable enclosed to have been conspicuously sparse.[9]

There were irrefutable arguments in favour of enclosure, a foremost one being that the owner or occupier retained complete control of his land, without the necessity of having constant reference to the activities of his neighbours. In the case of arable land he was not tied to a system of crop rotation common to an entire parish, and which might not suit his own individual requirements. In the case of pasture land such arguments derived added emphasis from the wretched condition of some of the fen commons, over which a large number of commoners exercised grazing rights. These commons were supposed to encourage idleness by providing the bare necessities adequate to support life. Also their indiscriminate stocking with every variety of domestic beast and fowl generated diseases of all kinds. Such a system offered unlimited scope for trespass, and led to frequent quarrels and litigation. Grunty Fen near Ely was a case in point. This common contained 1,300 acres, of which 400 were corporation land and hence private property. The remaining 900 acres were used as common by persons having grazing rights in Ely, Stretham, Wilburton, Wentworth and Witchford, to name but a few of the parishes represented. All claimed the right of grazing a miscellaneous variety of beasts on the common, 'without stint or limitation of number, which are generally turned loose, and left usually without keepers, to shift for themselves . . . In consequence of this negligence and ill management, the cattle, for want of shelter, and being thus exposed to the inclemency of the weather . . . suffer greatly.'[10] James Bentham complained of the losses the commoners sustained 'by frequent trespasses and encroachments on each other'. 'Not one in ten' of the commoners derived any advantage from it.[11] The more disciplined cultivation of the adjoining corporation lands obviously stood out in marked contrast to this disorder, and may have initially provoked Bentham to campaign for the division and enclosure of the common.

That the fen lands before enclosure were not realising their full potential is apparent from the example of Peterborough Fen. This consisted of about 7,000 acres of 'fine level land, of a soil equal to any perhaps in the Kingdom of Great Britain, and susceptible to the highest cultivation'.[12] The fact that it was dangerous to stock in its existing waterlogged state did not prevent its being depastured by the horses, cattle and sheep of thirty-two parishes in the Soke of Peterborough. 'Considering the present mode of management,' wrote James Donaldson, 'it is impossible that any advantage can arise to the persons having right therein.' But in his opinion the land, if properly drained, enclosed and tilled, would yield considerable crops, and be capable of employing from 1,300 to 1,400 labourers.[13] The immediate rise in the value of the majority of the fen commons, once enclosed, was frequently spectacular. William Gooch quotes a number of examples in the southern Fenland. He found that in Doddington, for instance, improved drainage and enclosure had 'advanced the commons in this parish . . . in value from 2s to 30s per acre', whilst at Bottisham rents more than doubled: 'on prospect of enclosing, fen land advanced six-fold'.[14]

On the enclosed lands throughout the Bedford Level small lot cultivation was prevalent to an unusual degree, whilst the dearth of large estates in the locality obviated the possibilities of absorption by a more powerful neighbour. According to J. Bateman only 11 per cent of the county of Cambridge was occupied by estates which exceeded 10,000 acres;[15] in the fen region around Ely the proportion was considerably less. This low density of estates can be traced directly to climatic and scenic disadvantages. The general unattractiveness of the fens for residential purposes outweighed other considerations such as relative proximity to London, and the chance of acquiring cheap land whenever the floods threatened. Hence there was at many periods a comparative dearth of external investment in the area, because commercial and industrial magnates hesitated to sink their fortunes in a region so conspicuously uncongenial. Some members of the Bedford Level Corporation noted the difficulties of inducing settlement in the fens, 'with all the prejudices and all the unhealthiness which formerly attended such situations'.[16] Because the fens repelled rather than invited residence both farmer and labourer invariably lived in a neighbouring town or village, rather than on the land itself.[17] No peer had his principal estate in the region. Although the Earl of Hardwicke owned about 2,000 acres of fen, his seat was at Royston, just over the Hertfordshire border. The Duke of Bedford, it is true, had Thorney, but even his chief residential estates were in Bedfordshire and Devon. In a sense the fens to the south were almost as persistently shunned after the general draining as they had been in the days of St Guthlac.

It was the absence of estate building which gave an unusual

degree of prominence to the small landowner. Because the soil was rich and the yield per acre unusually high, the region attracted a host of small farmers and cultivators. From the lists of landowners in the Bedford Level, provided by J. G. Lenny, it would appear that a typical 'farm' during the earlier half of the nineteenth century was roughly in the region of 100 to 300 acres, whilst even allowing for the double, or even treble, appearance of some of the proprietors in more than one fen, smallholders owning less than 50 acres were very numerous. Hence in the parish of Manea, where the total acreage under cultivation was slightly over 4,410, of the sixty-six proprietors forty-five owned less than 50 acres, and of these, eighteen less than 20 acres. In Haddenham Level 106 of its 125 proprietors worked less than 50 acres of land, of whom seventy farmed less than 20 acres and forty-five of these less than 10 acres. Similarly the Bury and Upwood New Fen District was partitioned amongst forty-four cultivators, thirty of whom owned less than 10 acres, and not one of whom held over 100 acres.[18] The above examples are typical of the pattern of land tenure in relation to individual acreages farmed in the average fen parish after enclosure. The system encountered criticism in some quarters. 'I need scarcely say,' complained F. A. Ruston, 'that these occupations are altogether bad; they fearfully multiply the difficulties of management, and tend to increase the cost and diminish the profits of cultivation. These small ownerships, too, operate prejudicially to the labourer.' Ruston deplored the fact that, in the absence of any large landowners, there was no authority capable of ensuring adequate standards of accommodation, the labourer being 'driven to seek such a home as the village can offer, and, instead of being on the farm ready for his work, has, morning and evening, to walk to and fro, thereby increasing his own toil, and with no corresponding gain, but an actual loss to his employer'. According to Ruston 'the cottage accommodation which these villages afford is painfully insufficient. Families are ofttimes crowded into miserable, wretched hovels totally unfit for human habitation ... they must tend to foster every social evil'.[19] Indeed Thorney, a compact agricultural estate of 20,000 acres, was unique in the southern Fenland, whilst the village of Thorney represented the sole example of a planned estate village, for a long period the sole property of an occasionally resident landlord.

The various small pieces of adventurers' land, which comprised many of the individual holdings of fen, were usually grouped together to form a more or less undivided whole. In the case of the free lands it was more common for the holdings of one person to be scattered in different parts of the Level. There was a general overall tendency for the number of adventurers' land owners to increase, ie from 469 in 1697 to 501 by 1734.[20] Up to at least 1812 there was no very significant fluctuation in this total,[21] until at some point during the post-Napoleonic War period the number of owners approximately doubled.[22] Similar tendencies were undoubtedly to be found on the free lands. Transfers of land were numerous during the period of low prices and farming difficulties which accompanied the cessation of hostilities. The times were especially hard for small farmers who, because of their restricted technical and capital resources, had a merely limited capacity for survival. Those who had borrowed heavily during the war period were invariably badly affected because their debts, incurred at a time when prices were high, were accompanied by a burden of high interest payments, which it was difficult to meet at a time of rapidly falling price levels. The smaller freeholders, lacking the resources of their more fortunate neighbours with larger holdings, and exposed by their limited incomes to the full force of economic change, simply sold off a part of their land in order to obtain the capital essential for survival. A large part of the land seems to have been purchased by local men with alternative occupations, who seized the opportunity to acquire a few acres as an additional source of income.[23] There is no doubt that a considerable proportion of the smaller holdings were not genuine farm business units, but represented part-time occupations. This became a very prominent feature in the southern Fens. The example of Henry Martin, a farmer of Littleport, seems fairly typical. He and his grandmother also owned a shop; the shop and the farm were rated together and carried on as 'one general concern'.[24]

At this point it is interesting to define the general characteristics of the hundreds of landowners who collectively formed the Bedford Level Corporation. Some few of the adventurers' lands were institutional properties; for instance land was owned at different periods by such bodies as the March Charity School Trustees, the Wisbech and March Turnpike Trustees, the Bank of England, and some Cambridge colleges.[25] Amongst the individual proprietors we find a whole host of rural occupations represented, as fascinating as they are diverse.[26] In the last quarter of the seventeenth century, although landownership as a whole was markedly agrarian and local in character, there had also been a fairly constant infusion, however slight, of proprietors drawn from the ranks of London traders and professional men. London investment in the fens during the late seventeenth century was represented by such differing occupations as a clockmaker, a goldsmith, a tinplater, a draper, a wigmaker, a saddler, and by numerous members of the legal profession. The purely mercantile element was never very strong at any period, and in so far as it existed at all, largely local. Merchants who purchased fen land usually originated from such towns as Wisbech, Peterborough, Cambridge, Norwich, Brandon and Northampton. Apart from a small sprinkling of gentry and aristocracy, and a large number of farmers, graziers and associated occupations, owners of adventurers' land included grocers, blacksmiths, apothecaries, watermen, scriveners, drapers, an 'oylman', innkeepers, a handful of Bedfordshire widows, wheelwrights, farriers, carpenters, a 'fustian maker' of Godmanchester and a 'monger' of Kent.[27] At all periods the vast majority of the proprietors had their residence permanently within, or at least adjacent to, the Bedford Level.[28] From about the mid-eighteenth century, however, business and professional men living outside the area seem to have been even less strongly attracted by the opportunities to own fen land than hitherto. There were other reasons apart from deteriorating drainage.

In the seventeenth century land had been the only secure source of purely financial investment, but during the ensuing century its reputation in this context declined. The increasing security and scope of investment in the funds made stocks an acceptable alternative to land. From the eighteenth century land purchase in England on any large scale tended to be rather more exclusively for the social and residential benefits which its possession implied, and here the Bedford Level was at a permanent disadvantage, not solely on account of the environmental rigours of climate and terrain. This type of purchaser would require to buy land in the form of consolidated estates. These, as we have seen, were virtually non-existent in the southern Fenland, whilst the presence of innumerable small proprietors militated against their future creation. Where land was held in small parcels estate-building would necessarily be by dint of a laborious process of piecemeal acquisition. Also the incidence of heavy drainage taxes might have constituted an additional deterrent. In this connection it is interesting to note what the eleventh Duke of Bedford wrote of Thorney in 1897:

> In the period 1816–95 the taxation of Thorney has amounted to the sum of £614,714, and in addition the Dukes of Bedford have expended £983,640 on soil which was reclaimed by an ancestor from the inroads of the sea at the cost of £100,000. The taxation paid for eighty years has amounted to nine-tenths of the net income ... The average net income for the past twenty years, without taking the death duties into account, is only equal to $2\frac{1}{7}$ per cent interest on the capital outlay on new works.[29]

The large number of fen landowners who were town dwellers with alternative occupations meant that attention to business affairs would automatically prohibit many of them from farming their own land. In these cases it would be leased.[30] It is difficult to assess the proportion of land in the Bedford Level which was leased as against that farmed by occupying owners, particularly as there were no clear-cut divisions between owner occupiers and tenant farmers. Many of the former seem to have rented some land, often in fact renting more than they owned. William Wells, an Upwell farmer, is probably a fairly typical example. He farmed his own land and was also a tenant for 200 acres, which he rented from not less than four landlords.[31]

The advisability of long leases has been variously debated. Many writers considered that security of tenure was vital to a farmer if he were to invest money in developing the potentialities of his land to the full. A long lease of from fourteen to twenty-one years was for this reason often considered ideal.[32] Leases of adventurers' land up to the close of the eighteenth century were frequently granted for twenty-one-year terms. After this time there seems to have been a general decline in very long leases, periods of from seven to eleven or twelve years becoming more common.[33] After the French Wars the popularity of leasing fen land seems to have suffered a sharp decline.[34] Apart from a few isolated instances, as the Duke of Bedford's lands at Thorney, yearly tenancies became an obvious substitute for leases where an owner was reluctant to tie himself to a fixed rent at a period of unstable prices. Such tenancies did not necessarily imply insecurity of tenure, at least in the case of a good tenant.

Leases of adventurers' land are interesting in so far as they often contain detailed covenants prescribing the actual mode of farming the lands. In addition to the customary restrictions about selling manure and fodder off the land, and the conventional regulations concerning the repair of buildings and fences, maintenance of drains and upkeep of osier plantations, covenants relating to husbandry often bound the tenant to follow a stipulated five or six course rotation. William Gooch asserted, with some truth, that it was not until the last quarter of the eighteenth century that a convertible system of agriculture – which relied on the alternate use of fodder and corn crops to obviate fallowing, keep the soil in good heart and provide food for livestock – was generally employed in the fens. According to him the system previously followed was to 'crop the land as long as it would produce anything, then to let it be overrun with twitch (or couch) grass, to which all fen land is prone; and after it had rested a few years to break it up again, paring and burning it without care or discretion'.[35]

On the drained enclosed peat fen the process of paring and burning was introduced in the middle of the seventeenth century and remained the prominent feature of arable cultivation until the end of the eighteenth. The soil of the southern Fenland in general consisted of a deposit of peat, resting on clay. The peat was composed of the roots and fibres of about forty species of plant, in varying stages of decomposition, and was found in differing depths throughout the Level of from a few inches to 10ft or more. This land was turfed, and the turfs laid in small heaps until thoroughly dry, and then burnt. Arthur Young described how the process was carried out in the fen district of Suffolk:

> In these fens, the original surface is rough and unequal, from great tufts of rushes, etc called there *hassocks*. Some persons cut them with spades, at the expence of five or ten shillings an acre; others with the plough ... But opinions are, in general, that hand-work is the cheaper; in either case the hassocks are dried, heaped, burnt, and the ashes spread. After this they go over it again with a very complete and very effective tool called a fen-paring plough, the furrow of which is burnt.[36]

The alkali in the ashes helped to counteract the high acid content of the peat. The resulting soil produced heavy crops, although effects were invariably short-lived:

> This virgin soil, under such management, produced cole seed of most extraordinary fattening qualities, and perhaps there has never been any natural food that would compare with it, or that would in so short a time produce so much weight of mutton.[37]

The produce gathered in a good year more than compensated for two or three bad harvests:

> the produce of the fens, when dry, is so great and so much exceeding any other lands, that the growth of oats here governs in some measure the London market, and consequently has an influence on the whole Kingdom.[38]

Some land possessed such fertility that corn could be taken year after year without a fallow.

The cropping system which followed paring and burning usually consisted of coleseed the first year, followed by from two to four grain crops, with oats predominating, after which the land was converted to pasture for periods ranging from three to six or seven years, a practice which, although resulting in a severe loss of arable output, had the overriding advantage of conserving the peat. However individual farmers, 'impatient of the restraints of system', experimented with different crops and rotations.[39] Sometimes wheat, beans or clover were sown, with an occasional year of coleseed or grass to rest the land, and to enable the vegetation to rot and build up the peat again. Nevertheless contemporary writers have shown how small a proportion of the fens was being used for arable before the high prices of corn during the Napoleonic Wars gave an impetus to wheat production.[40] Between 1793 and 1815 the pace of enclosure was immensely accelerated. The process of breaking up the great commons was commenced in earnest, and increasingly large tracts of land were taken into arable cultivation.

Despite its many advantages paring and burning was often intensely criticised. Lord Orford attributed the poor crops which he observed in the vicinity of March to this mode of cultivation: 'They make use of burnt turf for manure, which is much disapproved by good husbandmen, as destructive to the natural soil.'[41] The main objections to paring and burning had their origin in the complaint that it reduced the soil and lowered the ground level. Since peat is almost entirely composed of vegetable matter the practice of burning obviously helped to lower the level of the land. For this reason leases of Bedford Level Corporation land usually restricted the process, frequently to once in seven, occasionally to once in fourteen years. To prevent immoderate burning, leases often contained the provision that land must be 'burnt to a proper Ash' and must not 'burn beyond the Soil and make large pitts therein'.[42] This did, in fact, represent a considerable danger. In dry seasons when

> the moisture of the earth is very low, the fire catches the soil below and causes what is called *pitting*, making great unsightly holes to the bottom of the moor which with great difficulty are extinguished. About thirteen years ago, a large common at Chatteris in the Isle of Ely, was thus burnt up, 16 or 18 inches deep to the very gravel.[43]

But whatever arguments were adduced against it, paring and burning was the cheapest and, in the opinion of many agriculturalists, the only effective way to cultivate the fens, which explains why the method persisted for more than 150 years after its first introduction in the mid-seventeenth century.

Up to the latter years of the eighteenth century a strong prejudice persisted against the use of the plough on the light fen soils. Therefore the amount of adventurers' land under a particular lease which could be ploughed in any one year was frequently restricted by its owner to a quarter of the total acreage rented, and in extreme cases to a tenth or even a twentieth. Infrequently the tenant was permitted to plough during the greater part of his term, except for the last three or four years when the land had to be laid down to grass. Infringement of these regulations carried the penalty of a heavy fine, ranging from £5 to £20 an acre – sometimes more – per annum.

The fundamental improvement in the cultivation of the fen lands consisted in the spread of more flexible crop rotations. In the Fenland as a whole the process was assisted by an alteration in the structure of the soil. With the continuing shrinkage and thinning of the surface layer the underlying clay came within easy reach of the plough in many districts by the close of the eighteenth century. It was found that the peat soil derived a greater consistency and solidity from its admixture with the heavier clay, which not only enriched the peat, balancing its acid content, but had the additional advantage of preventing too rapid an evaporation of moisture. The soil became so productive that in those areas where the clay was too deep for the plough the custom of digging for it became widespread. By 1830 the practice had become well established.[44] The process of claying consisted of cutting trenches at intervals, usually about 14yd apart and running parallel to each other: 'the clay is disinterred and spread over the land, and the black soil is returned to the trench'.[45] In those areas where there was no suitable clay it had to be carted on to the land from elsewhere. Where clay lay close to the surface the cost of the claying process was comparatively small, but where it lay several feet deep the expense was proportionately greater. The average cost of claying was calculated at between 30s and 50s per acre, which was still relatively cheap when considering the advantages.[46]

Claying very much more than doubled land values, which in some localities increased from £5 to £30 or even £50 an acre.[47] The peat lands became the 'most productive of soils yielding the most luxuriant crops of wheat, oats, coleseed and turnips',[48] whilst beans, potatoes and cabbages were increasingly cultivated. But it was on corn growing that claying had probably the most spectacular effect. The soil was now strong and rich enough to support heavy crops. In some places yield was doubled or even trebled. Even Holme Fen, near Whittlesey, formerly an 'immense reed shoal', had been so improved by claying that great crops of corn were being harvested by 1847.[49] The land in many localities was so rich that farmers could grow wheat, that most soil-exhausting of crops, for several seasons running without detriment. Wheat became the predominant crop in the Bedford Level, with a greater acreage yield than that of any other part of England. Whereas the national average was somewhere in the region of 24 bushels an acre, in the fens the average normal yield was between 26 and 30 bushels, in good years even increasing to 34. London and the industrial north furnished ready outlets for surplus produce, and to these rapidly expanding centres corn was exported in large quantities.[50]

The general increase in the prosperity of the southern Fenland was reflected in the upward movement of Bedford Level Corporation rents, from a total of £650 in 1800 to over £4,000 by the 1850s.[51] The corporation itself, no longer harassed to the same extent by its traditional financial difficulties, was able, in 1847, to discontinue taxation on those adventurers' lands still under its jurisdiction, whilst the latter years of the nineteenth century were characterised by a steady capitalisation of its surplus income.[52] But this prosperity had its grimmer aspects. The rich soil produced a luxuriant crop of weeds, and it was 'a constant labour to eradicate them . . . to accomplish this, resort has been had to what are popularly known as agricultural gangs'. The system gained an evil reputation in many localities for 'cruelty and slave-driving'. Children were widely employed, a practice which was sometimes justified on the dubious grounds that 'the earnings of these young people form a most important item in the family income, and can ill be spared'.[53] It is hardly surprising to find some writers looking back to the more carefree days of commoning, fishing and wildfowling with nostalgia.[54]

The difficulty of defining the specific crop rotation generally in vogue within the Bedford Level after claying lies in the fact that no regular or uniform system was adopted. Rotations varied not only between the North, Middle and South Levels, but also from parish to parish.[55] S. Jonas affirmed that:

> The plan pursued by the best farmers of the district is to fallow
> with rape or turnips ... to which a dressing of bones is applied ...
> The rape is fed off with sheep ... [and] is so strong and luxuriant
> and stands so high that the sheep eat as it were their way in ...
> sometimes wheat is sown after rape but generally oats.[56]

The most common rotations were (1) turnips or coleseed for arable grazing by sheep, (2) oats, (3) wheat, (4) seeds, (5) wheat; or (1) turnips or coleseed for oil or fattening sheep, (2) wheat, (3) seeds, (4) wheat, (5) beans, (6) wheat.[57] Such rotations, embracing improved grasses, legumes and root crops, served a number of purposes. They provided more fodder enabling the land to support increasing numbers of livestock, which in turn manured the soil. Heavier manuring raised the yields of all crops, with correspondingly more fodder to support even greater numbers of livestock, whose individual quality improved as a result of better nutrition. The cultivation of legumes and grasses also improved the soil.

Although there were many instances in leases of a specified crop rotation being enjoined upon the tenant, it is usual to find the more general provision that the land was to be farmed 'in a good husbandlike manner' and 'according to the customs of the country'. The imposition of specific general restrictions was nevertheless common. It became customary for a landlord to prohibit his tenant from taking above two successive corn crops from the soil without growing coleseed or turnips to be eaten by sheep on the land. The cultivation of some crops was absolutely forbidden, including mustard seed and 'other pernicious seeds' which exhausted the soil. The growth of coleseed as a standing crop was frequently banned. But even where progressive or prohibitive covenants were in force, and although heavy fines were imposed for their contravention, it is difficult to know how strictly they could be enforced in each individual case. At all events arable land gradually superseded pasture, so that there was very little temporary grass, whilst permanent pasture consisted mainly of 'wash' grazings, which were frequently flooded in winter.

A practice strictly prohibited or at least curtailed in leases was that of turf-cutting. From 3 to 5ft below the surface of the land was a hard, fibrous substance resting on the clay, and it was the custom to cut this into bricklike shapes and sell it for fuel. Prices varied, from 6s per thousand at Ely, 8s at Cambridge to 10s at Whittlesey.[58] Turf was widely used throughout the Bedford Level in preference to coal, and was hence a lucrative crop. On the debit side turf-cutting rendered the land useless for cultivation. In leases of adventurers' land it was usual for the landlord to restrict the quantity of turf which could be cut to the amount required by the tenant for his personal use. Often the land from which turf could be cut was rigidly defined. Heavy fines were imposed on any tenant who cut turfs in excess of the stated quantity, which was usually 20,000 annually 'for his own fireing and noe more'. In many instances tenants were prohibited from turf digging altogether.

Assisted by all these safeguards the prosperity of the southern Fenland continued to increase. Even though there is evidence that the two national agricultural depressions of the nineteenth century exerted an adverse effect in the Bedford Level, in both instances many fen farmers found a means of combating their worst effects. The situation was so bad after the Napoleonic Wars that the innkeepers and retailers of Ely in 1816 were moved to present a petition in parliament through Lord Osborne, seeking relief from the Inhabited House Duty and the Window Tax, because 'business had decreased beyond conception, from the distressed state of agriculture in the neighbourhood, upon which the population depend for their support'.[59] The great riots, in the course of which an armed mob terrorised the inhabitants of Ely, Littleport, Downham and neighbouring villages for several days in May 1816, are symptomatic of the distress of local agriculture. Rioting was not confined to labourers. It was claimed that 'many of the most conspicuous actors in the dark drama were above the lowest classes of society ... who possessed some property and something like an aspect of reputation'.[60] John Dennis, who was subsequently hanged, 'could not plead that his object was a rise in wages, for he was a man of some property', whilst another of the ringleaders, charged with inciting the mob, was described as a 'considerable farmer'.[61] In fact many local farmers were so badly affected by the depression that they abandoned their lands and emigrated.[62] Nineteen farms in the Isle of Ely were without tenants in 1815.[63] Owners of corporation land in a majority of instances solved their immediate problems by selling part of their land, or by mortgaging their property to local business and professional men. This alone explains their continued ability to meet, however tardily, the payment of the high drainage taxes in the teeth of savage deflation.

Mortgages also increased to some extent during the depression which occupied the last quarter of the nineteenth century and were accompanied by an overall decline in the value of the land. In the Cambridgeshire Fens the depression was felt 'very severely'. There was widespread distress among farmers; some were 'absolutely insolvent' and the rest 'greatly reduced in circumstances'.[64] Huntingdonshire fared no better. Here there were signs of the 'bad seasons and of the depressed state of agriculture'.[65] This 'Great Depression' seems to have constituted in the main a depression in wheat, associated with persistently adverse weather conditions in some areas, and with excessive imports from America. The rising living standards of the working classes, accompanied by changing patterns of food consumption, stimulating the demand for livestock as against cereal products, was another factor. Therefore it has been generally supposed that pasture farmers were less adversely affected by falling prices than were arable. The almost 50 per cent reduction in the rents of pasture land owned by the Bedford Level Corporation, falling from £1,403 in 1878 to £726 by 1896, is undoubtedly a reflection of the difficulties of those who farmed not only pasture but arable land also.[66]

Ernle's narrative leaves us in no doubt as to the severity of the depression throughout England: 'Since 1862 the tide of agricultural prosperity had ceased to flow; after 1874 it turned and rapidly ebbed.'[67] The general opinion is summarised by Halévy: 'If the position of industry was doubtful, about agriculture there could be no doubt. It was in an advanced state of decay.'[68] It is significant that the Duke of Bedford sold his Thorney estate at this time, shrewdly disembarrassing himself of an investment which was yielding little or no profit, although incurring a heavy expenditure. Depression inflicted suffering on the large corn

Plate 7 (above) An unusual scene in the fens: cattle grazing on the Hundred Foot (Ouse) washes; *(below)* a more conventional scene: potato planting at Whittlesey

Plate 8 (above) Problems of wind erosion: a dust storm at its height, seen from the Coveney–Downham road; *(below)* attempted solution: inter-row nurse planting of barley and onions, at the Arthur Rickwood Experimental Husbandry Farm, Mepal, Cambs

growers. However the fen farmers 'escaped many misfortunes which had befallen the occupier of strong obdurate clay'. Indeed they were not 'hit anything like so hard as those on other varieties of soil'.[69] Therefore in Cambridgeshire the fen acres did not lose anywhere near the value of land in the southern uplands of the county. Here there were 'large tracts where the deteriorated state of the land is painfully apparent to all, being practically worthless to owner and occupier alike, and scarcely able to be designated as cultivated'.[70] An important internal revolution was effected in the Fenland during the period of falling prices. Many were compelled by self-interest and the logic of their bank balances to change their systems, and a large number of fen farmers switched to market gardening and fruit growing, where the competition from foreign imports was negligible. Potatoes, it was said, had 'proved the making of the Fens and the mainstay of the Fen farmer'.[71] According to a statement made at a meeting of local farmers at Wisbech in 1894:

> there has been the means of enabling the people to escape from the depression. They are able to grow the best class of potatoes, vegetables, and fruit. The men in the marsh have been hit to some extent by prices, but are better off than other people occupying land.[72]

FARMING ACTIVITY IN THE NORTHERN FENLAND

Farming in the northern Fenland, up to the latter half of the eighteenth century, was characterised by the continued prevalence of the system of intercommoning, and by the predominance of pasture land over arable. The management of the common fens was subject to minute and detailed regulation, a first necessity if utter confusion were to be avoided. Despite the existence of some semblance of disciplined management chaos was prevalent enough. The common fens were stocked with every conceivable species of livestock, originally with no limits set to the numbers which could be grazed. Eventually as lords of the manor acquired a more sensitive awareness of their rights, it became increasingly the custom for villagers to pasture their stock subject to the payment of a specific rent, whilst numbers were restricted.

A code of laws had been drawn up during the reign of Edward VI, which remained fully operative in the Lincolnshire Fens until their enclosure from the latter part of the eighteenth century. The code consisted of seventy-two articles, primarily relating to branding and stocking. It contained many negative prohibitions and some positive instructions. Penalties were attached to a wide variety of offences, for example, putting diseased cattle on the fens; disturbing the cattle by baiting with savage dogs; leaving any dead animals unburied for more than three days, and taking or leaving dogs on the fens after sunset. No cattle were to be driven out of the fens during divine service on Sundays or holy days. No reed thatch was to be mown before it had two years' growth. Before being sent on to the common fens livestock were collected at certain defined places and marked, and again, on being taken off in the autumn, were brought to the same place to be claimed by their owners. Bailiffs were appointed to look after the stock. On the marshes of South Holland a marsh reeve was annually appointed, and a marsh shepherd, their wages being paid at the annual rate of 1s 6d for each horse and cow, and 3d for each sheep grazed on the commons. No swans', cranes' or bitterns' eggs, or any eggs apart from those of ducks or geese, could be brought out of the fen. No fodder was to be mown in the East or West Fens before Midsummer day. A code of seventeen articles was also devised, relative to fishing. The laws chiefly concerned the kind of nets allowed, and the manner of using them. There were other regulations. Because the preservation of the sea and river banks was a matter of fundamental importance rabbits were banned, under laws promulgated by the sewer commissions, from being kept on the banks; if found they were to be removed. Horses and cattle were also prohibited, and pigs unless ringed.[73] The difficulties of farming the unenclosed land may be judged from the fact that, in the Witham Fens, the sheep had frequently to be carried to their pastures in boats, and the cows swam from island to island. Large tracts of the Lincolnshire Fens were covered with water and thistles. The sheep were subject to the rot, and cattle plague caused immense devastation.

In 1794 the principal Lincolnshire commons were the East and West Fens (29,000 acres), Wildmore Fen (10,500 acres), and the

East and West Deeping Fens (15,000 acres). The management of the East, West and Wildmore Fens was reputedly superior to that of any others in the Lincolnshire Fenland. 'Yet,' wrote Thomas Stone, before the improvements carried out during the first half of the nineteenth century, 'they are extremely wet and unprofitable in their present state, standing much in need of drainage, are generally overstocked, and dug up for turf and fuel.'[74] The sheep and cattle depastured on these fens were frequently unhealthy and of an inferior breed, 'occasioned by the scantiness as well as the bad quality of their food, and the wetness of their lair. Geese, with which these commons are generally stocked . . . are often subject to be destroyed.' Usually the commoners neglected to remove their livestock from the fens during the autumn: 'but some of the worst of the neat cattle, with the horses, – and particularly those upon Wildmore Fen, – are left to abide the event of the winter season'. Cattle seldom survived the rigours of a harsh winter, whilst the horses were 'driven to such distress for food that they eat up every remaining dead thistle, and are said to devour the hair off the manes and tails of each other and also the dung of geese'. Arthur Young observed 'whole acres' in Wildmore Fen 'covered with thistles and nettles four feet high and more'. It was estimated that in one year alone 40,000 sheep – approximately one per acre – had rotted on the East, West and Wildmore Fens.[75]

The above descriptions, we are told, applied to the best regulated commons. Conversely the Deeping Fens may be taken as representative of the more typical management of Lincolnshire Fen commons. 'The occupiers,' wrote Thomas Stone in 1794:

> frequently, in one season, lose four fifths of their stock. These commons are without stint, and almost every cottage within the manors has a common right belonging to it. Every kind of depredation is made upon this land in cutting up the best of the turf for fuel; and the farmers in the neighbourhood, having common rights, availing themselves of a fine season, turn on 7 or 800 sheep each, to ease their inclosed land, whilst the mere cottager cannot get a bite for a cow; but yet the cottager in his turn . . . takes the stock of a foreigner as his own, who occasionally turns on immense quantities of stock in good seasons. The cattle and sheep, which are constantly depastured on this common, are of a very

unthrifty, ill-shapen kind, from being frequently starved, and no attention paid to their breed. Geese are the only animals which are at any time thrifty; and these frequently, when young, die of the cramp, or, when plucked, in consequence of the excessive bleakness and wetness of the commons . . . These commons are the frequent resort of thieves, who convey the cattle into distant Counties for sale.[76]

There is no doubt that the fen commons were grossly overstocked. At least forty-seven parishes claimed common rights in the East, West and Wildmore Fens. In 1784 West Fen alone was supporting 3,936 head of cattle: 'In dry years, it is perfectly white with sheep.'[77] Arthur Young noted how

> Mr Thacker, of Langrike ferry, has clipped 1,200 sheep on Wildmore; and yet he assured me, that he would rather continue at his present rent, and pay the full value for whatever might be allotted to his farm on an enclosure, rather than have the common right for nothing.[78]

Norfolk Marshland, consisting of what was termed 'the Fen' and 'Tilney Smeeth', was in a scarcely better condition. Here, in the pre-enclosure days, there were not less than 528 common rights:

> This great tract of land was . . . worth little: the Fen not above 1s an acre in reed, being two or three feet deep under water: the Smeeth was often under water, in parts to the amount of half; and then at the Midsummer often rotted the sheep that fed it.[79]

The state of the commons in the two Marshland parishes of Terrington St John and St Clement, before enclosure in 1790, was especially vulnerable to criticism. Here there were 868 acres of salt-marsh over which 118 owners exercised common rights. Before embankment and enclosure, 'The tract was worth less than nothing: being injurious by the commoners' cattle being often swept away by the tides.'[80]

There was an obvious need for improvement. Arthur Young in particular deplored the ill-effects – agricultural and moral – of the intercommoning system:

So wild a country nurses up a race of people as wild as the fen, and thus the morals and eternal welfare of numbers are hazarded and ruined for want of an inclosure... In discourse at Louth upon the characters of the poor, observations were made upon the consequences of great commons in nursing up a mischievous race of people; and instanced, that on the very day we were talking, a gang of villains were brought to Louth gaol, from Coningsby, who had committed numberless outrages upon cattle and corn; laming, killing, cutting off tails, and wounding a variety of cattle, hogs, and sheep; and that many of them were commoners on the immense fens of East, West, and Wildmore.[81]

The benefits to be derived from enclosing the fen commons were constantly enumerated, and probable increased land values assessed. Arthur Young estimated that the enclosure of the East and West Fens would increase their annual rental value by more than £22,000, from £4,173 to £26,343. The net gain anticipated from the enclosure of Wildmore Fen was about £9,000.[82] In practice these estimates proved to be reasonably accurate.

The agricultural defects of the common pasture system were quite as obvious in the northern as in the southern Fenland. So long as farming had been unprogressive, and population had remained stationary, the economic loss was comparatively unimportant. When the national demand for food threatened to outstrip the supply, the need for change became imperative. Arthur Young never failed to stress the underlying causes for the unprofitableness of many of the fen commons, in his estimation chiefly arising from the indiscriminate over-stocking, the direct outcome of 'different views of supposed interest':

> because human nature being in their various capacities anxious of property, some through avarice, or a wish to get rich at once, stock so largely as to injure themselves, and oppress the common; others, in the line of jobbing, put in great quantities of stock to sell again, which are altogether injurious to the farm commoner, who only stocks with what his farm produces.[83]

Young advocated enclosure on the grounds of greater employment for the poor and increased grain production, making possible a reduction in imports.

Delays in enclosing the northern Fenland were in large measure due – as in the southern Fens – to the dogged resistance of the commoners. A considerable disincentive towards enclosing was that common land was not subject to crippling drainage taxes. In some fen parishes there were also frequent disputes about the share due to the lord of the manor. The sheer magnitude of the task further obstructed the pathway of improvement. Many tracts of common were for long left unenclosed, because the extravagant cost threatened to absorb the possible profits of the undertaking. But despite disputes and setbacks the general benefit was very apparent.

The movement had proceeded slowly. Holland Fen was drained and enclosed by an act passed in 1767. Some smaller fens were enclosed at the same period, bringing a considerable tract of land into cultivation. The greater part of the long reach of predominantly peat fen, extending from Tattershall to Lincoln was reclaimed and enclosed during the late eighteenth century: 'This is a vast work, which in the whole, had drained, enclosed, and built and cultivated, between 20 and 30 square miles of country . . . Its produce before little, letting for not more than 1s 6d an acre, now for 11s to 17s an acre.'[84] The steep appreciation of land values was a characteristic accompaniment of enclosure. In the mid-eighteenth century enclosed land in Deeping Fen was let at from 7s to 8s per acre, and sold for about £3 an acre. Some of it was in so poor a state that it could not be let or sold at any price. After enclosure in 1801 selling and letting values rose to £20 and £1 an acre respectively.[85] Similarly in Holland Fen, soon after enclosure, the average annual acreage value was 27s; the previous value had been negligible – if Arthur Young is to be believed 'nothing at all'.[86] However there seem to have been few instances where the benefits of enclosure were more apparent than at Long Sutton in South Holland. By an act of 1788 almost 4,000 acres of common land had been enclosed. Previously rents had averaged 5s an acre. After enclosure they soared to between 30s and 50s: 'about half of it is ploughed . . . there is now more livestock kept than before, and of a much better kind; though above 2,000 acres have been ploughed up to yield an enormous profit'.[87] It was the same story in Norfolk Marshland. After enclosure and the accompanying drainage improvements had been effected, the Smeeth rents rose to £3 an acre and the fen rents to 25s.[88]

The incessant accretion of land along the coast between Boston and Wisbech meant that the draining and enclosure of salt-marshes was a continuous process. In Long Sutton 10,000 acres had been reclaimed from the sea by the close of the eighteenth century, and by an act of 1792 more than 5,000 acres in the parishes of Spalding, Moulton, Whaplode, Holbeach and Gedney were enclosed.[89] The initial cultivation of this type of land posed several problems. At first many crops would not flourish, due to excessive salinity in the soil. Arthur Young thought that 'the land should be pastured for three years after excluding the sea, after which ploughing will succeed without hazard'. In his view salt-marsh, having been brought into full cultivation, represented some of the richest land in England. He was eloquent in his praise of reclamation and enclosure efforts in the Lincolnshire Fens:

> it will appear that there is not probably a county in the Kingdom that has made equal exertions in this very important work of draining. The quantity of land thus added to the Kingdom has been great; fens of water, mud, wild fowl, frogs, and agues, have been converted to rich pasture and arable worth from 20s to 40s an acre: health improved, morals corrected, and the community enriched. These, when carried to such an extent, are great works, and reflect the highest credit on the good sense and energy of the proprietors.[90]

In the northern Fenland the two kinds of land involved, broadly, two types of management. On the reclaimed salt-marshes, defended from the sea by great banks, the land was chiefly arable although some pasture was in evidence. The ploughed land yielded heavy crops of beans, wheat and oats, and in addition was utilised for arable grazing by sheep. In the inland parishes of the region rich grazing land was to be found, although after enclosure there is indication of a considerable conversion of pasture to arable. In the seventeenth century William Camden's *Britannia* had described how Tilney Smeeth in Norfolk Marshland was a famous feeding and breeding ground for cattle and sheep,[91] whilst in 1700 the 30,000 acres of Norfolk Marshland gained 'more Profit by Grazing than Plowing'.[92] Following drainage and enclosure the land produced great crops of mustard, wheat and oats: 'About 30,000l. a year is added to the produce of the Kingdom, by this most beneficial undertaking.'[93] Before their enclosure in 1790 the salt-marshes of Terrington had yielded very little in the way of arable produce. After enclosure and ploughing the land was producing wheat, oats, coleseed, and some beans: 'None of it laid to permanent grass.'[94] In Deeping Fen, formerly devoted to rearing livestock, immense corn crops were harvested, whilst woad, flax, cole, beans, and corn were being grown 'upon the rich arable of Holland Fen'.[95] But corn here was of an inferior quality, due to 'the extraordinary fertility giving such a luxuriance of straw'. South Holland, at one time predominantly utilised for the breeding of cattle and horses, was also producing heavy crops of wheat and oats after enclosure.[96] Potatoes were widely cultivated, especially in the Spalding area. However grazing still remained a major occupation in the Deeping and South Holland Fens. On the fens adjacent to the river Witham, in the vicinity of Boston, were some of the finest grazing lands in England: 'these will carry in summer a bullock to an acre and a half, besides four sheep an acre; and two sheep an acre in winter'.[97] But even here hemp, flax, beans, wheat and oats were being cultivated in increasing quantities by the early part of the nineteenth century.

As regards modes of agriculture, the practice of paring and burning was almost as sharply criticised in the Lincolnshire Fenland as in the Bedford Level, for identical reasons. Yet Arthur Young was convinced of the benefits to be gained from this method of cultivation, especially as 'burning a second time is not frequent'. It was difficult for landowners to obtain fair rents unless paring and burning were permitted, and although Arthur Young found considerable prejudice entertained against the system, on the whole farmers were adamant that 'their profit depended on it'.[98] Claying was another practice widely adopted here, as in the Bedford Level. On land that had been clayed wheat quickly became the foremost crop. It is significant that whereas 72,964 quarters of corn were sold in Boston market in 1829, five years later this had increased to 131,370. One farmer, who recollected to have heard that wheat was formerly imported to Spalding, actually exported 30,000 quarters from the locality in 1835.[99] It was recorded how

There is a great deal more wheat grown in the fens of Lincolnshire than there used to be some years ago; the corn grown in the fens of Lincolnshire some years back was principally confined to oats; the land is brought into a better state of cultivation, and now the returns of oats have fallen off, and the returns of wheat considerably increased.[100]

Leases in the Lincolnshire Fenland were a considerable rarity. In the fens of Norfolk they were much more common, although restricted in the majority of cases to seven or nine year terms.[101] In Lincolnshire, fen land was let as a rule on annual tenancies. When leases were granted they generally ran, as in Norfolk, for not more than nine or ten years, usually for considerably less. But the covenants relative to cropping were very easy and seldom enforced: 'if a tenant farms fairly he may do as he likes'.[102] Arthur Young assessed the absence of leases, especially in difficult areas like the fen districts, as a grave disadvantage:

> Upon soils so rich that there is nothing to do, the want of them cannot be material; but upon all others, where liming, marling, draining, fencing, etc. are demanded, the want of a lease will often be the want of improvement... nothing will be so well done upon an uncertain tenure, as with security.[103]

On the other hand W. H. Wheeler thought that tenants, in their own view at least, had 'all the fixity of tenure they require and on the whole a very friendly relationship exists between all classes on the land'.[104]

The northern, like the southern, Fenland was never dominated by any large territorial owners. There were few attractions to induce a large landowner to live in the district. This was an area where small freeholders, often working less than 20 acres of land, constituted a dominant class. It was estimated that at least half of the land in the fen parishes of Lincolnshire consisted of small freeholds, with their owners in many instances supplementing their incomes by such secondary occupations as thatching, hedging and ditching, or 'by assisting the neighbouring farmers at harvest, and in doing work that requires skill'.[105] Arthur Young was not convinced that the system was a good one. In his view the owners of very small farms worked much harder than labourers for insignificant rewards:

it is much to be questioned, whether the mass of human happiness is not considerably lessened by such occupations. As to the effect of them on the cultivation of the Kingdom, no doubt can be entertained of its evil tendency; and I have had very many opportunities of remarking it in the course of my journey through this country.[106]

But Arthur Young was undoubtedly too severe in his judgement, for the system certainly did not lack advantages. The crops principally grown, apart from wheat, were potatoes, cabbages, celery and bush fruits. During the Great Depression, when very many larger farmers were ruined, 'these little Freeholders held on; very few went under'.[107] Their survival was in large measure due to the preponderance of family labour and more attention to smaller products than corn growing. The achievement was the more remarkable as farming was particularly hard-hit in the fen parts of Lincolnshire. Land values depreciated rapidly. An arable farm of 300 acres at Spalding, purchased in 1876 for £19,000, could not, in 1894, find a purchaser for £23 an acre. Another peat farm, this time of 461 acres, was sold in 1892 for £13 an acre; seven years previously it had been purchased for £65 an acre.[108]

As in the Bedford Level a switch in the type of crops grown saved the area from complete disaster. The evidence relating to south Lincolnshire is conclusive enough. Here there were sweeping changes, as individuals doggedly geared themselves to weather the economic storm. In the fen districts around Spalding, where wheat and beans had formerly been the great staples, mustard, turnips, potatoes, cabbages, carrots, celery, rhubarb and asparagus were increasingly grown, chiefly for export to London and northern markets. The cultivation of fruit, flowers and bulbs made a spectacular advance. There was a marked upward surge in the rents of this land; they rose considerably above the normal for the rest of Lincolnshire. In the locality of Spalding this trend was particularly marked. Here rents of ordinary farms seldom rose above £2 an acre, whilst rents of market-garden land soared to over £4, with early potato land fetching up to £5. It is apparent that many market gardeners were in a superior position to weather the worst effects of the depression, and were 'doing pretty well, notwithstanding decreased profits from home and foreign competition'.[109]

10

The Final Triumph?

FROM STEAM TO DIESEL

SINCE the mid-seventeenth century up to recent times the story of fen drainage and flood protection, as we have seen, has for the most part been that of the draining of those meres and fens which remained after Vermuyden's project had been completed; the construction of additional new cuts; and the further development of the internal, or field-to-river, drainage system of the region. With the advent of the steam-engine the use of windmills had been virtually discontinued throughout the Fenland. There were a few instances of windmill retention, as for example at Soham Mere in Cambridgeshire, where a windmill was still operating in 1938.[1] But such cases were exceptionally rare. Steam replaced wind engines almost everywhere.

The last century or so has witnessed many changes in fen pumping. After 1851 the more efficient centrifugal pump gradually superseded the scoop-wheel. Changes also were effected in the steam-driven plants themselves, and the beam and old low-pressure engines were gradually replaced by more modern types. The steady surface shrinkage has remained a persistent problem, and has meant that even those individual fens which had originally boasted a natural drainage often had to have ultimate recourse to pumping. This occurred at Methwold Fen in Norfolk, where a steam pump was finally erected in 1883 as a last desperate attempt to cope with the steadily worsening floods. It brought about a temporary alleviation of the difficulties rather than a permanent solution. The Fen continued to sink so rapidly that the pump was soon rendered completely ineffective. By 1913 it was estimated that the land had fallen between 5 and 6ft during the previous fifty years, and a second pumping station had to be erected.[2]

The steadily lowering surface of the Fenland, above all in the peat zone, has entailed constant adjustments in lift, whilst the modern practice of deepening the drains to lower the surface gradient of the water and to provide greater capacity has further contributed to this trend. By 1913 the average lift had increased to over 15ft, an increase of almost 6ft since the first introduction of steam.

The first diesel pump to be erected in the Fenland was in the Methwold and Feltwell District in 1913, and before very long diesel and electric had entirely supplanted steam. Between 1913 and 1938 lifts were further increased, to as much as 21ft in the Littleport and Downham, Swaffham and Bottisham Districts, and up to 26ft in the North Side District of Wisbech. Because of the increased capacity of many of the main arterial drains it often became possible, by about 1938, for the size of the pumps to be decreased, from a maximum of 42in with a capacity of 150 tons per minute to 24in with a capacity of 70 tons per minute.[3] The smaller unit has sometimes been considered to be more economical, although obviously the argument has not always been applied. When the new pumping station was constructed at Wiggenhall St Germans in 1934 it consisted of three pumping sets each with a discharge capacity of 1,000 tons of water per minute and each driven by a 1,000hp diesel engine.

The introduction of diesel engines constituted a further decisive advance in pumping methods. The weight per unit horse-power is considerably below that of steam. Therefore less heavy foundations are required, a great advantage in a region where firm ground can rarely be guaranteed. Also the transport of coal over rough tracks to the pumping stations – almost invariably sited at an inconvenient distance from a hard road – represented a weighty problem. From the technical standpoint diesel engines have the great advantage that they can be started up quickly at short notice, and are much more suitable than steam-engines for intermittent running. Pumping for drainage is mainly seasonal and always spasmodic. With a steam-driven plant steam had first to be raised in boilers, long before pumping could begin. When the pump had ceased work the fires had to be banked or drawn until the plant was required again. All this incurred an unnecessary fuel consumption and often the employment of additional labour.

Although diesel-driven pumps came rapidly to the fore, the period following World War I did not bring prosperity to the farmer, and many drainage districts were unable or unwilling to spend money on modernising their plants and drainage systems. But despite many difficulties the years between 1930 and 1939 saw a general, if slow improvement in fen drainage, as plants which were out-of-date were gradually replaced by more modern installations. With the threat of war this work assumed an altogether new importance, and many districts which had not previously attempted to keep their plants up-to-date decided to install new ones under the government aided schemes which were introduced in 1937. No less than sixty-two pumping stations were erected during World War II, at a cost of £416,000, and improving an area of 283,000 acres.[4] The effect of these efforts was to increase very materially the peak discharge from pumps delivering drainage water into the main river systems in times of high flood.

Taking all things into consideration there seems little doubt that the switch from steam to diesel and electric has constituted yet another distinct contribution to the increasing prosperity of the region. But the more efficient drainage has greatly accelerated the rate of surface shrinkage and wastage, which in turn has necessitated a constant lowering of drains to keep them functioning effectively. At times the financial burden has seemed intolerable.

IMPROVEMENTS IN DRAINAGE ADMINISTRATION

The late nineteenth century witnessed attempts to solve the administrative problems for long associated with Fenland drainage. During the early part of the twentieth century the first active steps were taken to reach a practical solution. The situation had long called for drastic action and was particularly acute in the southern Fenland, where the gradual financial collapse of the

Bedford Level Corporation had in the past encouraged the formation of an increasing number of small authorities. By 1850 the corporation's responsibilities were confined to the maintenance of a few of the major channels and sluices, whilst the Bedford Level consisted of an increasingly complex network of small, self-governing drainage districts, each one making its own fiscal, administrative and technical arrangements quite independently of the others. Co-operation between these statutory districts, whilst being a first essential, was virtually non-existent: 'each only solicitous for the welfare of their own territory, and jealous of spending money that might benefit their neighbours, or more especially the navigation of the rivers'.[5] Not until the early twentieth century was any attempt made to rationalise their structure in relation to each other and to a wider authority.

Meanwhile the disintegration of the Bedford Level Corporation continued at a pace which, if not fast was at least inexorable, and not even significantly arrested by undoubted improvements in its financial position. Unfortunately these had come too late to be of much use. As we have seen the North Level had been partially removed from its control in 1753.[6] Since that time, whilst retaining its authority over the adventurers' lands in the district north of Morton's Leam, the corporation had there commuted its general powers of taxation for a fixed tax. After 1810, when a separate body of commissioners was created to superintend the upkeep of the Middle Level rivers and drains, the control exercised by the corporation over this region also became largely nominal.[7] Even in the South Level – the corporation's last stronghold – much of its authority had, by 1830, been eroded by the activities of the Eau Brink and South Level commissioners. But it was after 1850 that the almost complete disintegration of the corporation occurred. The collapse when it came, like all necessary evils which have been staved off for an indefinite period, was sudden and almost catastrophic. In 1857 the corporation surrendered the last vestiges of its power in the North Level,[8] and five years later, not without a considerable struggle, the Middle Level was fully incorporated as a separate commission.[9] The severance was total, embracing property, finance and administration. The corporation, at least in its existing form, seemed by general consensus of opinion to have outlived its usefulness almost everywhere. Even its Governor, the Earl of Hardwicke, favoured total dissolution, bitterly observing that matters had 'arrived at the state prophesied by Wells long ago . . . that the division of the Level would ultimately tend to separate interests of so strong a character that the interests of the Corporation would be obliterated in the struggles that would take place'.[10] It is true that to render the corporation even partially capable of administering the drainage of an extensive area like the Bedford Level sweeping reforms would have been required, involving a thorough reorganisation of its constitution and financial structure, particularly in relation to the establishment of a more flexible taxation system and the provision of an adequate income. At the time – if such a solution were considered at all – this might have seemed hardly a practical concept, savouring too much of a patching-up operation, and it was probably thought a simpler matter to dissolve the corporation altogether. Nevertheless whilst advocating a complete dissolution, the inescapable influence of a long tradition prompted Lord Hardwicke to plead:

> we do insist upon it as a right that the Corporation may when it puts itself to death be permitted to make a will which is to be strictly just in itself guarding all those interests which they have had entrusted to their hands from the time of the great Duke of Bedford.[11]

It was a valid point and the executors attended to it. The Middle Level Separation Act was passed in 1862, and its provisions, which continued to safeguard the drainage interest, actually came into force in April 1864. But the corporation was not dissolved. Until 1920 it remained in existence to defend, often with surprising tenacity, the last remnants of its authority in the South Level.

By 1920 the situation was entirely chaotic. Subdivision of responsibility had advanced to so unrealistic a stage that there were eighty-three separate drainage authorities wholly or partly within the Great Ouse drainage area alone, together with twelve main channel and outfall authorities. Responsibility for the maintenance of the Ouse banks was divided between not less than six separate sets of commissioners.¹² Such anomalies in the administration were productive of appalling confusion, since no clear policy could be formulated from the large number of conflicting projects undergoing consideration or actually in operation.

The outstanding difficulty of the past has been the lack of a single controlling authority and the absence of co-operation amongst existing authorities. Conflict of interest was everywhere apparent; every project encountered great opposition from some source or other. Criticisms of existing arrangements and suggested solutions have embodied a discordant compendium of many voices. Such a situation entailed incessant and heavy expense. It was estimated that the legal and parliamentary costs incurred by the endless feuds which accompanied attempts to improve the river Nene had amounted to more than £100,000 by the close of the nineteenth century.¹³ The need for co-operation was repeatedly urged, and many advocated the establishment of authorities to be responsible for the entire length of main rivers to eliminate the clash of conflicting interests. In 1874 Sir John Coode, when summarising the major difficulties associated with the Nene, had stressed the desirability of forming 'one general Conservancy, having control over the whole tidal compartment'.¹⁴ J. H. H. Moxon's recommendations relating to the Great Ouse had gone a stage further:

> I certainly should suggest, that to carry out any improvements, it would be most desirable that there should be one central body ... who should have power over the whole river. At the present moment, what with one governing body and another – with divided action, and conflicting interests – the proper drainage of the Fens appears almost hopeless.¹⁵

W. H. Wheeler thought the number of private acts of parliament in force in relation to the Witham, Welland, Nene and Great Ouse 'extraordinary'. He deplored a situation where the 'number of jurisdictions which have control over the river or the banks has accumulated till at times it is almost impossible to define their powers and rights'.¹⁶ The ill effects of divided administration throughout the Fenland cannot be too much emphasised. Wheeler recommended the establishment of greater centralisation, whilst avoiding, as far as possible, too great an interference with existing arrangements:

> What is wanted is the consolidation of all these smaller trusts, and the uniting them by representatives sent to one common Conservancy Board, which should have control over the main river and its banks from its source to the sea, leaving the management of the interior drainage to the trusts already in existence, or, where none exist, to others formed under the powers of the Land Drainage Act.[17]

R. F. Grantham added his voice to the general clamour, attributing lack of improvement in the Fenland rivers mainly to the 'complication of authorities'.[18]

Although some effort was made in the direction of a more centralised administration there were inevitably delays in establishing conservancy boards on the lines advocated by Wheeler. The difficulties inherent in the introduction of a fair rating system proved at this period to be an insuperable obstacle. A major stumbling block arose over the question of rating the upland communities, hitherto largely exempt from the heavy drainage taxes which had at times constituted a considerable burden on many Fenland farmers. In 1877 it was suggested that the most equitable arrangement would be to levy the rates 'over the whole area of a watershed, the lands and houses below the flood level being rated at a higher amount than those above it, and other graduations and exceptions being made to meet particular cases'.[19] But at this stage the whole business seemed bedevilled with endless complexities. The upland interests opposed any attempt to draw them into the taxation net with bitter hostility; there was a further repetition of this situation in 1879. In that year the Rivers Conservancy Bill had proposed to divide the catchment basin of each river into lowland, midland and upland areas. These were to be rated in a 'diminishing ratio according to their respective altitudes'.[20] The bill was defeated by the efforts of the midlanders, however, 'who next to the owners of the lowlands would have to pay the largest rates'.[21] There were other difficulties. Lack of money had always been a great problem in the Fenland due to the total absence of any really large towns or industrial complexes. This meant that the burden of drainage taxation fell directly on the shoulders of the landed interest, a circumstance which was considerably offset, however, by the far greater productivity of the land when compared with other areas.

At length, in 1920, after widespread local agitation, the area drained by the Great Ouse and its tributaries was established as a separate and distinct drainage district.[22] As the Bedford Level Corporation's entire field of jurisdiction fell within the scope of the Land Drainage Act it had consented to the inclusion of its few remaining powers with those of the newly constituted Ouse Drainage Board. With the final transfer of its assets, liabilities and duties its existence was terminated. It had survived the vicissitudes of 237 years of difficulty and had played, for much of its history, a dominant role in the struggle to maintain the drained Level. The functions of the South Level, Denver sluice and Ouse Banks commissioners, together with those of the Ouse Outfall and Lower Ouse Drainage Boards were also transferred to the new authority. This arrangement represented a decisive step forward in the direction of a more centralised drainage administration throughout the Fenland.

Yet another advance was made in 1927 when a royal commission was appointed to examine the working of drainage authorities throughout England and Wales. In the report on its findings the commission recommended the establishment of conservancy boards, each with exclusive control over a main river, and empowered to levy rates over the whole of their respective catchment areas.[23] These recommendations embodied the central theme of the Land Drainage Act of 1930, which resulted in the creation of the Catchment Boards of the Witham and Steeping, Welland, Nene and Great Ouse. This act represents a considerable milestone in Fenland drainage administration. For the first time in history a single authority was established to be responsible for the whole catchment area of each major river system, and to be the over-riding voice in drainage matters throughout the whole area of the uplands from which it gathered its waters, and the lowlands through which it discharged them. Each Catchment Board was fully representative. One member was appointed by the Minister of Agriculture, at least two-thirds of the rest by county councils and county borough councils lying in the catchment area, and the remainder represented the Internal Drainage Boards responsible for the drainage of the low-lying lands within the region. These boards were the successors to the tangle of local drainage authorities that had grown up during past centuries. Each was responsible for the drains and main ditches in its own locality. The Catchment Boards were financed by a levy upon the rates and by special contributions from all the Internal Drainage Boards throughout the entire catchment area. Although there were still some anomalies this reorganisation represented a vast improvement on previous arrangements. It treated each river as a single entity rather than as a series of unrelated sections, was representative, and rates were levied with maximum fairness. It is interesting to note that in the case of the internal boards the basis of rating was on the Schedule 'A' value for income tax purposes of the land and premises in a particular district. This was considered to be more equitable than the traditional mode of taking the acreage basis.

By an act of 1948 the Catchment Boards were replaced by River Boards which, although invested with completely new responsibilities for fisheries and the prevention of water pollution, operated on identical lines so far as land drainage was concerned. The Welland and Great Ouse River Boards were destined to accomplish two of the most important drainage schemes to be executed in England during the past 300 years. It remains to give some account of the events leading up to these vast undertakings.

THE GREAT OUSE AND WELLAND FLOOD PROTECTION SCHEMES

Although modern pumping plant, driven first by steam and then by diesel engines or electric motors, went a long way towards solving the problem of fen drainage, the danger of widespread inundation had never entirely receded. The upland floodwaters were still experiencing difficulty in reaching the sea. The volume of these floodwaters seems to have increased considerably during the nineteenth century, and in 1876 Mr Hardy Wells penned an irascible letter to the *Cambridge Independent Press* on the subject. He argued that the land drainage improvements executed in the higher catchment areas were responsible for the present poor state of Fenland drainage, because these had the effect of discharging more water into the rivers with greater force:

> The upland country has done quite enough to ruin the Fens without dictating to them now what they shall do. It was never intended when the adventurers cut the hundred feet that the upland proprietors should carry out in Huntingdonshire, Cambridgeshire and Bedfordshire a system of subsoil drainage which rapidly casts upon their neighbours millions of tons of water, with a force which is unnatural by the side of the former natural downflow of the ... rivers.[24]

From the late nineteenth century the state of the Fenland rivers once again became the subject of much critical debate. Repeated attempts to improve their outfalls had brought very little overall benefit, more especially in the interior of the region. These outfalls were still very far from perfect. That of the Ouse was particularly defective, so that the 'low water of spring-tides did not fall to as low a level as in former years'.[25] Much harm was done by flushing mud from the various fleets and creeks adjoining King's Lynn harbour, which resulted in acute silting of the channel to seaward. The Nene and Welland outfalls were obstructed by silt. It was a similar story on the Witham. Here, despite the completion of extensive outfall works between 1880 and 1884 – which included the enlargement of the Grand sluice near Boston, the excavation of a new outfall cut further to seaward, and a thorough dredging of the existing channel up to Boston – the interior seems to have undergone scant improvement. Although the drainage of some parts nearer the coast benefited from the reduction in the low-water level, large tracts around Lincoln were frequently inundated.[26] But the Fenland outfalls, although admittedly unsatisfactory in a number of respects, were yet considerably better than they had been in the past. In view of the enormous efforts and capital expended on them the results seemed exceptionally disappointing.

In the past outfall works had exerted immediate, if invariably short-lived, effects. Projects on the river Nene during the first half of the nineteenth century had achieved such a significant improvement in the North Level that land values soared.[27] The benefits of outfall improvement on the Great Ouse also had been felt inland as far as Huntingdonshire and throughout the entire South and Middle Levels by effecting a widespread reduction in water levels.[28] Yet, at the commencement of the twentieth century flooding still occurred in the South Level with disturbing frequency. According to R. F. Grantham the condition of large areas was 'deplorable . . . at least 5,000 or 6,000 acres are waterlogged for want of a better system of drainage'.[29] In the Nene drainage area W. H. Wheeler had earlier drawn attention to the frequent inundation of thousands of acres inland. Even the streets of Peterborough were flooded 'and people driven from their houses'. He found the Welland, also, ill-adapted to carry off rain-water with sufficient speed to avert periodical disaster: 'The banks which protect the fens are constantly being broken, owing to the channel being overfull and the fens flooded.'[30] In July 1880 thousands of acres had been affected, with the town of Stamford and many nearby villages awash, 'the water rising to a height of 3 and 4 feet in some of the houses'. Wheeler concluded that although 'floods so calamitous are exceptional, yet their frequency and the large area of land thrown out of cultivation, are sufficient to demand that such alterations should be made in the river, as the main outfall of the drainage of the district, as to render it efficient for its discharge'.[31] Sidney Preston called attention to the extreme futility of outfall improvements under existing conditions:

> It must, of course, be admitted that it is right in principle to commence the improvement of any river from the outfall and to work upwards. At the same time, it is useless to obtain a perfect outfall if the upper lengths and branches of the river are in such a state that the water from the lands to be drained cannot reach the outfall quickly enough.

In this context he was highly critical of the Great Ouse:

> It seems to me . . . this is the case in the present instance. With the construction of the Eau Brink, Marsh and Vinegar Middle Cuts, a good deal was done to improve the outfall which, although it might be still further improved, may still be said to be fairly good. What, however, has been done in the past for the upper reaches of the river?[32]

What indeed? Sir John Rennie and Robert Stephenson had previously laid great emphasis on this point when reporting on the progress of the outfall works below King's Lynn in February 1855. They referred to the further lowering of the water up to Denver sluice, stressing however the need to adapt the internal drains to the improved outfall to derive advantage to the fullest extent.[33] Unfortunately very little effort had been made in this direction, and the condition of the Great Ouse and its tributaries steadily deteriorated. In 1879 the highly questionable dredging activities of the Denver sluice commissioners at Magdalen Bend was made the butt of innumerable criticisms. They were 'dredging up the mud and allowing it to drop into the river again, instead of putting it into barges and depositing it on the banks. – They simply raised the mud and passed it on to their neighbours.' The Lynn Council thought it 'a pity the Commissioners should act in such a manner when the stuff was so much needed on the banks'.[34] Further inland the Hundred Foot river was choked by 'moorbeds or boulders of rushes'.[35] It was considered desirable to dredge the channel to a uniform depth to eliminate existing variations, which ranged from $2\frac{1}{2}$ to 10ft. Since the days of Vermuyden there had in fact been no cessation in the complaints about the Hundred Foot. Although it had shortened the channel of the Ouse it had never exercised the looked-for effects. Its capacity was considered to be far too small:

> The new channel had not scoured to itself a deep and regular bed in that long lapse of time; on the contrary, it has become choked and unnavigable at times . . . far from being a better river, many eminent engineers, and amongst them the late Mr Rennie, have proposed to restore the river to its ancient course.[36]

Mr J. Abernethy's report on the Hundred Foot river in 1876 to the Ouse Floods Committee of St Ives had found its capacity, even when dredged, hopelessly insufficient to discharge the floodwaters. Of the rest of Vermuyden's drainage works, the demolition of Denver sluice and the deepening and embanking of the existing rivers to admit the greatest possible inflow of the tide to scour the channels had been ceaselessly advocated. Denver sluice was 'worse than nothing'; 'the worst of remedies inflicting an immense injury both to Drainage and to Navigation'.[37] In Telford's opinion 'it ought never to have existed, and should be removed'.[38]

But criticism of the Fenland rivers was by no means confined to the Great Ouse. Many sections of the Lark and Little Ouse came under fire for being impeded with weeds and reed-beds. On the Welland also there were few grounds for complacency. The river suffered from an exceptional disadvantage in that at Spalding, near its point of discharge into the Wash, the channel was very confined, and compressed the floodwaters in their passage through the town. A similar difficulty was experienced on the Nene where the 'insufficient and tortuous' waterway at Wisbech did little to facilitate the clearance of floodwater through the area.[39] J. H. H. Moxon had deplored the numerous obstructions in the channel.[40] A mile below Peterborough there was a 'miserably small bridge of three wooden arches' through which 'all the water of Northamptonshire' had to pass. He noted that the waterway through Wisbech was so extremely confined that it was known locally as 'the Bottleneck' on account of its 'puny width'. But these were by no means the total of the difficulties complained of: 'to crown all, just below the bridge there still remains under water the stone foundation of a sort of sluice which formerly existed, and which is also most appropriately named "The Throttle". Here, instead of running off quickly to sea, the waters swirl and eddy, by no means improving the chances of the upland country running off its waters in flood time.'

Although it was universally accepted that something would have to be done to remove these impediments and improve the channel, the problem of finance remained an insurmountable obstacle, whilst Sir John Coode was firmly convinced that the benefit to be derived from any major works would hardly justify the colossal expense.[41] There was ample scope for improvement everywhere, but the form that improvement should take became the subject, as with all fen projects, of intense arguments.

On the Nene, that most daunting of rivers, something concrete was at last done. Here from 1931 extremely important works were undertaken by the newly-formed Nene Catchment Board, whose achievement was the more remarkable since it had inherited a river in what seemed to be the final stages of decay. Within a few years a near miracle had been wrought. Between Northampton and Peterborough many cuts were made in order to straighten the river and eliminate sharp bends. The channel between Wisbech and Northampton was deepened and cleared of weeds over a distance of more than 80 miles. The dredging scheme from Wisbech to Peterborough had particular significance in that it provided an ample waterway for the discharge of floodwater, and material excavated by the dragline dredgers was used to form a cradge bank to prevent water, except in abnormal conditions, flowing into the Nene washlands, an area of about 3,500 acres extending from Peterborough to Guyhirne. The improved channel could now easily discharge the water of a relatively minor flood, leaving the washlands empty to deal with any major inundation. This balancing reservoir now acts as a protection for the lower reaches of the river and saves the whole area from what might otherwise be devastating flooding. In addition the famous – or infamous – Northey Gravels near Peterborough (a long shoal of exceedingly hard material stretching practically across the waterway, and creating a serious hazard to drainage and navigation alike) were dynamited out of the river, hence inducing a free flow of water approximately 10ft deep. At the same time the Dog-in-a-Doublet lock and sluices were constructed on the Nene between Peterborough and Guyhirne to control the flow and levels of the water. Also many banks were repaired and strengthened. At Wisbech, where the bottleneck in the existing channel retarded the floodwater discharge, dredging to attain greater depth could only be undertaken after both sides of the river had been piled for a distance of about $2\frac{1}{2}$ miles with concrete piles 23ft long in order to support the banks. Above all the Catchment Board built the magnificent Tydd pumping station near Sutton Bridge, which was capable of discharging $10\frac{3}{4}$ million gallons of water per hour when working to full capacity.

So far as the Great Ouse was concerned Sidney Preston may well have been right in recommending that the effects of overhauling the present system should be observed before any attempt was made to inaugurate expensive new undertakings.[42] Unfortunately nothing tangible was done to remedy existing defects, whilst at the theoretical level attention continued to be almost exclusively directed to outfall improvement, with a fine disregard for conditions inland. It was this 'preoccupation with the outfall' which, in the opinion of Mr W. E. Doran, chief engineer of the Great Ouse Catchment and River Boards, had 'played no small part in the lack of technical progress with the fen flood problem during the past fifty years'.[43] The real problem still awaiting a solution on the Ouse was the protection of the South Level from flooding by the failure or overtopping of the river embankments. The situation was not improved by the presence of Denver sluice which, during high tides when the sea doors were closed, bottled up the landwaters in the rivers and drains of the entire system, effectively blocking their discharge out to sea and ensuring their overspill into the fens. An added cause for concern was that the Ouse washlands, despite their relatively large capacity, could not always contain the floodwaters pouring into them. When these washlands were full, as well as the old channel of the Ouse through Ely and Littleport, an acute conflict arose between the need to discharge the former at Welmore or the latter at Denver. The fact that there was more water coming down the two branches than could be discharged below Denver lay at the root of the trouble. In fact the South Level was the area mainly threatened in times of high flood. Here there were many miles of flood bank, vulnerable to attack by the water at every point. Sir Alexander Gibb emphasised that 'the safeguarding of the South Level against flooding is the crux of the whole problem of flooding in the Fens and that a satisfactory solution of the South Level problem would in effect be a solution of practically the whole problem of the basin of the river Ouse'.[44]

The most obvious remedy, ie heightening and strengthening the banks to an extent where they could not be overtopped or breached, has been made impossible by a number of factors. The most vital of these is the continued sinking of the fens. When Vermuyden first built his flood banks they needed to be only a few feet higher than the surrounding land.[45] But as this sank steadily lower the banks sank with it and had to be continually heightened. As a result some of these flood banks towered, by the twentieth century, as much as 20ft above the fens, but without having significantly increased their safe margin above high flood level in the rivers. In past years effort has been principally concentrated on the attempt to keep pace with the rate of sinking of the embankments. In the 1950s it was estimated that an annual expenditure of about £120,000 was required to achieve this objective in the South Level,[46] whilst over the previous thirty-five years £1½ million had been expended.[47]

There were other difficulties. A notable one was that the banks could not be heightened too much at any one time, or indefinitely, in an area where the earth is too soft to furnish stable foundations able to support heavy weights. No matter how strong the upper portion of the bank may be, if the foundations are weak there is the danger that when a river is in flood the whole of the clay top of the bank may be pushed outwards by the weight of the water and slide over its base into the fen. The original drainers could not possibly have foreseen the result of their activities. Had they done so they would no doubt have left more room, both at the front and rear of the banks, for future heightening operations. As things are, further heightening is very difficult in many places, due to the presence of roads, buildings and drains, which prevent widening at the base, whilst past heightening of the banks has resulted in their becoming too high in relation to their base width. There was the added problem of seepage. Certainly the practice, widely employed since the nineteenth century, of digging a deep trench along the embankment ridge and filling it with clay, represented a great improvement, as the clay in effect formed a waterproof wall through which no water could seep. But where the banks rested on a peat foundation seepage occurred at the base whenever they were subject to high water-levels. Apart from the fact that this seepage was objectionable in itself, and had to be pumped back again into the river, the banks frequently failed through 'blowing-out' at the toe.

As the flood problem could not be solved by heightening and strengthening the banks the sole remaining solution was the reduction of floodwater levels in the rivers. A possible method was to enlarge the Great Ouse and its tributaries to provide greater capacity, and especially the tidal river below Denver, at least to the extent where Denver sluice could discharge at a sufficiently low level for the South Level to be freed from danger at all times. This solution was rejected on the grounds that enlargement would result in increased silting, since the force of the current would be eroded at times of low water. Conversely it could be argued that the dispersion of the Ouse waters amongst a number of comparatively smaller, often weed-infested channels, such as the Old Bedford and Hundred Foot rivers, was having that effect anyway, and that velocity is dependent on depth as well as slope.

Meanwhile suggestions for outfall improvement were demonstrating a uniform tendency to become more ambitious and increasingly complex. Many individuals now favoured the erection of an intermittent barrage at Freebridge, above King's Lynn harbour, for the dual purpose of excluding salt water and silt from the channel and of utilising the storage above the barrage in time of flood. An alternative proposal was to protect the channel with training walls until it terminated in such deep water that no silt could be expected to enter. Towards the end of October 1938 Sir Alexander Gibb & Partners were consulted by the Association of Internal Drainage Authorities within the South Level and their report appeared the following January. They pointed out that

> Any attempt to enlarge or deepen parts of the tidal channel of the Ouse (short of carrying training banks far out into the estuary to the point where sea water is clear of silt) is likely to result in partial failure and disappointment. On the other hand, the expense of a complete scheme with training banks a distance of 6 miles into the Wash estuary would be very great and the results uncertain.[48]

Referring to outfall improvements 'with the idea of creating in the river at Lynn a lower general level at low water of tides than now obtains' Sir Alexander Gibb was 'satisfied that any scheme of this kind can at best only have a slight effect in safeguarding the Fen area against flooding, and might actually be detrimental'. The barrage solution he rejected on the obvious grounds that it would cause heavy silting downstream and would encounter strong opposition from the harbour authorities at King's Lynn, pointing out that 'the exclusion of the tide does not in fact provide a complete remedy for the troubles'.[49] Nevertheless determined supporters of the barrage project have since deplored its rejection, despite the very obvious drawbacks. One Ely resident was subsequently moved to complain:

> For many years there have been advocates of a great Barrage near or below King's Lynn to cut off the tides and incidentally the silt passing up to choke the rivers, but this does not seem to find favour largely because of the opposition anticipated from the Borough of King's Lynn who through the centuries of fen drainage have been the bitter opponents of so many schemes calculated to benefit the fens.[50]

Sir Alexander Gibb's proposal was for the construction of a new relief channel running from Denver to Magdalen Bend, designed to ensure the prompt evacuation of all floodwater coming down the Ouse between Littleport and Denver. This was a crucial area, for through this channel poured the combined floodwaters of the river Cam, Soham Lode, and the rivers Lark, Little Ouse and Wissey. He further recommended the establishment of a pumping installation at the head of this new channel, to be operated, however, only on the occasion of an exceptional flood. The capital cost of the works was estimated at £649,000; the annual running and maintenance costs were expected to be small.

But although this scheme had a number of merits, notably cheapness, it was argued that it would afford insufficient relief to the South Level. Objections to Sir Alexander Gibb's proposals included the considerable expense of maintaining a large pumping station at Denver which would be required only during heavy floods. Furthermore the floodwater from the uplands would continue to flow through the fens and, as the embankments would continue to sink with the wastage of the land, further extensive work would become necessary in the future.

Unable to grope their way through such a morass of conflicting proposals and objections the River Great Ouse Catchment Board called in Sir Murdoch MacDonald & Partners to advise them. A report was issued in July 1940, and the need for urgency in tackling the problem was stressed. The banks were 'very obviously incapable of meeting the really big storm which inevitably will come one day and which will bring a major disaster in its train if preparation is not made to cope with it'. It was remarked how 'the inhabitants of the South Level are accustomed to living on the brink of disaster. At present . . . parts of the River Wissey banks are 1ft under maximum flood level, ie they have a freeboard of minus 1ft!'[51] Adopting the remedy first advocated by Vermuyden in 1638 plans proposed by Sir Murdoch MacDonald & Partners consisted of intercepting the upland waters in their passage through the fens. This involved constructing a canal, or cut-off channel, through the hard skirtland round the eastern edge of the fens, picking up the rivers Cam, Lark, Little Ouse and Wissey, as well as the upper portions of the various lodes. In addition it was suggested that there should be a new relief channel cut from Denver to St Germans. The scheme also provided for the straightening of the Magdalen Bend in the tidal river, and for washlands to be established in the Stoke Ferry Fen area for the storage of floodwaters during periods of high tide.

These suggestions possessed considerable merit. The existing rivers would become ordinary drainage channels, carrying only the local pumped water and as much of the upland water as was required for special amenities such as navigation and irrigation. The South Level would be relieved of all danger from breaches in its river embankments, and this would be the case under present conditions and also, it was hoped, when the fens sank to their lowest levels in the future. Maintenance of the existing embankments would be reduced to a minimum. The main disadvantage was cost, estimated at that time at close on £4 million. In view of the heavy expense the Catchment Board declared that the scheme could not at the present be wholly carried out, and that effort should be concentrated on the relief channel from Denver to St Germans to relieve the pressure of floodwater piling up to dangerous levels inside the Great Ouse river system. Unfortunately no immediate steps to implement these proposals could be taken due to the continuance of World War II, but work proceeded on the preparation of designs and plans. In the immediate post-war years the shortage of materials, manpower and large contractors' plant, coupled with economic uncertainties, further delayed the operation. Then came disaster, as Sir Murdoch MacDonald & Partners had predicted it would.

The 1947 winter had been phenomenally harsh, with well above average falls of snow and rain. Normally much of this would have sunk into the ground, and the rest would have been discharged out to sea by the rivers. In the winter of 1947 very little of this rain and snow could sink into the soil, because the whole of England was gripped by frost. In the fens the great drains were frozen solid and blocked with snow-drifts. Until the thaw came, a vast part of the rainfall which had fallen in the form of snow was held where it had fallen. With the thaw, however, the amount of water seeking outlet was far greater than the rivers could contain within their banks. Heavy rain immediately after the thaw and continued rain for the following month, with winds of hurricane force at the critical period, all in unusual combination, made flooding inevitable. The situation was considerably worsened by ice, which hampered the working of the pumping stations; also by the disintegrating effects of frost on the clay of which the flood banks were largely composed.

In March the melted snow began to run off into the rivers. Conditions around 13 March were remarkable. Many of the smaller tributary streams and drains were still blocked with ice; all were surcharged due to the excessive flow of water. The rain and melted snow collected at any low points on the land, or flowed swiftly along depressions towards the river valleys, following any route, roads, even across fields, along which there was a sufficient fall. On the eastern side of the fens the waters rose by about 8ft in four days, and some 10,000 cu ft of water per second was flowing into the Fenland river system on that side. From the Witham to the north came little trouble. There was considerable flooding in Lincoln itself, but the valuable farmlands through which the river flows were little damaged. The Nene, owing to the reinforcement and improvement which had been carried out to the flood banks in previous years, stood the test magnificently, even though it carried a far greater volume and intensity of floodwater than had been experienced for more than a century. Also elaborate preparations had been made in anticipation of the thaw. The entire length of the river had been drawn down to a very low level; the washlands between Peterborough and Guyhirne were empty, and the water-level in Morton's Leam had been lowered to the minimum level permitted by the tide. All the gates at the Dog-in-a-Doublet sluice were fully raised to allow for a maximum flood discharge; the setting of these gates was not to be altered for thirty-one consecutive days.

The volume of floodwater passing down the Nene was colossal. According to some typical data published on the March 1947 flood discharges in other rivers, the pro rata flow in the river Nene was exceeded only by that of the Yorkshire Ouse. At the Wansford gauging station near Peterborough a discharge of 285 million gallons per hour (12,700 cusecs) was recorded on 18 March, a figure far in excess of any previously recorded:[52]

Date	Discharge in gallons per hour	Cusecs
January 1939	125,000,000	5,570
October 1939	80,500,000	3,590
February 1940	135,000,000	6,040
March 1941	71,000,000	3,170
18 March 1947	285,000,000	12,700

Flood protection works executed on the Nene during previous years were thoroughly tested by the high water-levels. It is remarkable that no floodwater from the river entered the protected areas, which were saved from serious and prolonged inundation. It was not so with the Welland and Great Ouse.

The Welland Catchment Board was fully alive to the danger represented by the bottleneck in the river at Spalding, where a number of buildings and roads were inconveniently sited in close proximity to the channel. The water could not be discharged through that reach of the river in sufficient volume to drain away a heavy flood in the upper reaches. A scheme had been approved some years previously to divert much of the river water in a by-pass channel round the town, but World War II had terminated all progress. The result of this check near the mouth of the river was that in flood times large quantities of water were impounded in the Crowland and Cowbit washlands. In March

1947 it was not long before the washland near Crowland was filled to capacity with 6 million tons of water. In the meantime great blocks of ice fretted away the tops of the flood banks, carving holes in them which had to be hastily plugged with sandbags. This situation prevailed until about midday on Friday 21 March, when the eastern bank failed at a point about $1\frac{1}{4}$ miles north of Crowland. The water-level was then about 20ft above the level of the adjacent fen land, and a breach about 180ft wide formed rapidly, through which the floodwater from the river Welland swept into the North Level. The timely decision of the North Level commissioners to regulate the flow of floodwater to the pumping stations to avoid putting these out of action, coupled with the prompt execution of measures to confine the flood to as small an area as possible, did much to alleviate the disaster. The level of the gates at certain of the control sluices was raised by the addition of timbers. Stone was deposited in the New South Eau to form a dam, to block the eastward advance of water from the breach. Timbers were placed to raise the level of the sluice at Clough's Cross for the purpose of controlling the flow of water to the pumping station at Tydd to avoid flooding the engine house. Drains were blocked and roads and culverts sandbagged in whichever direction there was a natural fall for the floodwater. By these means some measure of control was obtained. Fortunately the Tydd pumps functioned magnificently. They were called upon to work continuously night and day for six weeks. Their contribution towards averting a major flood disaster in the North Level and South Holland districts cannot be overestimated.

The worst floods occurred along the Great Ouse and its tributaries, with breaches in the Wissey and Little Ouse, as well as in the main river itself. The banks of the river Lark held, but by a narrow margin. Gale force winds whipped up the water into great waves, which were dashed against the sagging embankments. At Over the waves were 'breaking across the top of the bank like the waves of the sea breaking across the quay of some fishing port'.[53] The huge breach in the barrier bank of the Great Ouse at Over Fen was the most serious in the entire Fenland. Yet ironically this was a bank that had given less anxiety than most.

It was 12ft wide at the top, built of solid clay, and had never been overtopped or breached within living memory. Now a 50yd gap was torn in the bank, and the waters swept through it across Over Fen, where they began eating away at the southern flood bank of the Old West River from the rear. That bank gave also and the water poured into the Hill Row and Haddenham Fens. A total of 57,000 acres of Fenland eventually lay under water, in some cases to a depth of 7 or 8ft. But things could very well have been worse. High tides did not complicate the situation. Winds

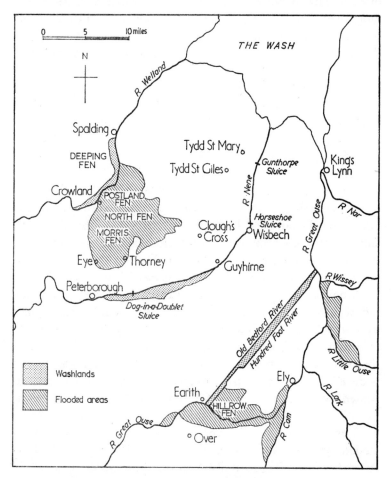

FIGURE 12. The flooded Fenland: March 1947

did not blow in a direction which could force the tides in at higher levels and for longer periods. And it was doubtless fortunate that, in the southern Fenland, the bank blew out at Over rather than lower down in the Hundred Foot river, where the results of breaching, by releasing the pent-up water in the washlands, would have been more serious, and the breach more difficult to repair.

When the floods were over came the work of collating the flood discharge records and estimating the magnitude of the disaster. The cost of repairing the damage was heavy, assessed at more than £200,000 in the South Level alone. Considerable sums were spent on strengthening the north bank of the Welland and the banks of the river Glen, and on making good the North Level bank where the waters had overflowed the Great Postland, North and Morris Fens. The Welland Catchment Board now pressed ahead with the scheme of constructing a by-pass channel to eliminate the bottleneck in the Welland at Spalding, to improve the discharge of floodwater out to sea. This was carried out as part of the River Welland Major Improvement Scheme, executed between 1947 and 1957, and involving some form of improvement from the outfall almost up to Stamford. The scheme included widening, regrading and raising the flood banks of the tidal channel from Fosdyke Bridge to Marsh Road. Between 1948 and 1953 the important Spalding Coronation Channel was constructed, effectively diverting the main body of water away from the centre of the town. The tidal Marsh Road sluice, situated upstream of the confluence of the Coronation Channel with the old Welland channel, cut off the tidal water, whilst maintaining a constant level of fresh water in the town of Spalding and further upstream. At the same time the channel between Locks Mill and the Folly River through the Cowbit and Crowland washes was widened to increase flood-carrying capacity. This was accompanied by the construction of a new cradge bank and weirs at Four Mile Bar and Crowland Bridge to enable the washes to be used as a reservoir whenever necessary. The scheme also included the widening and regrading of the old Maxey North Drain from the Folly river to Lolham Bridges, the material excavated being used to construct flood banks to prevent any further over-

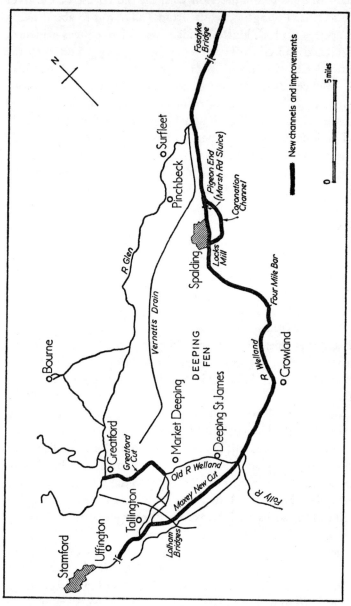

FIGURE 13. The River Welland Major Improvement Scheme 1947-57

flowing of the adjacent land. A new channel was excavated from Lolham Bridges to the junction with the old course of the river Welland near Tallington, whilst from Tallington to about half a mile upstream of Uffington Bridge the old river was widened, straightened and embanked. Finally between 1955 and 1957 the Greatford Cut was made from Market Deeping to Greatford. This new channel, cut across country, consists of a shallow, embanked waterway varying from 17 to 24ft wide, with control sluices at Greatford. The channel is designed for operation in flood periods to discharge the floodwaters of the Glen, which in the past have often inundated large tracts of arable land in the locality. The channel relieves the overtopping and overloading of the Glen banks through the Bourne Fen, Pinchbeck and Surfleet area, which has constituted so great a problem in the past.[54]

So much for the important works executed on the Welland; so far as the Great Ouse was concerned it was obvious that Sir Murdoch MacDonald's scheme, far from being too large as had been suggested in 1940, was now too small in view of the new flood records, and it was accordingly modified to provide for a flood of even greater dimensions than that of 1947 coinciding with a spring tide. The scheme ultimately executed provided for a cut-off channel, $27\frac{1}{2}$ miles long, starting from the river Lark at Barton Mills in Suffolk, and carrying the waters of the Lark, Little Ouse and Wissey round the edge of the fens to join the proposed relief channel at Denver. The old course of the river between Ely and Denver would continue to receive the waters of the Cam and various minor waterways, as well as the discharges from the pumping stations. Provision was made for the Ouse to be widened and deepened from Denver to the mouth of the Cam. Meanwhile the original design of the relief channel required modification, so as to increase its discharge capacity from the original 6,300 cusecs to the new figure of 10,000. The consulting engineers proposed to achieve this objective by extending the channel for a further $1\frac{1}{4}$ miles to enter the tidal Ouse a short distance above King's Lynn. The width of its lower section was increased from 175 to 200ft, whilst the higher section above Magdalen Bend was deepened. This would enable a satisfactory

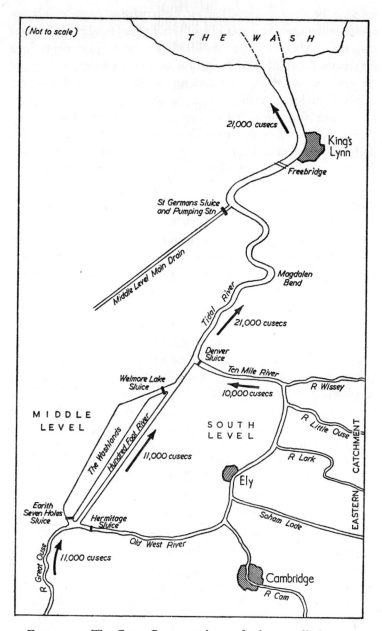

FIGURE 14. The Great Ouse: maximum freshwater discharges required in times of extraordinary flood, as 1947

level to be obtained at Denver, even with a considerably increased discharge, and would also benefit the Hundred Foot river and the washlands. The freeboard on the embankments in a maximum flood allowed for would be from 4 to 5ft at Ely and 7ft near Denver.[55] Two dangers remained: that these freeboards would be reduced gradually as the embankments settled, both in themselves and through the shrinking of the peat layer below them, and also that this reduction in freeboard might coincide with a flood of even larger dimensions than that of 1947. Therefore provision was made for future sinking of the South Level river embankments, when the freeboard would become inadequate in many places, by a proposed large low-lift pumping station at Ely, with a barrage across the river at that point, so that water-levels south of Ely could be maintained at a safe limit. It was envisaged that the construction of the pumping station and barrage would be delayed until some future date, when conditions would render them essential.[56]

It was decided that for work of this magnitude parliamentary sanction would be necessary, and here the project ran into trouble. It was distinctly unfortunate that the Catchment Board saw fit to press ahead with the undertaking without first consulting the interests of those bodies most likely to be affected by it, pleading in extenuation that the 1947 floods had underlined the need for urgent action. As might have been predicted the Flood Protection Bill elicited a great clamour from various opposing interests. The Church Commissioners presented a list of grievances, principally relating to the compulsory acquisition for the works of land owned by the Commission. The Ely Urban District Council lodged protests about the acquisition of land near the cathedral for digging clay, which would not only interfere with public footpaths, but also 'ruin one of the best views of the cathedral by introducing into the landscape an unsightly scar, right across the lower part of the view'. But these were comparatively minor matters and a compromise was soon reached. The most serious opposition came from the navigation interest, of which the King's Lynn Conservancy Board was the most prominent representative. The board was concerned about the possible effects of a high flood discharge, concentrated into short periods, on the shipping channel in the Wash. Fears were expressed that a greatly increased volume of water might erode the bed and banks of the river at King's Lynn and threaten the safety of quays and other riverside structures, whilst great quantities of silt would be swept out into the Wash and might obstruct the shipping channel. The Conservancy Board's case received support from the British Transport Commission, fearful of the consequences of possible silting at the docks' entrance as well as in the shipping channel itself. Various trading interests within the port were equally concerned about the loss of navigation facilities.[57] Remedial works were considered highly essential and the Conservancy Board was prominent in the campaign for an extension of the existing training walls into the Wash for the purpose of utilising the scouring action of the water to the maximum by confining the currents in a fixed channel to assist in the removal of silt.

The Catchment Board countered these suggestions by arguing that the Wash was not their problem but that of the King's Lynn port authorities; that the navigation channel was tortuous and impermanent; that a situation in which they were to be held responsible for the constant vagaries of nature would be intolerable, and that the Flood Protection Scheme would not in any way alter the total amount of water flowing off the catchment. It would merely flow faster during a flood than formerly and with an increased freshwater scouring effect from King's Lynn to the sea.[58] Finally the Catchment Board suggested that the navigation interest was trying to obtain 'at the public expense the execution of works which . . . would be beneficial for navigation but unnecessary from the point of view of land drainage'.[59]

A detailed summary of the various conflicting arguments would be tedious. It is sufficient to note that although the King's Lynn Conservancy Board was unsuccessful in getting its proposals accepted in the Commons, at a subsequent hearing in the Lords their efforts were crowned with success. A clause for the safeguarding of navigation was inserted in the Flood Protection Bill, prohibiting the use of the relief channel for flood discharge purposes until protective works had been carried out within the port of King's Lynn. At a later date the engineer of the Great

Ouse River Board, Mr W. E. Doran, gave vent to profound exasperation:

> What an ironical situation! After ten years of work and delays, the Board, having produced a scheme to deal effectively with the worst floods on record and having apparently freed itself from the shifting sands of the Wash, was confronted with the old training wall nightmare reappearing in new guise, not as a drainage scheme this time, but as a scheme for the protection of navigation. Would the sands of the Wash still have power to strangle the drainage of the fens?[60]

In the light of the very real dangers confronting the South Level inhabitants the interminable feud between the Catchment and Conservancy Boards presented a singularly unedifying spectacle. Although the Flood Protection Act received the Royal Assent in 1949 it was not until 1953 that disagreements with the Conservancy Board were finally resolved and work could begin.

The undertaking included several important structural works. The cut-off channel itself is carried in concrete syphons when it passes underneath the Lark, Little Ouse and Wissey. Connections have been made with the Little Ouse and Wissey by sluices, by means of which the full flow or part of it is diverted into the cut-off channel instead of passing through the South Level. A Head sluice has been constructed at Barton Mills, but at the downstream end at Denver the cut-off has a free discharge into the relief channel. There are sluices at the head and tail of the relief channel. The Head sluice admits floodwater from the old Ouse flowing round Ely into the relief channel. It is built of reinforced concrete and has three openings, each 30ft wide, controlled by vertical-lift steel sluice-gates operated by electric motors. The Tail sluice controls the discharge of the floodwater into the tidal river. This sluice has seven openings each 30ft wide by 22ft high, and controlled by a power-operated vertical-lift steel gate and an automatic steel flap-gate. The structure is supported on concrete piles driven into the hard clay.

An important feature of the Flood Protection Scheme has been the use of willow and brushwood mattresses, and slag pitching for bank protection work at bridge sites on the tidal river Ouse. A total of 118,000 sq yd of pitching and 120,000 sq yd of mattress

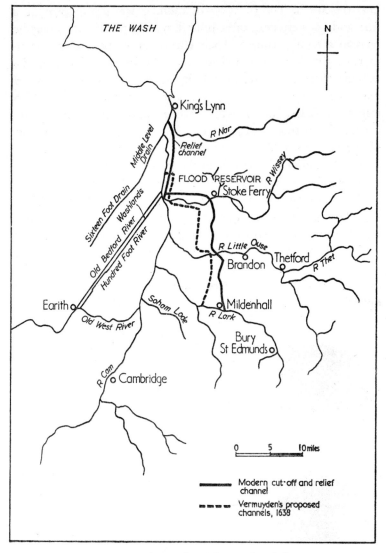

FIGURE 15. The Great Ouse Flood Protection Scheme 1954–64: compared with Vermuyden's scheme of 1638

work were included in the contract. In addition, £600,000 was expended primarily on an extension of the west training wall out into the Wash. The function of training walls is to provide a firm and not very permeable boundary so that the waters may be held in a regular course. Their effects, as we have seen, are to increase the depth of the channel and hence the velocity of the current; to give a degree of stability, to carry the general flow off seawards, and also to annul, or at any rate reduce, silting which might otherwise occur when masses of eroded material are carried downstream.[61] In this context, despite the initial doubts of the Catchment Board, the Flood Protection Scheme has undoubtedly derived benefit from the improved outfall, which has considerably facilitated the discharge of floodwater out to sea.

The entire project was completed by the Great Ouse River Board by September 1964, and at a total cost of £10,452,000. The annual value of the crops harvested from the fens was estimated at £20 million in 1949.[62] After more than three hundred years of effort Vermuyden's original scheme at last appeared to be operating with complete success in the South Level. A cautious optimism seemed justified.

Epilogue – The Fenland Present and Future

MUCH has been accomplished in the Fenland during the past three centuries. The threat of future flooding on any large scale appears to have receded, and the rich fen soils continue to yield abundant crops, apparently justifying the vast expense and effort which have contributed to this achievement. In 1664 Colonel William Dodson had expressed the hope that 'the charge of those fen lands may not exceed the profit'.[1] Today a great question mark still hangs over the fens. Paradoxically a problem which now remains is not so much flooding as over-draining.

Now that the problem of flooding has receded, that of the continued surface shrinkage of the land has come inexorably to the fore, as vast acreages are threatened with the ultimate destruction of the peat. This will involve the use of entirely new agricultural techniques, designed to retain, in the highest degree possible, the existing productivity of the soil. To what actual extent these will be successful it is of course too early to judge. But apart from this certain changes and proposals are going forward or are under investigation, whose ultimate impact on the Fenland is uncertain. It remains to examine these factors in closer detail.

ADMINISTRATION: THE ANGLIAN WATER AUTHORITY

Under the provisions of the 1963 Water Resources Act new River Authorities took up their duties on 1 April 1965. So far as land drainage and flood prevention were concerned their responsibilities were identical to those exercised by the now defunct

River Boards. They were simply invested with wider powers in other fields. But continued development has not ceased even with the establishment of River Authorities. The significance to the Fenland drainage interests of the proposals to create ten Regional Water Authorities throughout England and Wales in April 1974 has been much debated. So far as land drainage was concerned existing arrangements had proved completely adequate. The River Authorities had encountered no problems in this connection, and it was at no time suggested that they were ill constituted or poorly equipped to deal with land drainage. In this context no need existed for their responsibilities in this highly specialised field to be handed over to another type of organisation; rather the reverse was true, especially as it was not even partially for land drainage purposes that the new Water Authorities were originally conceived.

In a densely populated country like England, with smaller resources of water in relation to its population than any of its European neighbours, the increasing use of water for both domestic and industrial purposes is now posing major problems, which it will require considerable effort to solve. It has been argued that substantial and increasing capital investment would be needed to increase supplies of water to keep pace with greater demand, to treat this enlarged volume of water after use, and to reduce the present degree of pollution of rivers and coastal waters. In the government's view there was an urgent need for Regional Water Authorities with a clear sense of purpose, able to take a comprehensive and long-term view of all the relevant aspects of water management, and at the same time capable of taking successful and cost-effective action to safeguard water supplies and protect the environment. The government was convinced that the changes were essential if water supplies were to be safeguarded and if the quality of water in rivers and estuaries was to be improved or even maintained.[2] Therefore it was envisaged that the new authorities would be responsible for the planning and co-ordination of all water services within their areas, and would draw up a long-term water plan for their regions within the framework of a national plan.

Briefly, the Regional Water Authorities are concerned with the development and control of water resources, the distribution of water in bulk and its supply to consumers, the control of water quality, the treatment of sewage, the administration and improvement of fisheries, and the management of canals and inland navigations; all these in addition to the administration of land drainage, including flood protection and sea defence. The land drainage functions of the River Authorities had, it has been argued, objectives fundamentally different from those of the functions of the Water Authorities, involving different problems, and the exercise of different techniques.[3] The proposals outlined above generated widespread fears that the Water Authorities, because of other, extremely onerous commitments, may not have the same concern for land drainage that the River Authorities had had.

The Fenland comprises part of the area which has been placed under the jurisdiction of the new Anglian Water Authority. This area is exceptionally large, extending from north of the city of Lincoln to Southend-on-Sea. It embraces the whole of the areas hitherto administered by the East Suffolk and Norfolk, the Lincolnshire, the Welland and Nene, and the Great Ouse River Authorities, and includes the greater part of the area formerly under the jurisdiction of the Essex River Authority. The main objection to the Water Authorities assuming the land-drainage functions of the River Authorities – ie that it would remove the exercise of these functions from any effective local control, with the danger of their becoming submerged in the other work to be dealt with – seems particularly relevant in the case of East Anglia. Through over-centralisation there is a danger of everything becoming too complex and of procedures being congested.

The need to safeguard drainage interests led the Fenland, and other River Authorities with responsibilities in this field, to submit recommendations for the establishment of autonomous land-drainage bodies, comparable with the River Authorities in territorial extent and organisation, and retaining their well-tried financial system.[4] Support for their efforts came from other interested bodies, for example from the King's Lynn Conservancy Board, which in a memorandum to the Ministry of Agriculture cast some doubt on the ability of the proposed new monoliths to

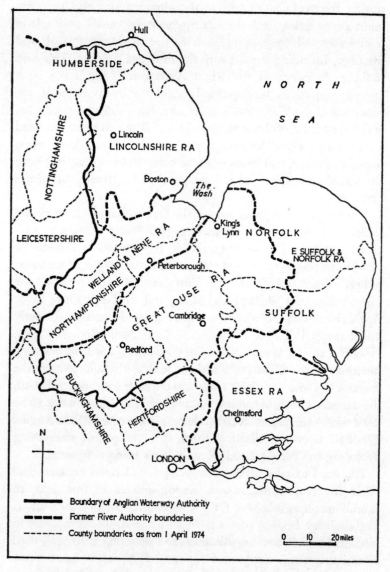

FIGURE 16. Boundaries of the Anglian Water Authority

perform all their far-reaching functions effectively. The board was

> gravely concerned about the possibility of the vital responsibilities which the Great Ouse River Authority have as the land drainage authority for the maintenance of the tidal river outfall at the Port of King's Lynn and in the Wash Approaches being transferred to the proposed Regional Water Authority 5. The new authority would have such extensive, important and crucial responsibilities in other areas as would ipso facto preclude the Regional Water Authority from acquiring and exercising the necessary local knowledge and experience acquired by the Great Ouse River Authority over the past 41 years.
>
> The size of the proposed new Regional Water Authorities seems to preclude adequate local representation and efficient administration at local level . . .[5]

A compromise has now been achieved, whereby a statutory Regional Land Drainage Committee, responsible to the Anglian Water Authority, has been established, which in turn delegates considerable powers to local Land Drainage Committees, set up for each of the River Authority areas. Provided that delegation arrangements can be made to work out as well in practice as in theory, no special problems or difficulties are foreseen. In fact it is hoped that land drainage will continue to be administered on much the same basis as before, certainly for a time. Past events have, of course, proved that where land drainage is concerned no satisfactory substitute has so far been found for the expedient of establishing a single, completely autonomous authority to undertake sole responsibility for individual or related groups of catchment areas. Any provision or arrangement lacking these constituent elements would be bound to represent a retrograde step.

THE WASH: ESTUARY STORAGE PROJECTS

To meet the expected heavily increased demands for water in the central area of south-east England by the end of the present century a number of schemes have been considered, which inevitably have implications for fen drainage. Proposals have been made from time to time to build a barrage across the Wash so as to exclude the sea from a part or all of the area and to allow fresh water to collect by gravity behind the barrage. On the other hand Binnie & Partners – the consulting engineers appointed by the Water Resources Board to carry out the engineering investigations – commenced a feasibility study into the possibility of establishing comparatively small embanked, or bunded, reservoirs on the fringes of the inter-tidal area. Barrage schemes in the sense of a complete damming off on some line across the Wash are not recommended, and are indeed considered to be superfluous if the reservoir plan is carried out.[6] Even a limited barrage enclosing a part of the Wash area would be costly to build and maintain, whilst a barrage enclosing the entire Wash is thought to be beyond the capabilities of existing engineering technology.

Ultimate development envisages four reservoirs, situated just off the south-west shore of the bay between the Welland and Great Ouse outfalls. These would be built in stages, so that the rate of capital outlay would approximate to the rate of increase in demand, and the cost to the consumer be kept to the minimum. The reservoirs would cover in all an area of about 25,000 acres, ie about 15 per cent of the total Wash area. They would be filled by tunnel or pipeline from points on the four major Fenland rivers just upstream of the ports, tidal sluices being constructed at these points. To replace the diminished current in the Great Ouse and Nene, caused by the abstraction of fresh water, proposals have been made for a sea-water intake to be pumped into the rivers at a given point, and used to flush out the outfalls, which may otherwise become silted impeding both navigation and land drainage. No salt-water transfer-intakes seem to be contemplated for the Welland or Witham.

A water conservation scheme involving reservoirs would not necessarily inhibit any further reclamation of land. The reservoirs would start some distance to seaward of the present margin of reclaimed land. The area actually occupied by the reservoirs would obviously not be available for reclamation, but increased silting might occur in their vicinity, and particularly between them and the existing shore-line. This could be reclaimed, possibly for recreational, certainly for agricultural use. The effect of the proposed reservoirs on the existing arrangements for sea defence is considered to be more favourable than otherwise. A

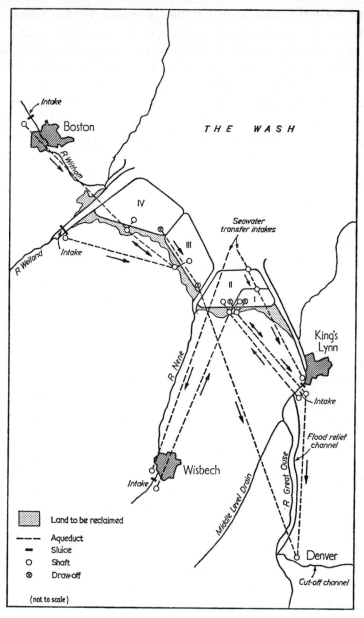

FIGURE 17. The Wash: scheme for estuary storage reservoirs

reduction in overall expenditure might be expected, because of the reduced length of the coastline involved. A major barrage, conversely, would almost certainly increase sea defence costs.

Land drainage would inevitably be affected by any scheme for developing water-storage in the Wash. A barrage would induce a change of river regime from one controlled by the tides to one controlled by reservoir level, which would impede discharge through gravity outfalls. Admittedly the rivers would be non-tidal and maintenance work due to scour and bank-slip would be less. Siltation of river channels would be reduced and the cost of dredging maintenance would also be minimal. On the debit side the absence of tidal flow would mean an increase of weed growth which could reduce flood-carrying capacity.

The effect of bunded reservoirs would depend to a large extent upon the point at which tidal penetration is cut off by the proposed new sluices. Also a scheme which would exclude the tide from extensive areas of the bay, but without the protection of a shore-to-shore barrage, would involve the possibility of siltation of the areas remaining open to the tide, which must obstruct land-drainage and navigation. Siltation of the tidal reaches of the Fenland rivers is a matter for detailed study, but could be caused by smaller tidal currents due to any reduction in the length of the tidal reach. It could be affected by a reduction in the freshwater flow and by interference with sediment movement in the shallow areas of the Wash due to the construction of reservoirs near the river outfalls. It is considered that these outfalls might be maintained either by extending the tidal reach seawards by building full-height training walls out to deep water, or by a combination of limited training wall construction and dredging. The problems are many, but fortunately it is implicit in the recommendations of the consulting engineers that no scheme will be entertained which gives any indication of being unsatisfactory from the viewpoint of either land-drainage or the navigation of the Wash ports. At all events the future of the estuary is uncertain, and until all studies are completed it is unlikely that any further works will be executed in the area.

EPILOGUE – THE FENLAND PRESENT AND FUTURE

SOME PROBLEMS IN FENLAND AGRICULTURE

Throughout the Fenland the twentieth century has seen a continued advance in the acreage under arable cultivation. In Norfolk Marshland, where the fine, silty soils favour their production, sugar beet and potatoes are the great staples, with wheat and barley also being widely grown. The coastal marshes have similarly expanded their arable acreages at the expense of pasture, the range of crops being comparable to those found in Marshland. In the Lincolnshire silt zone also pasture land has slowly receded before the advancing arable tide.

The black peat fens, stretching from Norfolk, through Cambridgeshire and Huntingdonshire into Lincolnshire, are exceedingly fertile. Their high organic content makes them eminently suitable for an intensive arable system. Because they are easily worked at all times of the year they are ideal for producing early crops. The great staples here are cereals, sugar beet, potatoes, celery, carrots and onions, but a large number of other crops are grown on a limited scale. With few exceptions, only on the washlands, the islands, and in paddocks attached to farmhouses is grassland now to be found in quantity, and even here as much land as possible is being ploughed. Any tradition of livestock farming in the peat fens has dimmed with the passage of time.

Farms vary enormously in size; many boast only a few acres, and are run on a part-time basis. About two-thirds are less than 50 acres, although the region contains some very large farms of several thousand acres. The intensive cropping practised in the fens still requires large numbers of workers, although with advancing mechanisation their number is of course decreasing, whilst future trends will undoubtedly be towards an increase in the size of individual holdings, and hence towards a reduction in their number.

The continuing loss of depth in peat soils remains the major problem. Initially this wastage was simply the shrinkage of the spongy peat mass as water was abstracted from it by drainage. In recent times real loss of soil material has occurred. This is a much slower and more insidious process whereby oxidation of plant-remains leads to a wastage of the peat. The more efficiently the land is drained and cultivated the faster is the wastage rate, and already this inexorable process has converted roughly one-third of the original 345,000 acres of drained peat fen into what is known as skirtland, ie an organic plough layer over mineral subsoils, varying in texture from silty clay to fine sand. It has been estimated that the loss of a further 24in of peat during the next thirty years or so will result in the conversion of three-quarters of existing peat soils into skirtland.

Continued shrinkage will ultimately lead to a situation where it is the mineral fen floor which is being farmed, and the nature of that floor varies very considerably. It is unfortunate that with the carving up of the great commons by enclosure in the late eighteenth and early nineteenth centuries, and the continuing advance of arable cultivation since then, little has been done to prevent the Fenland peats from being cropped without a planned or constructive strategy to conserve them. The farmers, resigned apparently to the fact that peat is a shrinking asset, have been concerned simply to work it while it remained, and any remedial measures have been dictated solely by current expediency. As the peat wastes there will inevitably be an increase in the variability of soil texture and depth. A decrease in crop yields is highly probable. Some soils may very possibly go out of arable production, and on others farmers will doubtless modify the present cropping system if the soil forces them to do so. A fairly recent estimate by the Soil Survey of England and Wales put the area of Fenland in Cambridgeshire, West Suffolk and South Norfolk that was at risk from severe erosion damage at over 90,000 acres. This land has a maximum layer of peat topsoil of 3ft and with an estimated wastage of $\frac{1}{2}$in to $\frac{3}{4}$in in a year all of it is in danger of undergoing the change from peat to skirtland in the foreseeable future. In many cases – one estimate is of 120,000 acres – the change has already occurred. Farmers who were once on easily workable peat or peaty loam, capable of growing virtually any high return root and vegetable crop, are now faced with fields of quite heavy soil, and a far more restricted rotation. They are already experiencing considerable difficulty in finding sufficient peat soils for growing wide row celery and late harvested carrots. The fen farmers' present success in producing high value cash crops in very large quantity per acre is, of course, entirely dependent on the continuance of the peat top soil.

There is no doubt that the problem is a pressing one. Farmers who are working on a thin layer of peat over clay subsoils could be faced with a complete change of policy once the skirtland becomes established, but they would still be able to farm a reasonable arable rotation. The position is less certain in those eastern fens where the underlying soil is sand, gravel or chalk. In some of the fens near Lakenheath there is nothing under the peat but pure sand. Much of this sand could be almost infertile, and this would mean at best putting the land down to permanent pasture and at worst being faced with a swing to forestry or some other very low-return system. Once these fens are denuded of their peat perhaps only renewed flooding would restore complete fertility to the soil. Since grass is the only crop which can be grown on peat without ultimately destroying it, it is surprising that the more enlightened system followed in the eighteenth century of putting land down to pasture for several years after a period of arable cropping has not been adhered to. The argument has persisted that it would hardly be good business to graze land capable of producing such high yields of valuable cash crops. At this point it seems not irrelevant to remember that at the beginning of the seventeenth century, before the general draining, Methwold Fen in Norfolk was fairly typical in its ability to support 1,700 sheep, up to 400 milch cows, whilst feeding in addition 'working horses, and bred store of young cattle, which were kept on the common in winter, time out of mind'.[7]

However a partial return to pastoral farming cannot be entirely discounted, and is in fact the solution most generally favoured in the Netherlands. In the Methwold Fens this trend is already visible. The peat here is very light and hence particularly susceptible to erosion. Consequently ley grass now occupies between one-fifth and three-quarters of the total farm acreage. The grass is used in a number of different ways: for dairy cows, semi-intensive beef production, sheep, and herbage seed production. This is not to suggest that there is, as yet, any general movement in the direction of conversion to pasture throughout the peat fens. In the Isle of Ely, for example, the acreage of rotational grassland is 1,371 out of a total of 188,000 acres. Nevertheless for many farmers the writing seems to be on the wall.

But apart from the danger of some land going out of effective cultivation the peat shrinkage has other, very grave, implications. As the peat wastes the ground water-table comes closer to the surface, a circumstance which poses a totally different type of drainage problem than any hitherto encountered. Vast sums of money will be needed to lay new under-drainage systems to supplement the existing drains and pumps.

An important factor for the future is the work that is being done, notably by the Arthur Rickwood Experimental Husbandry Farm, in connection with soil mixing, because hopefully this technique will reduce the rate of peat loss.[8] Instead of waiting for oxidation, wind erosion, and other natural sources to remove the peat layer, the process involves mixing the last remnants of the peat with a similar depth of mineral subsoil, with the aim of creating an even, deep organic loam. In 1966 Dr A. N. Ede began experiments with his single-bladed raiser-mixer, which has enabled mixing to be done on a field scale. This has now been developed even further, and subsequently large-scale field trials have been carried out using a three-tined raiser-mixer. It is hoped that this process, by removing some of the peat to a less well aerated zone will reduce overall wastage, create a situation of soil stability, and maintain crop yields for a longer period than natural degeneration would allow. Of experiments carried out so far results have not been uniformly conclusive. Many years will be needed before an assessment of the true position can be made. However it is thought that the resulting mixed soil should be capable of retaining some peat elements and providing a stable soil for at least a further thirty years.

It is interesting to note that the soil-mixing technique, although originally devised to counter wastage in the peat fens, has also been employed in the Holbeach Marsh district of Lincolnshire, in this case to turn heavy warp land into a much more free-working silty loam. In this area of Lincolnshire, where land has been reclaimed from the marshes, there can be as much as 3 to 4ft of heavy silt over the sand. The process of raising the sand and mixing it with the topsoil has undoubtedly made the soil more workable, and has increased the crop rotational scope and potential of the land.

But the problems here are indeed somewhat different from those encountered in the peat zone, where the topsoil, as well as shrinking is literally blowing away. In East Anglia strong winds are most common during April and May, but damaging winds can occur as early as March and as late as June. The light and friable peat is easily picked up by these winds which sweep across the flat countryside for the most part unchecked by hedgerows or other forms of windbreak. Large dust clouds are formed, which rise into the air and can often be seen for many miles. Areas where the peat is still deep are the worst affected, as the shallower peat, which has an admixture of other soils, presents a surface which is more stable and resistant to blowing. Dust storms have become worse during the present century, and are now an annual event in the peat fens. Frequently they are local in character; sometimes they extend for miles. Although in all cases most of the soil is redistributed rather than destroyed, redistribution is usually in an undesirable pattern, with a proportionate loss in soil, fertiliser, seed and time. If the seeds have already germinated the abrasive particles of dust damage the young growth, roots are exposed, and if the storm is severe, dislodged. In prolonged high velocity winds transpiration losses can be harmful; the plants fail to thrive causing yield reductions and delay in reaching maturity. This of course plays havoc with programmed marketing. At the same time drains and ditches are choked, and the cost of cleaning out can constitute a heavy burden. This has to be done immediately in case heavy rain should follow and fields become waterlogged through impeded drainage. The work of weeks may be destroyed in a few hours. It is quite usual for farmers to make two or three spring sowings, often forfeiting some of the most vital weeks of the growing season.

Over the years farmers have devised systems to try to reduce the effects of wind both on soil and crops.[9] These systems include applying tar or co-polymerised emulsions to hold down the soil; pulling up a ridge when a blow is imminent; and more sophisticated techniques of drilling protective crops up the rows.

Inter-row nurse crops of barley or mustard have been tested between drilled crops of sugar beet and onions. Eventually the nurse crop is destroyed. If left too long this is physically difficult – notably in the case of fast-growing mustard – without damaging the protected crop. Needless to say, the fact that none of these systems have been widely or readily adopted in the past proves that they were considered either too expensive, ineffective, or extremely difficult to manage. Nevertheless more efficient methods are continually being developed. Another solution is to use a 'knubby' seed bed, ie one where the soil has not been worked to too fine a tilth. Shelter belts, a common form of wind-break, have never been employed on a sufficient scale to be of much use. It is true that many trees suitable for this purpose – for example conifers – do not grow easily in peat and never attain a tenacious root-hold. Others, as willow and poplar, are not fully in leaf when they are most needed. Farmers argue that, if planted in sufficient depth to be effective, trees will occupy valuable farm land, and harbour small animals and birds. Also shelter belts give protection for only a limited distance in relation to their height; the wind at the end of this distance blows with renewed force. A more certain remedy is to mix clay with the surface peat, provided that a suitable type is within easy reach of the surface or can be imported into the area at an economic price. This remedy, as we have seen, has been applied with considerable success in many localities since about 1830. But clay is not to be found in all areas of the peat fens. Also the process of claying can be highly expensive, although its effects are reasonably durable.

It will be seen that many problems still confront the Fenland. As expenditure on drainage works and advanced agricultural techniques rises, and profits from much of the soil fall, any future balance-sheet could possibly be weighted against the region. In 1629 the Commissioners of Sewers for Suffolk had drawn attention to the point that

> they have no surrounded grounds that lie long under water, but only such as are sometimes overflowed for a short time, which overflowing much enricheth those grounds, so that more draining would be very hurtful to them. These grounds . . . cannot be spared or bettered by the industry of the undertakers.[10]

It would be somewhat ironical if after centuries of drainage effort and expense large areas of the Fenland were ultimately to go either partially or almost wholly out of effective cultivation; if the remedy were in fact to prove no better, or worse, than the original disease.

Notes

CHAPTER 1 (*pages* 9–29)

1. C. W. Goodwin, *The Anglo-Saxon Version of the Life of St Guthlac* (1848), p 21 and Felix, *Vita Guthlaci* (W. de Gray Birch, *Memorials of St Guthlac of Crowland* [1881], p xliv).
2. Goodwin, op cit.
3. Birch, op cit, p 17.
4. Goodwin, op cit, p 29.
5. Lord Macaulay was a modern supporter of this theory. See *History of England*, III, C. H. Firth (ed) (1914), p 1349.
6. H. Petrie and J. Sharpe (eds), *Monumenta Historica Britannica* (1848), pp liv, lx.
7. Bede, *Historia Ecclesiastica*, Lib IV, cap 19. See also W. Dugdale, *History of Imbanking and Drayning* (1772 ed), p 185.
8. Goodwin, op cit, p 21.
9. Birch, op cit, pp xi–xii.
10. W. Elstobb, *An Historical Account of the Great Level of the Fens* (1793), p 276.
11. F. R. Chapman, *Sacrist Rolls of Ely*, I (1907), p 87.
12. See *Fenland Notes and Queries*, VI (1905–6), p 256.
13. S. B. J. Skertchly, *The Geology of the Fenland* (1877), p 52.
14. See the following papers by G. Fowler: 'Fenland Waterways, Past and Present. South Level District', Parts I–II, *Proc Camb Antiq Soc*, XXXIII (1933), p 108; XXXIV (1934), p 17; 'The Extinct Waterways of the Fens', *Geog Journ*, LXXXIII (1934), p 30.
15. See British Museum, Lansdowne MSS 60/34.
16. S. B. J. Skertchly noted that the boundary between the peat and silt zones was indecisive, 'for the peat thins out insensibly along its borders'. See op cit, p 129.
17. E. A. R. Ennion, *Cambridgeshire, Huntingdonshire and the Isle of Ely* (1951), p 80.
18. W. Gooch, *Agriculture of the County of Cambridge* (1813), p 246.
19. Skertchly, op cit, p 132.

20. Ennion, op cit, pp 69–70.
21. A. Burrell, *A Briefe Relation discovering Plainely the true Causes why the great Levell of the Fenns in the Severall Counties of Norfolk, Suffolk, Cambridge, Huntingdon, Northampton and Lincoln Shires have been drowned and made unfruitful for many years past* (1642), p 5.
22. C. Vermuyden, 'A Discourse' (1642), printed in S. Wells, *The History of the Drainage of the Great Level of the Fens, called Bedford Level* (1830), II, p 342.
23. Ibid.
24. Ibid.
25. D. Defoe, *A Tour through the Whole Island of Great Britain*, I (1724), p 114.
26. H. C. Darby (ed), *A Scientific Survey of the Cambridge District* (1938), p 20.
27. W. Dodson, *The Designe for the Perfect Draining of the Great Level of the Fens* (1665), p 5.
28. Skertchly, op cit, p 124.
29. Burrell, op cit, p 5.
30. W. Camden, *Britannia* (1637), p 481.
31. See for example C. W. Phillips, 'The Present State of Archaeology in Lincolnshire', Part II, *Archaeological Journal*, XCI (1934), pp 123–4: 'While not categorically denying that some parts of this bank may have had a Roman origin it must be pointed out there is not a shred of evidence for this . . . a medieval origin seems to be indicated.'
32. See A. K. Astbury, *The Black Fens* (1958), p 183. A central argument of this work is that all watercourses dug during the Roman Occupation were not drains but transport canals. This conclusion rests on the supposition that the condition of the Fenland was so good at this period that no drainage works of any description were necessary. Such an assumption hardly derives unqualified support from the facts. In fact the author asserts elsewhere (p 6) that 'the tides, even after they had almost ended their task of dropping silt wholesale over the northern fens, continued before and during the Roman Occupation to press far up the fen rivers, bearing with them great quantities of silt eroded from coasts near the mouth of the Wash . . . Inland this silting of river channels led to even greater flooding.'
33. S. H. Miller and S. B. J. Skertchly, *The Fenland Past and Present* (1878), p 142.
34. Dugdale, op cit, p 16. Miller and Skertchly's arguments support Dugdale's theory: 'it is very improbable that the cowed and enervated Britons would have undertaken such a great national work after the departure of their conquerors'. Op cit, p 144.
35. This point is discussed by T. C. Lethbridge in 'The Car Dyke,

The Cambridgeshire Ditches and the Anglo-Saxons'. See *Proc Camb Antiq Soc*, XXV (1935), pp 94–6.
36. Birch, op cit, p 19.
37. See P. H. Blair, *Roman Britain and Early England 55 BC–AD 871* (1963), p 120 for a discussion of this point.
38. Ibid, p 121.

CHAPTER 2 (*pages* 30–49)

1. W. Dugdale, *History of Imbanking and Drayning* (1772 ed), p 171.
2. See H. C. Darby, *The Domesday Geography of Eastern England* (3rd ed 1971), p 95.
3. D. J. Stewart (ed), *Liber Eliensis* (1848), p 4.
4. Bede, *Historia Ecclesiastica*, Lib IV, cap 19. See also H. M. Chadwick, *Origin of the English Nation* (1924), p 8.
5. *Victoria County History of Northamptonshire*, I (1902), pp 250–1. See also E. Miller, *The Abbey and Bishopric of Ely* (1951), pp 10–12.
6. T. Arnold (ed), *Memorials of St Edmund's Abbey*, I (1890), p 6.
7. Dugdale, op cit, p 179.
8. Ibid, p 210.
9. See S. Wells, *Bedford Level*, II (1830), pp 1–7.
10. W. G. Hoskins and H. P. R. Finberg, *Devonshire Studies* (1952), p 217.
11. Dugdale, op cit, p 179.
12. William of Malmesbury, *De Gestis Pontificum Anglorum* (Rolls Series, 1870), ed N. E. S. A. Hamilton, p 322.
13. W. H. Hart and P. A. Lyons (eds), *Cartularium Monasterii de Ramesia*, II (Rolls Series, 1884/86/93), p 192.
14. W. O. Ault, *Court Rolls of the Abbey of Ramsey* (1928), p 117.
15. F. W. Maitland and W. P. Baildon (eds), *The Court Baron* (Selden Society, 1897), p 122.
16. H. T. Riley (ed), *Ingulph's Chronicle of the Abbey of Croyland* (1854), p 385.
17. British Museum, Additional Charters, No 39599.
18. Maitland and Baildon, op cit, p 122.
19. BM, Additional Charters, No 39894.
20. Dugdale, op cit, p 244.
21. *Ramsey Cartulary*, I, p 79. See also BM, Additional Charters, No 39595, where the Abbot of Ramsey, in 1279, was accused of enclosing common pasture. There are many similar examples at this period.
22. *Chronicon Abbatiae Ramesiensis*, p 8.
23. William of Malmesbury, op cit, pp 326–7.
24. *Chronica Maiora*, III, p 570.
25. H. C. Darby, *The Medieval Fenland* (1940), p 52.
26. Dugdale, op cit, p 262.

27. Ibid, p 169.
28. Ibid.
29. Patent Rolls, 10 Edw III, pt II, m 8d.
30. See Wells, op cit, p 6.
31. H. T. Riley (ed), op cit, pp 443-4.
32. Dugdale, op cit, p 299.
33. Ibid, p 262.
34. Ibid, p 254.
35. Ibid, p 203.
36. Ibid, p 327.
37. Ibid, p 281.
38. Ibid, p 254.
39. Ibid, p 258-9.
40. Public Record Office, Duchy of Lanc Misc VII/7.
41. Dugdale, op cit, p 317.
42. C. T. Flower, *Public Works in Medieval Law*, I (Selden Society, 1915), p 274.
43. *Ramsey Cartulary*, I, p 216.
44. See Flower, op cit, pp 269, 273-4.
45. Dugdale, op cit, p 194.
46. Parts of Ingulph's *Historia Croylandensis* were used as evidence to defend the rights of the monastery of Crowland in the various lawsuits in which it became embroiled from the twelfth century. Therefore much of Ingulph's original narrative may have been distorted or even fabricated by later writers to strengthen the monastery's case. See W. G. Searle, *Ingulf and the Historia Croylandensis* (Camb Antiq Soc 1894).
47. Dugdale, op cit, p 263.
48. See Wells, op cit, p 82.
49. W. Camden, *Britannia* (1637 ed), p 495.
50. Close Rolls, 18 Ric II, m 33.
51. Dugdale, op cit, p 244.
52. *Ramsey Cartulary*, II, p 216.
53. BM, Additional Charters, No 33072.
54. *Fenland Notes and Queries*, III (1897), p 191.
55. Maitland and Baildon, op cit, p 109.
56. Miller, op cit, p 94 et seq.
57. Red Book of Thorney, f 460 (Cambridge University Library).
58. H. T. Riley (ed), *Ingulph's Chronicle of the Abbey of Croyland* (1854), p 107.
59. W. Elstobb, *An Historical Account of the Great Level of the Fens* (1793), p 79.
60. See H. G. Richardson, 'The Early History of Commissions of Sewers', *English Historical Review*, XXXIV (1919), p 389.
61. Patent Rolls 42 Hen III, m 14d.

62. For an examination of the conditions which led to the creation of Sewer Courts, and an account of their main functions and procedure see H. C. Darby, *The Medieval Fenland* (1940), pp 155-68 and *The Draining of the Fens* (1956 ed), pp 1-5. See also S. and B. Webb, *English Local Government. Statutory Authorities for Special Purposes* (1922), pp 17-24.
63. N. Walker and T. Craddock, *The History of Wisbech and the Fens* (1849), p 112.
64. See the Acts of 18 Hen VI c 10 (1439); 23 Hen VI c 9 (1444); 12 Edw IV c 6 (1472) and 4 Hen VII c 1 (1488) in this connection.
65. 6 Hen VI c 1 (1427).
66. See the *Reading of . . . Robert Callis upon the Statute of 23 Hen 8 cap 5 of Sewers* (1824 ed), pp 115-25.
67. Wells, op cit, p 6.
68. Dugdale, op cit, p 328.

CHAPTER 3 (*pages* 50-78)

1. According to L. E. Harris, *Vermuyden and the Fens* (1953), p 17, there is no evidence to suggest that due to the Dissolution 'an intelligent and co-ordinated drainage system was destroyed, and the story that the drainage of the Fens suffered a disastrous setback by the dissolution of the monasteries is one of those easy generalisations which have slipped into history without much inquiry'. See also *V. C. H. Hunts*, III, p 256.
2. *Calendar of State Papers Domestic*, Eliz I, XCIX, 38 (1574).
3. *Letters and Papers. Hen VIII*, IX, p 380.
4. W. Camden, *Britannia* (1637 ed), p 491.
5. Acts of the Privy Council, 2 March 1596, p 537.
6. I. Casaubon, *Ephemerides* (1611), II, p 871.
7. H.C., *A discourse concerning the drayning of fennes and surrounded grounds in the sixe counteys of Norfolke, Suffolke, Cambridge, with the Isle of Ely, Huntingdon, Northampton, and Lincolne* (1629).
8. See S. Wells, *Bedford Level*, II (1830), p 62.
9. W. Elstobb, *An Historical Account of the Great Level of the Fens* (1793), pp 200-1.
10. Camden, op cit, p 529.
11. R. Holinshed, *The Historie of England* (1587), III, pp 1222-3.
12. W. Dugdale, *History of Imbanking and Drayning* (1772 ed), p 277.
13. Public Record Office, LR 2, 256, f 210.
14. For an account of population distribution in the Holland region of south Lincolnshire see Joan Thirsk, *Fenland Farming in the sixteenth century* (University College, Leicester, Occasional Papers 1953), pp 10-13.

15. 'Sir Clement Edmond's Report' and 'Mr Atkyns's Reports' (1618). Both printed in S. Wells, *Bedford Level*, II (1830), pp 60 et seq.
16. W. Dugdale, op cit, p viii.
17. 43 Eliz I, c 11 (1600).
18. 4 Jas I, c 13 (1605/6).
19. Wells, op cit, p 65.
20. British Museum, Lansdowne MSS 84/32.
21. *CSPD*, Jas I, XIX, 47 (1606).
22. *CSPD*, Eliz I, CCXLI, 114 (1592).
23. Ibid, CCXXIV, 97 (1593).
24. Acts of the Privy Council, XXVII, pp 275, 367.
25. BM, Lansdowne MSS, 87/4.
26. *CSPD*, Jas I, VIII, 99 (1604).
27. 4 Jas I, c 13 *for the draining of certain Fens and low Grounds in the Isle of Ely, subject to hurt by surrounding . . . commonly called . . . the Ring of Waldersea and Cooldham.*
28. W. Dugdale, *History of Imbanking and Drayning* (1772 ed), p 352.
29. *CSPD*, Jas I, XVIII, 102 (1606).
30. See Wells, op cit, p 43.
31. *CSPD*, Jas I, XCIX, 51 (1618).
32. T. Badeslade, *The History of the Ancient and Present State of the Navigation of the Port of King's Lyn, and of Cambridge, and the rest of the trading Towns in those parts* (1725), p 31.
33. *CSPD*, Jas I, CXVII, 78 (1620).
34. Ibid, CXII, 61; CXVII, 15 (1620).
35. Ibid, CXXVIII, 105 (1622).
36. Badeslade, op cit, p 33.
37. C. Vermuyden, 'A Discourse' (1642). See S. Wells, *Bedford Level*, II (1830), p 340.
38. *CSPD*, Chas I, CLXI, 34 (1630).
39. Printed in S. Wells, op cit, pp 98–110.
40. *CSPD*, Chas I, CLXXI, 30 (1630).
41. J. H. Wiffen, *Memoirs of the House of Russell*, II (1833), p 149.
42. Cambridge Record Office, R.59.31.36.5 (c): 'Instructions, Forms of Procedure, Rules and Regulations of the Bedford Level Corporation' (1814).
43. CRO, R.59.31.9.1: Proceedings of the Adventurers (1646).
44. See the 'Indenture of Fourteen Parts' 1631, printed in Wells, op cit, p 113.
45. Ibid, pp 111–20.
46. Dugdale, op cit, p 409.
47. *CSPD*, Chas I, CLXXIII, 29 (1630).
48. Ibid, CLXXV, Nov 1630.
49. Ibid, Council of State, XXV, 13 (1652).
50. 43 Eliz I, c 11 (1600).

51. See 'The Indenture of Fourteen Parts' 1631. Wells, op cit, pp 111–12.
52. 'The Lynn Law' 1630. See Wells, op cit, p 102.
53. Vermuyden, 'A Discourse' (1642). See Wells, op cit, p 360.
54. Ibid, p 349.
55. See H. C. Darby, *The Draining of the Fens* (1956 ed), pp 41–2.
56. *CSPD*, Chas I, CCCLVII, 152 (1637).
57. 'St Ives Law of Sewers', printed in Wells, op cit, p 240.
58. Vermuyden, 'A Discourse' (1642). See Wells, op cit, p 340.
59. Dugdale, op cit, p 413.
60. Ibid, p 414.
61. A. Burrell, *Exceptions against Sir Cornelius Virmudens Discourse* (1642).
62. See, for example, W. E. Doran, 'Cornelius Vermuyden, the draining of the Fens, and recent developments' in *Proc Anglo-Netherlands Soc* (1943–4), p 33 and L. E. Harris, *Vermuyden and the Fens* (1953), pp 136–8.
63. Vermuyden, 'A Discourse' (1642). See Wells, op cit, p 344.
64. Ibid, p 349.
65. Ibid, p 363.
66. Ibid, p 348.
67. Ibid, p 342.
68. Ibid, p 363: 'The three Rivers of Mildenhall, Brandon, and Stoke, must bee made one river, and to that end Mildenhall must be brought into Brandon, and both into Stoke, and all into Ouse.'
69. This was the 'Pretended Act' of 1649, so-called after the Restoration.
70. Vermuyden, 'A Discourse' (1642). See Wells, op cit, p 360.
71. Badeslade, op cit, pp 85, 87
72. Wells, op cit, p 361.
73. Ibid, p 365.
74. See *The Case of the Proprietors of the South Level of the Fens* (nd, c1793).
75. J. Vetch and J. Washington, *Norfolk Estuary Bill 1849. Report to the Lords Commissioners of the Admiralty* (1849), p 12.
76. Dugdale, op cit, p 409.
77. CRO, R.59.31.9.1. Proceedings of the Adventurers (1646), and Wells, *Bedford Level*, I (1830), p 131.
78. BM, K.816.m. 8/13: *The humble Petition of Col. Samuell Sandys* (nd, c1662).
79. Wells, op cit, II, p 340.
80. Wells, op cit, I, p 354 and BM, K.816.m. 8/12: *The Answer of the Petitioners against the Pretended Act of 1649* (nd, c1662).
81. BM, K.816.m. 8/12: *A Narrative of the Dreyning of the Great Level of the Fens* (nd, c1662).

82. *CSPD*, Council of State, XXXIX, 97 (1653).
83. According to William Dodson the cost of draining the southern Fens had amounted to 'five or six hundred thousand pounds'. See 'The Designe, for the perfect draining of the Great Level of the Fens' (1665), printed in Wells, op cit, II, p 441.
84. BM, K.816.m. 8/12: *A Narrative of the Dreyning of the Great Level of the Fens* (nd, c1662).
85. T. Fuller, *History of the University of Cambridge* (1665), Section V.
86. M. A. E. Green (ed), *Cal Proc Committee for Advance of Money 1642–56* (1888).
87. See G. Scott Thomson, *Life in a Noble Household 1641–1700* (1937), p 50.
88. CRO, R.59.31.9.3: Proceedings of the Adventurers (1653).

CHAPTER 4 (*pages 79–91*)

1. T. Badeslade, *The History of the Ancient and Present State of the Navigation of the Port of King's Lyn, and of Cambridge, and the rest of the trading Towns in those parts* . . . (1725), p 53.
2. *Calendar of State Papers Domestic*, Chas I, CLXXXVII, 76 (1631).
3. Preamble of the Act of 15 Chas 2, c 17 (1663), 'for settling the Draining of the Great Level of the Fens'.
4. Samuel Fortrey was one of the six Bailiffs from 1663, and in 1684 became a conservator and the surveyor of the Middle Level. His family, who were merchants, originated from South Brabant. Samuel Fortrey seems to have enjoyed a reputation for 'commercial sagacity', his treatise, *England's Interest and Improvement Consisting in the increase of the store, and trade of this Kingdom* (1663) earning him the approval of the Chairman of the East India Company. See *Fenland Notes and Queries*, IV (1900), pp 352–7.
5. C. Vermuyden, 'A Discourse' (1642). See S. Wells, *Bedford Level*, II (1830), p 340.
6. 15 Chas 2, c 17, XXVI. The navigation was to be preserved 'as the same was in the said sixth year of the said King Charles the First', ie 1630.
7. See 'The Report of the Committee of the Board . . . to enquire into the general liability of the Corporation'. Printed in Wells, op cit, p 765.
8. Cambridge Record Office, R.59.31.9.8. Proceedings of the Adventurers (1656).
9. CRO, R.59.31.11.1: Corporation Orders. London (1663).
10. R.59.31. Petitions (1665–70).
11. R.59.31.11.7: Corporation Orders. London (1673).
12. R.59.31.10.2: Conservators' Proceedings. Ely Series (1674).
13. R.59.31.11.14 (1693).

14. *CSPD*, Council of State, XXXIX, 97 (1653).
15. See Wells, op cit, p 768.
16. R.59.31.10.10–11: Conservators' Proceedings. Ely Series (1708–10).
17. R.59.31.10.19 (1737).
18. C. N. Cole, *A Collection of Laws which form the Constitution of the Bedford Level Corporation* (1761), p xlvii.
19. *Fenland Notes and Queries*, VI (1904–6), p 293.

CHAPTER 5 (*pages* 92–114)

1. In 1667, as a purely temporary measure, the Fen Office was sited on the ground floor of No 3 Tanfield Court, Inner Temple, but shortly afterwards premises were obtained at Serjeant's Inn. The Fen Office remained here until its removal to Ely in the mid-nineteenth century. See L. Tebbutt, 'The Fen Office, Ely', *Proc Camb Antiq Soc*, XXXVIII (1938).
2. Few records of the Adventurers have survived for the period prior to 1663. The most important manuscript sources for the early years are the 'Proceedings of Earlier Courts' 1362–1737 (12 volumes), which include 'Proceedings of the Adventurers' 1646–1662. See Cambridge Record Office, R.59.31.9.
3. British Museum, Lansdowne MSS 722, 29–38: Sir William Dugdale's diary of 'Things observable in our Itinerarie begun from London 19 May 1657'.
4. John Evelyn, *Diary*. 22 July 1670.
5. See G. Scott Thomson, *Life in a Noble Household 1641–1700* (1937), pp 152–3. Miss Scott Thomson observed that 'Thorney presently began to supply Woburn with produce on a scale which made what had been sent before seem a mere trickle.'
6. Cambridge Record Office, R.59.31. Petition addressed to the Bedford Level Corporation (1669).
7. T. Fuller, *History of the University of Cambridge* (ed 1840), Section V.
8. From a poem at the end of *The History or Narrative of the Great Level of the Fens, called Bedford Level* (1685).
9. G. Leti, *Teatro Britannico* (1683), I, p 317.
10. CRO, R.59.31: Petitions (1693).
11. R.59.31.9.12: Proceedings of Earlier Courts (1688).
12. R.59.31: Petitions (1682).
13. See W. Dodson, 'The Designe, for the perfect draining of the Great Level of the Fens' (1665). Printed in S. Wells, *Bedford Level*, II (1830), p 427.
14. In this connection it is significant that when the landowners of Haddenham Level complained that their lands had been per-

petually flooded for seven years, yielding 'little or no Profit', their explanation of the disaster was that the rivers 'lie higher than the Lands'. See BM, Add MSS 5819,89 (Feb 1726/7).

For an account of the peat shrinkage see S. H. Miller and S. B. J. Skertchly, *The Fenland Past and Present* (1878), p 160: 'From the time the desiccation of the fens commenced, the drainage began to deteriorate in consequence primarily of the shrinkage of the peat which reduced the slope of the ground.'

15. Dodson, op cit. See Wells, op cit, p 446.
16. A. Burrell, *A Briefe Relation discovering Plainely the true Causes why the great Levell of the Fenns . . . have been drowned . . . many years past* (1642): introduction.
17. Dodson, op cit. See Wells, op cit, pp 430–1.
18. Ibid, p 432.
19. CRO, R.59.31.11.72.21 (1674).
20. R.59.31.A.
21. R.59.31.10.13.1 (1726).
22. R.59.31.11.7.15–17 (1673).
23. R.59.31.11.15 (1697–8).
24. T. Badeslade, *The History of the Ancient and Present State of the Navigation of the Port of King's Lyn, and of Cambridge, and the rest of the trading Towns in those parts . . .* (1725), p 94.
25. D. Defoe, *A Tour through the Whole Island of Great Britain*, II (1724), p 151.
26. CRO, R.59,31.11.38: *Standing and General Orders of the Bedford Level Corporation* (1814), p 2.
27. R.59.31.11.16.18: *Corporation Orders*, London (1699–1716).
28. P. Bateson, *An Answer to some Objections by Hatton Berners Esq* (1710), p 11.
29. Defoe, op cit, p 151.
30. C. Vermuyden, 'A Discourse' (1642). See Wells, op cit, p 363.
31. Dodson, op cit. See Wells, op cit, p 431.
32. Ibid, p 432.
33. W. Elstobb, *An Historical Account of the Great Level of the Fens* (1793), p 199.
34. See *Fenland Notes and Queries*, V (1903), p 165.
35. 43 Eliz I, c 11 (1600).
36. J. Bentham, *The Claim of Taxing the Navigations and Free Lands for the Drainage and Preservation of the Fens Considered* (1778), p 32.
37. See *The Anti-Projector; or the history of the fen project* (c1646).
38. See Elstobb, op cit, pp 200–2. The inhabitants living on the east side of the Cam had petitioned the Lord Chancellor 'to be excused from contracting with the undertakers for draining the fens, their lands being worth 10s to 20s per acre, and not having been overflowed for twenty years past'. *Calendar of State Papers*

Domestic, Jas I, CXVII, 114 (1620). There are many similar petitions.
39. *CSPD*, Chas I, CCCXC, 89 (1638).
40. CRO, R.59.31.9.2 (1649): Proceedings of Earlier Courts.
41. *CSPD*, Council of State, XXXVI, 9 (1653).
42. CRO, R.59.31.11.7.26: Corporation Orders, London (1674).
43. See W. M. Palmer, 'The Fen Office Documents', *Proc Camb Antiq Soc*, XXXVIII (1938), pp 116–18, for a detailed account of the riot.
44. CRO, R.59.31.11.20 (1722).
45. See for example R.59.31.10.25. Conservators' Proceedings (1753).
46. W. Elstobb, *Report on the State of the Navigation between Clay Hithe and Denver Sluice 1778* (1779), p 15.
47. Badeslade, op cit, p 53.
48. Ibid, p 52.
49. Ibid, p 69.
50. Ibid, p 67.
51. Ibid, p 65.
52. Ibid.
53. Ibid, p 82.
54. See *The Case of the Proprietors of the South Level of the Fens* (nd, c1793), p 2. Thomas Badeslade had enlarged on this point at some length: 'in the Winter Season, when the *Bedford* Land-Floods came down the New *Bedford* River, which they constantly did do every wet Winter with great Rapidity, as bringing with them the River, Springs and downfal Waters of many Counties; the Sluice Doors were forceably kept shut by these Waters rising against them for Weeks together, so that the Waters in the *South* Level on the other side the Sluice, could not get through, but were penn'd in, and made to swell and overflow the Lands; insomuch that the *South* Level became more surrounded now in Winter, than ever it was before the erecting these Sluices'. See *Navigation of ... King's Lyn, and of Cambridge ...* (1725), pp 81–2.
55. Wells, op cit, I (1830), p 646.
56. CRO, R.59.31.11.7: Corporation Orders. London (1673).
57. W. H. S. Jones, *History of St Catharine's College* (1936), p 170.
58. CRO, R.59.31.11.14 (1693).
59. R.59.31.10.6 (1694).
60. R.59.31.11.15 (1696).
61. R.59.31.10.7 (1696).
62. R.59.31.6.B (1696/7).
63. C. Morris, *The Journeys of Celia Fiennes* (1949), p 154.
64. R.59.31.11 (1701).
65. Defoe, op cit (1724), I, p 114.

66. Badeslade, op cit, Abstract.
67. Ibid, p 87.
68. Ibid, p 91.
69. T. Neale, *The Ruinous State of the parish of Manea, in the Isle of Ely* (1748), pp 17–18.
70. CRO, R.59.31.10.8 (1701).
71. BM, Add MSS 5819,89 (Feb 1726/7).
72. These statistics have been extracted from the account books of the Bedford Level Corporation. See CRO, R.59.31.19.38–86 (1699–1750).
73. See 'The Report of the Committee of the Board . . . to enquire into the general liability of the Corporation' (1810). See Wells, op cit, II, p 768.

CHAPTER 6 (*pages* 115–43)

1. Cambridge Record Office, R.59.31.5.22 (1814).
2. British Museum, 816.m. 8/22: *Standing Orders of the Bedford Level Corporation* (1711–12), p 2.
3. CRO, R.59.31.6.A: Letter of 22 June 1693.
4. Ibid.
5. R.59.31.5.D (1700).
6. R.59.31.6.A: Letter of 29 Dec 1720.
7. Ibid: Letter of 20 Dec 1720.
8. R.59.31.5.H (1730).
9. R.59.31.10.31.15 (1772).
10. R.59.31.9.12.201 (1715).
11. R.59.31.13.A.1.56 (1846).
12. R.59.31.10.19.36 (1740).
13. See S. H. Miller and S. B. J. Skertchly, *The Fenland Past and Present* (1878), pp 8–9.
14. *Commons Journals*, XXXVI (1777), p 299.
15. CRO, R.59.31.9.12.72 (1698).
16. R.59.31: Petitions (1732).
17. J. Bentham, *The Claim of Taxing the Navigations and Free Lands for the Drainage and Preservation of the Fens Considered* (1778), p 26.
18. *CJ*, XXXVI (1777), p 298.
19. BM, Add MSS 5819,89 (Feb 1726/7).
20. CRO, R.59.31.10 (7 April 1727).
21. R.59.31.11 (2 March 1727).
22. 13 Geo I, c 18.
23. 27 Geo II, c 19.
24. C. N. Cole, *A Collection of Laws which form the constitution of the Bedford Level Corporation* (1761), p xxix.
25. 11 Geo II, c 34.

26. 14 Geo II, c 24.
27. T. Neale, *The ruinous state of the parish of Manea, in the Isle of Ely* (1748), pp 14–15.
28. 31 Geo II, c 18.
29. 33 Geo II, c 32.
30. See Cambridge Record Office, 283 and 297 for the Minute Books, Rate Books, accounts etc of the Burnt Fen, Middle Fen, Feltwell, and Littleport and Downham districts.
31. 27 Geo II, c 19.
32. CRO, R.59.31.10.24 (1751).
33. Ibid.
34. R.59.31.14.1 (ii): 'Extracts as to the Taxes laid at different periods' (nd).
35. 27 Geo II, c 19.
36. *Commons Journals*, XXVI (1753), p 922.
37. 27 Geo II, c 19.
38. See Cole, op cit, pp xxx–xxxi.
39. S. Wells, *Bedford Level*, I (1830), p 664.
40. The Corporation had defined the boundaries of the three Levels by an edict of 1697, hence officially ratifying Vermuyden's arrangements. See CRO, R.59.31.11.38: Standing and General Orders and Resolutions of the Corporation (1814), p 4.
41. Cole, op cit, p xxix, and Wells, op cit, p 661.
42. Miller and Skertchly, op cit, pp 157–8.
43. CRO, R.59.31.11.29 (1768).
44. R.59.31.10.31 (1773).
45. J. Wing, *An Inquiry into the State of the Revenues of the North Level* (1778), p 6.
46. *A Series of Letters of the First Earl of Malmesbury*, I (1870), pp 91–2.
47. BM, Add MSS 5819,89 (1773).
48. CRO, R.59.31.37.5: *The Bedford Level Corporation Petition presented to the House of Commons* (Feb 1777), p 156.
49. The *Norfolk Chronicle*, 19 Feb 1774.
50. A. Young, *Agriculture of the County of Suffolk* (1794), pp 31–2.
51. J. Golborne, *Report upon the Middle and South Levels* (1777), p 8.
52. CRO, R.59.31. Petitions (1782).
53. Bentham, op cit, p 10.
54. Ibid, p 15.
55. CRO, R.59.31.37.5 (1777).
56. BM, 710 K. 25(2): Anon, Letter 'To the Gentlemen Merchants and Navigators concerned in the Navigation from Cambridge to Lynn' (Nov 1778).
57. *Eau Brink Drainage: Residue of the Evidence* (1795), p 260.
58. J. Bentham, *Considerations and Reflections on the Present State of the Fens near Ely* (1778), p 4.

59. G. Maxwell, *Agriculture of the County of Huntingdon* (1793), p 24.
60. J. Bentham, *Considerations and Reflections* . . ., p 4.
61. BM, Add MSS 5821, 14a.
62. J. Bentham, *Considerations and Reflections* . . ., p 3.
63. CSPD, Eliz I, XL, 72 (1566).
64. Ibid, Jas I, CCLXXXIII, 58 (1602).
65. W. Dugdale, *History of Imbanking and Drayning* (1772 ed), p 205.
66. Ibid, p 206.
67. Sir Philibert Vernatti was a party to the 'Indenture of Fourteen Parts' 1631, adventuring for one share, ie the draining of 4,000 acres. See S. Wells, *Bedford Level*, II (1830), p 111 et seq.
68. *CSPD*, Chas I, CCLXXIX, 96 (1634).
69. Ibid, CCLXII, 30 (1634).
70. See W. H. Wheeler, *A History of the Fens of South Lincolnshire* (2nd ed 1896), p 207.
71. *CSPD*, Chas I, CCXXXVII, 9 (1633).
72. Dugdale, op cit, p 419.
73. C. Vermuyden, 'A Discourse' (1642). See S. Wells, *Bedford Level*, II (1830), p 347–51.
74. *CSPD*, Chas II, XXIV, 116 (1660).
75. 22 Chas II, c 15, *An Act for settling the Draining of the Fens in Lincolnshire called Deeping Fens*.
76. See Wheeler, op cit, p 34.
77. 2 Geo II, c 39.
78. 34 Geo III, c 102.
79. 5 Geo III, c 86.
80. 2 Geo III, c 32.
81. Wheeler, op cit, p 156.
82. T. Pennant, *Tour in Scotland* (1771), p 9.
83. T. Cox, *Magna Britannia*, III (1724), p 296.
84. Norfolk County Record Office, Minute Book of the Norfolk Court of Sewers (1753–63), p 58. This represents a typical entry.
85. C. B. Andrews (ed), *The Torrington Diaries*, II (1935), p 229.
86. 41 Geo III, c 128.
87. A. Young, *Agriculture of the County of Lincoln* (1799), p 223.
88. Sir G. Heathcote, *Thoughts of a Lincolnshire Freeholder* . . . (1794), p 14.
89. A. Young, op cit, pp 117, 235.
90. W. Chapman, *Observations on the Improvement of Boston Haven* (1800).
91. A. Young, *Annals of Agriculture*, XLIII (1805), p 543.

CHAPTER 7 (*pages* 144–61)

1. Throughout the Fenland the major floods were almost invariably caused by breaches in the river banks. See W. Gooch, *Agriculture*

NOTES

  of the County of Cambridge (1813), pp 208–9 and J. M. Heathcote, *Reminiscences of Fen and Mere* (1876), p 97.
2. C. T. Flower, *Public Works in Medieval Law*, I (Selden Society, 1915), p 311.
3. W. Dodson, *The Designe for the perfect Draining of the Great Level of the Fens* (1665), p 18.
4. W. Dugdale, *History of Imbanking and Drayning* (1772 ed), p 177.
5. Ibid.
6. Bedford County Record Office, FN 1255: 'Some Thoughts on the Case of Lynn-Regis, in Relation to their Port and Trade' (nd, early 18c), p 502.
7. See T. Badeslade, *The History of the Ancient and Present State of the Navigation of the Port of King's Lyn* . . . (1725), pp 109 et seq for Colonel Armstrong's *Report . . . of the State of the Fens, and the Port of Lyn* (1724).
8. Badeslade, op cit, pp 56–7.
9. Ibid, p 82.
10. Ibid, pp 56, 85.
11. Ibid, p 91.
12. J. Rennie, *Report concerning the Improvement of Boston Haven* (1800).
13. See C. Kinderley, *The Present State of the Navigation of the Towns of Lyn, Wisbeach and Spalding* (1721).
14. N. Kinderley, *The Ancient and Present State of the Navigation of the Towns of Lynn, Wisbeach, Spalding and Boston* (1751).
15. C. Labelye, *Result of a Particular View of the North Level of the Fens. Taken in August, 1745* (1748), p 9.
16. N. Kinderley, op cit, p 73.
17. N. Walker and T. Craddock, *The History of Wisbech and the Fens* (1849), p 172.
18. S. Wells, *Bedford Level*, I (1830), p 720.
19. See for example J. A. Clarke, 'On the Great Level of the Fens', *Journ Roy Agric Soc*, VIII (1848), p 88.
20. 35 Geo III, c 77.
21. Dodson, op cit, p 18.
22. T. Stone, *General View of the Agriculture of the County of Huntingdon* (1793), pp 8, 13.
23. R. Parkinson, *General View of the Agriculture of the County of Huntingdon* (1811), p 21.
24. C. Vancouver, *Agriculture of the County of Cambridge* (1794), pp 25, 36, 151.
25. T. Stone, *Agriculture of the County of Lincoln* (1794), pp 18, 22.
26. C. Vancouver, op cit, p 149.
27. A. Young, *Annals of Agriculture*, XLIII (1805), p 557.
28. J. Rennie, *Report and Estimate on the Improvement of the Drainage and Navigation of the South and Middle Levels* (1810), p 3.

29. W. Watson, *An Historical Account of the Ancient Town and Port of Wisbech* (1827), p 356.
30. Cambridge Record Office, R.59.31.37.5.21-2 (1777).
31. See CRO, R.59.31.19.54-69 (1715-30) and E. W. Gilboy, *Wages in Eighteenth Century England* (1934), pp 8 et seq, 92 et seq, and 148 et seq. Between 1715 and 1730 labourers' day wages in the southern Fenland rose on occasions to 2s 6d., whereas in London, according to Gilboy, labourers' wages in 1735 were 2s on average, and about 1s 6d in other parts of England.
32. That this difficulty was a very real one is apparent from the diary of James Golborne, Superintendent of the Bedford Level. See CRO, R.59.31.7.14. His entry for 10 July 1798 reads: 'In the Morning went to Salters Lode Sluice, where I met Mr Gotobed, who Informed me that he at that time could not produce hands enough to attempt to hang the new doors there, and repair that Sluice; we therefore agreed to put it off until the latter End of Harvest when Hands might be Obtained for both Purposes.'
33. See CRO, R.59.31.7.11 (1795) and R.59.31.7.14 (1799).
34. R.59.31.19: Account books of the Bedford Level Corporation 1715-1813. Up to the late eighteenth century wages paid by the Corporation to day labourers never exceeded 2s 6d. Subsequently these rose steadily until by 1813 the wages of labourers working on the barrier banks had undergone a relatively massive increase to 4s or even 5s per day, plus a daily allowance of 6d for ale.
35. R.59.31: Petitions (1822).
36. J. Bentham, *The Claim of Taxing the Navigations and Free Lands for the Drainage and Preservation of the Fens Considered* (1778).
37. Eau Brink Drainage: Minute Book of the Commissioners of Navigation (1820-37).
38. The Earl of Hardwicke, *Observations upon the Eau Brink Cut with a Proposal* (1793), p 22.
39. Young, op cit, pp 149-50.
40. T. Telford, *Life of Thomas Telford . . .* (1838), p 105.
41. Report on the Outfall of the River Nene, August 1821, p 4.
42. Wisbech Corporation Minute Books, 23 April 1822.
43. Ibid, 6 Dec 1826.
44. Walker and Craddock, op cit, p 465.
45. W. H. Wheeler, *Tidal Rivers* (1893), p 212.
46. W. H. Wheeler, *A History of the Fens of South Lincolnshire* (1896 ed), p 304. See also 'Fascine Work at the Outfalls of the Fen Rivers, and Reclamation of the Foreshore', *Min Proc Inst Civ Eng*, XLVI (1876), pp 61-80.
47. 52 Geo III, c 108.
48. 7 and 8 Geo IV, c 79.
49. 50 Geo III, c 125.

50. F. A. Ruston, *The Fen Country* (1870), p 19.
51. Walker and Craddock, op cit, p 191.
52. 7 and 8 Vict, c 56.
53. 11 and 12 Vict, c 104.
54. F. J. Gardiner, *History of Wisbech and Neighbourhood* (1898), pp 338-47.
55. W. H. Wheeler, 'The River Witham and its Estuary', *Min Proc Inst Civ Eng*, XXVIII (1868), pp 69-70.
56. W. H. Wheeler, 'The Conservancy of Rivers: the Eastern Midland District of England', *Min Proc Inst Civ Eng*, LXVII (1882), pp 211, 219.
57. Ibid, p 220.

CHAPTER 8 (*pages 162-82*)

1. A. Young, *Annals of Agriculture*, XLIII (1805), pp 545, 547, 557.
2. T. Neale, *The ruinous state of the parish of Manea in the Isle of Ely* (1748), pp 12-13, 15.
3. P. Bateson, *An Answer to some Objections by Hatton Berners Esq* (1710), p 10.
4. J. Rennie, *Report and Estimate on The Improvement of the Drainage and Navigation of the South and Middle Levels* (1810), pp 5-6.
5. Boulton and Watt Collection, J. Watt to W. Swansborough, 6 Aug 1814, cited in R. L. Hills, *Machines, Mills and Uncountable Costly Necessities* (1967), p 32.
6. J. Rennie, Letter Books, II, p 340.
7. T. Stone, *Agriculture of the County of Lincoln* (1794), p 67.
8. Young, op cit, p 569.
9. R. Parkinson, *Agriculture of the County of Huntingdon* (1811), p 23.
10. See Hills, op cit, pp 75-6.
11. T. Wing, *Considerations on the Principles of Mr Rennie's Plans for the Drainage of the North Level* . . . (1820), p 22.
12. Boulton and Watt Collection, J. Rennie to Watt, 14 July 1820. See R. L. Hills, op cit, p 87.
13. J. Glynn, 'Draining land by Steam Power', *Trans Roy Soc Arts*, 51 (1838), p 3.
14. See J. A. Clarke, 'On the Great Level of the Fens', *Journ Roy Agric Soc*, VIII (1848), p 93.
15. S. Jonas, 'On the Farming of Cambridgeshire', *Journ Roy Agric Soc*, VII (1847), p 69.
16. J. A. Clarke, *Fen Sketches* (1852), pp 247-8.
17. S. Jonas, op cit, p 64.
18. J. A. Clarke, op cit (1848), p 121.

19. J. Glynn, op cit, p 16.
20. W. H. Wheeler, *A History of the Fens of South Lincolnshire* (2nd ed 1896), p 380.
21. Ibid.
22. Ibid, pp 380–1.
23. J. A. Clarke, op cit (1852), p 249.
24. W. Wells, 'The Drainage of Whittlesea Mere', *Journ Roy Agric Soc*, XXI (1860), pp 135–6.
25. S. H. Miller and S. B. J. Skertchly, *The Fenland Past and Present* (1878), p 165.
26. Wheeler, op cit, p 380.
27. J. M. Heathcote, *Scoopwheel and Centrifugal Pump* (1877), p 12.
28. J. Rennie, *Report concerning the Drainage of Wildmore Fen, and of the East and West Fens* (April 1800); *Second Report* (Sept 1800).
29. 41 Geo III, c 35.
30. The 'Farmers Magazine' (Feb 1807), cited from S. Smiles, *Lives of the Engineers*, II (1862), p 163.
31. Ibid, p 164.
32. Cambridge Record Office, R.59.31.19.A.3 (1809).
33. R.59.31.19.A.15–22 (1821–8).
34. R.59.31.19.A.19–20 (1825–6).
35. S. Wells, *Letter to His Grace the Duke of Bedford . . . on the works in the . . . One Hundred Feet River* (1828), p 10.
36. J. H. H. Moxon, 'The Floods of the Lower Ouse', *Abs Proc and Trans Beds Nat Hist Soc* (1877–8), p 30.
37. CRO, R.59.31.9.A.19–31 (1825–38).
38. W. Gooch, *Agriculture of the County of Cambridge* (1811), p 247.
39. W. Gooch observed that before puddling was adopted the water had soaked 'through all fen banks every year in every district, and when the water-mills have lifted the waters up out of the fens into the rivers in a windy day, a great part of the water soaks back through the porous banks in the night upon the same land again', which 'drowns the wheat in winter, washes the manure into the dykes, destroys the best natural and artificial grasses, and prevents the fens from being sown till too late in the season'. Op cit, p 246.
40. W. Bower, *Statement as to the Drainage and Levels of the Fens North of Boston* (1814).
41. J. A. Clarke, *Fen Sketches* (1852), p 251.
42. W. Cobbett, *Rural Rides*, II (eds G. D. H. and M. Cole [1920]), pp 626–43.
43. S. Jonas, 'On the Farming of Cambridgeshire', *Journ Roy Agric Soc*, VII (1847), p 68.
44. J. A. Clarke, 'On the Great Level of the Fens', *Journ Roy Agric Soc*, VIII (1848), pp 132–3.

45. Eau Brink Drainage. Minute Book of the Navigation Commissioners (1838–73).
46. N. Walker and T. Craddock, *History of Wisbech and the Fens* (1849), p 464.
47. Ibid.
48. W. H. Wheeler, *Tidal Rivers* (1893), pp 400–1.
49. N. Kent, *Agriculture of the County of Norfolk* (1795), p 18.
50. See *A Short Demonstration That Navigation to Bedford is for the Benefit of Bedfordshire* (nd, c1720).
51. A. Young, *Agriculture of the County of Lincoln* (1813), p 454.

CHAPTER 9 (*pages* 183–210)

1. 15 Chas II, c 17.
2. Tax Act, 20 Chas II, c 8.
3. *Fenland Notes and Queries*, VII (1909), pp 115–16.
4. 20 Chas II, c 8.
5. Cambridge Record Office, R.59.31.11.38: Standing and General Orders and Resolutions of the Corporation (1814), p 62.
6. 15 Chas II, c 17.
7. See the Enclosure Prevention Act of 1 Jas II, c 21.
8. *The History or narrative of the great level of the fenns called Bedford Level* (1685), p 59. (Published anonymously, but later attributed to Samuel Fortrey.)
9. See W. E. Tate, 'Cambridgeshire Field Systems', *Proc Camb Antiq Soc*, XL (1939–42), pp 56–8, 72 et seq.
10. J. Bentham, *Considerations and Reflections on the Present State of the Fens near Ely, with a Proposal for Enclosing and Dividing the Common called Gruntifen* (1778), p 7.
11. Ibid.
12. J. Donaldson, *Agriculture of the County of Northampton* (1794), p 30.
13. Ibid.
14. W. Gooch, *Agriculture of the County of Cambridge* (1813), pp 67, 74.
15. J. Bateman, *The Great Landowners of Great Britain and Ireland* (1873).
16. CRO, R.59.31: Petitions (1811).
17. F. A. Ruston, *The Fen Country* (1870), p 27.
18. J. G. Lenny lists landowners and acreages according to parishes. See *Particulars referring to a Plan of Part of the Bedford Level and Lands Adjacent ... Surveyed 1828–1834* (1844).
19. Ruston, op cit, p 27.
20. CRO, R.59.31.18.7.E and R.59.31.18.8.G: Tax Rolls of 1697 and 1734.
21. R.59.31.14.2: 'Mr Sassery's List of Owners of adventure land' (nd, c1805–12).

22. See the Corporation Lot Book of 1828 in S. Wells, *Bedford Level*, II (1830), pp 692–754.
23. R.59.31.1: Register of Conveyances (1649–1815) and R.59.31.3: Register of Conveyances and Leases (1816–1920).
24. C. Johnson, *An Account of the Ely and Littleport Riots in 1816* (2nd ed 1948), p 38.
25. S. Wells, *The Lot Book of the Bedford Level Corporation . . . Corrected to November 1840* (1841).
26. CRO, R.59.31.1–3: Register of Conveyances and Leases (1649–1920).
27. Ibid.
28. Ibid. See also R.59.31.14.2. (v): 'List of voters and their residences' (nd late 18c or early 19c).
29. The Duke of Bedford, *A Great Agricultural Estate. Being the Story of the Origin and Administration of Woburn and Thorney* (1897), pp 48–9.
30. CRO, R.59.31.2–3: Register of Conveyances and Leases (1664–1920).
31. *Eau Brink Cut. Residue of the Evidence* (1795), p 55.
32. See W. Gooch, op cit, p 40.
33. CRO, R.59.31.2: Register of Leases (1664–1815).
34. R.59.31.3: Register of Conveyances and Leases (1816–1920).
35. W. Gooch, op cit, pp 105–6.
36. A. Young, *Agriculture of the County of Suffolk* (1794), p 30.
37. F. A. Ruston, op cit, p 24.
38. A. Young, *Annals of Agriculture*, XLIII (1805), p 560.
39. Ruston, op cit, p 25.
40. G. Maxwell, *Agriculture of the County of Huntingdon* (1793), p 24. See also A. Young, *Annals of Agriculture*, XLIII, p 282.
41. J. W. Childers, *Lord Orford's Voyage round the Fens in 1774* (1868), p 57.
42. CRO, R.59.31.2: Register of Leases (1664–1815).
43. A. Young, *Agriculture of the County of Lincoln* (1799), p 247.
44. S. Wells, *Bedford Level*, I (1830), p 442.
45. J. M. Heathcote, *Reminiscences of Fen and Mere* (1876), pp 90–1.
46. P. Pusey, 'Some account of the Practise of English Farmers . . .', *Journ Roy Agric Soc*, II (1842), p 406. See also J. Card, *English Agriculture in 1850–1* (1852), p 181.
47. R. Parkinson, *Agriculture of the County of Huntingdon* (1811), p 301. See also J. A. Clarke, 'On the Great Level of the Fens', *Journ Roy Agric Soc*, VIII (1848), p 100.
48. Clarke, op cit, p 92.
49. Ibid, p 101.
50. *Minutes of Evidence Taken before Select Committee on Agricultural Distress March 1836*, 7830.

51. CRO, R.59.31.19: Account Books (1800–60) and R.59.31.22: Rent Books (1830–60).
52. R.59.31.19.A.38–44 (1860–1900).
53. Ruston, op cit, pp 27–8.
54. J. A. Clarke, *Fen Sketches* (1852), pp 262–71.
55. Clarke, op cit (1848), pp 96 et seq.
56. S. Jonas, 'On the Farming of Cambridgeshire', *Journ Roy Agric Soc*, VII (1847), p 70.
57. CRO, R.59.31.3: Register of Conveyances and Leases (1816–1920).
58. Gooch, op cit, p 176.
59. Johnson, op cit, p 9.
60. Ibid, p 10.
61. Ibid, p 60.
62. Ibid, p 9.
63. See Lord Ernle, *English Farming Past and Present* (6th ed 1961), pp 322–3.
64. *Royal Commission on Agriculture: Report by Mr Druce* (1881), p 364.
65. Ibid (1882), p 40.
66. CRO, R.59.31.22: Rent Books (1878–96).
67. Lord Ernle, op cit, p 377.
68. E. Halévy, *A History of the English People in the Nineteenth Century*, V (2nd ed 1951), pp 293–4.
69. R. H. Pringle, *Royal Commission on Agriculture: Report on Bedford, Huntingdon and Northampton* (1895), pp 12, 34.
70. A. W. Fox, *Royal Commission on Agriculture: Report on Cambridgeshire* (1895), p 25.
71. Pringle, op cit, p 34.
72. Fox, op cit, p 26.
73. W. H. Wheeler, *A History of the Fens of South Lincolnshire* (1896 ed), pp 36–8.
74. T. Stone, *Agriculture of the County of Lincoln* (1794), pp 18, 22.
75. A. Young, *Agriculture of the County of Lincoln* (1813), pp 253–4.
76. Stone, op cit, p 22.
77. Young, op cit, p 258.
78. Ibid, pp 253–4.
79. A. Young, *Agriculture of the County of Norfolk* (1804), p 138.
80. Ibid, p 173.
81. Young, *Lincoln* (1813), pp 254, 255.
82. Ibid, p 260.
83. Ibid, p 261.
84. Ibid, p 274.
85. Ibid, p 269.
86. Ibid, p 48.
87. Ibid, p 98.
88. Young, *Norfolk* (1804), p 138.

89. 33 Geo III, c 116.
90. Young, *Lincoln* (1813), p 281.
91. W. Camden, *Britannia* (1637), p 481.
92. T. Cox, *Magna Britannia*, III (1724), p 296.
93. Young, *Lincoln* (1813), p 138.
94. Young, *Norfolk* (1804), p 173.
95. Young, *Lincoln* (1813), p 140.
96. Ibid, p 139.
97. Ibid, p 204.
98. Ibid, pp 117, 284.
99. *Minutes of Evidence Taken before Select Committee on Agricultural Distress, March 1836*, 8115–19, 9602–3.
100. Ibid, 9602–3.
101. Young, *Norfolk* (1804), p 48.
102. Wheeler, op cit, p 424.
103. Young, *Lincoln* (1813), p 64.
104. Wheeler, op cit, p 424.
105. Ibid, p 414.
106. Young, *Lincoln* (1813), p 44.
107. Wheeler, op cit, p 422.
108. Ibid, p 424.
109. A. W. Fox, *Royal Commission on Agriculture: Report on Lincolnshire* (1895), pp 19–20, 105, 106.

CHAPTER 10 (pages 211–42)

1. H. C. Darby (ed), *A Scientific Survey of the Cambridge District* (1938), p 194.
2. E. G. Crocker, 'The Drainage of the River Ouse Basin', *Min Proc Inst Mech Eng* (1913), pp 821–4.
3. H. C. Darby (ed), op cit, p 195.
4. W. E. Doran, 'Drainage during the War'. Reprinted from *Water and Water Engineering* (March/April 1945), p 11.
5. W. H. Wheeler, 'Fascine Work at the Outfalls of the Fen Rivers, and Reclamation of the Foreshore', *Min Proc Inst Civ Eng*, XLVI (1876), p 62.
6. See the First North Level Act, 27 Geo II, c 19.
7. 50 Geo III, c 125.
8. 20 and 21 Vict, c 109.
9. See the Middle Level Separation Act, 25 and 26 Vict, c 188.
10. *Middle Level Drainage and Navigation Bill. Minutes of the Evidence*, July 1862, p 6.
11. Ibid, p 7.
12. See schedules attached to the Land Drainage Act (Great Ouse) of 10 and 11 Geo V, c 122.

13. W. H. Wheeler, 'The Conservancy of Rivers: the Eastern Midland District of England', *Min Proc Inst Civ Eng*, LXVII (1882), p 225.
14. J. Coode, *River Nene, Thorney Lordship, and Proposed Dock, etc, at Wisbech: Report to His Grace the Duke of Bedford* (1874), pp 53–4.
15. J. H. H. Moxon, 'The Floods of the Lower Ouse', *Abs Proc and Trans Beds Nat Hist Soc* (1877–8), p 33.
16. W. H. Wheeler, op cit (1882), p 226.
17. Ibid, pp 226–7.
18. R. F. Grantham, 'The Present Conditions of Arterial Drainage in some English Rivers', *Min Proc Inst Civ Eng*, CCII (1917), p 265.
19. *Report of the Royal Commission on Land Drainage in England and Wales* (1927), Appendix III, p 51.
20. R. F. Grantham, op cit, p 263.
21. Ibid.
22. By the Land Drainage Act of 10 and 11 Geo V, c 122 (Great Ouse).
23. *Report of the Royal Commission on Land Drainage in England and Wales* (1927), pp 45–6.
24. King's Lynn Public Library. Norfolk Estuary Company records: Drainage Inquiry (1914), p 40.
25. E. G. Crocker, 'The Drainage of the River Ouse Basin', *Min Proc Inst Mech Eng* (1913), p 809.
26. R. F. Grantham, op cit, p 259.
27. See N. Walker and T. Craddock, *The History of Wisbech and the Fens* (1849), p 465.
28. S. Smiles, *Lives of the Engineers*, II (1862), pp 168–9. See also King's Lynn Public Library, Norfolk Estuary Company records: Drainage Inquiry (1914), pp 37–8.
29. R. F. Grantham, op cit, p 254.
30. Wheeler, op cit (1882), pp 209, 219.
31. Ibid.
32. S. Preston, *Report on the River Ouse*, p 14.
33. Norfolk Estuary Company records: Drainage Inquiry (1914), p 13.
34. Ibid, pp 31–2.
35. Ibid, p 41.
36. J. Vetch and J. Washington, *Norfolk Estuary Bill 1849: Report to the Lords Commissioners of the Admiralty* (1849), pp 13, 17.
37. Eau Brink Drainage: Minute Book of the Navigation Commissioners (1820–37), p 85.
38. *Eau Brink Navigation. Mr Telford's Report* (1825), p 2.
39. Coode, op cit, p 51.
40. Moxon, op cit, p 30.

41. Coode, op cit, p 51.
42. See Preston, op cit.
43. W. E. Doran, 'The Great Ouse Flood Protection Scheme. Drainage and Engineering Works in the Fens'. Reprinted from *The Dock and Harbour Authority* (April/May 1956), p 4.
44. Sir Alexander Gibb & Partners, *Report to the Association of Internal Drainage Authorities within the South Level on Measures for Securing Safety from Flooding in the South Level* (January 1939), p 3.
45. W. Dugdale, *History of Imbanking and Drayning* (1772 ed), p 415.
46. Doran, op cit (1956), p 2.
47. *Great Ouse River Board: The Official Opening of the Tail Sluice of the Great Ouse Flood Protection Scheme* (1959), p 5.
48. Sir Alexander Gibb & Partners, op cit, p 8.
49. Ibid, p 4.
50. *The Battle of the Banks* (Ely Rotary Club, 1947), p 8.
51. Sir Murdoch MacDonald & Partners, 'The River Great Ouse Flood Protection Scheme'. Reprinted from *The Engineer* (Sept 1942), pp 10–11.
52. River Nene Catchment Board, *Report on the Floods of March 1947* (1947), pp 1–2.
53. *Harvest Home. The Official Story of the Great Floods of 1947 and their Sequel* (HMSO 1948), p 37.
54. River Welland Catchment Board, *The River Welland Major Improvement Scheme* (1957).
55. River Great Ouse Catchment Board: Minute Books, VI (1946–9), pp 148–9.
56. W. E. Doran, 'The Fight for the Fens'. Reprinted from *Water and Water Engineering* (June 1948), p 10.
57. House of Commons Session 1948–9. River Great Ouse (Flood Protection) Bill. Petitions of the King's Lynn Conservancy Board, the British Transport Commission, the West Norfolk Farmers' Manure & Chemical Co-operative Co Ltd, and the Boal Quay Wharfingers Ltd.
58. House of Commons Session 1948–9. River Great Ouse (Flood Protection) Bill. Evidence of the River Great Ouse Catchment Board.
59. House of Lords Session 1948–9. River Great Ouse (Flood Protection) Bill. Petition of the King's Lynn Conservancy Board.
60. Doran, op cit (1956), p 6.
61. House of Commons Session 1948–9. Opposition evidence of the King's Lynn Conservancy Board.
62. Ibid. Evidence of the River Great Ouse Catchment Board.

EPILOGUE (*pages* 243–57)

1. W. Dodson, 'The Designe, for the perfect draining of the Great Level of the Fens'. Printed in S. Wells, *Bedford Level*, II (1830), p 432.
2. *Reorganisation of Water and Sewage Services: Government Proposals* (HMSO Dec 1971).
3. River Authorities – Reorganisation: Land Drainage. Memorandum of Submissions of 7 River Authorities (February 1972). I am greatly indebted to Mr J. S. Bissett, Clerk of the Great Ouse River Authority, for allowing me access to this information.
4. Ibid.
5. Memorandum of Representations by the King's Lynn Conservancy Board, East Coast – River Great Ouse – The Wash (March 1972).
6. *The Wash: Estuary Storage: Report on the Desk Study* (HMSO 1970), p 26.
7. W. Elstobb, *An Historical Account of the Great Level of the Fens* (1793), pp 200–1.
8. See J. Smith, 'Soil Mixing to Preserve Fen Peats', *Agriculture* (Dec 1969), pp 612–16. See also J. Smith, R. Wickens and S. J. Richardson, 'Soil Mixing in the Fens'. Printed in the Arthur Rickwood Experimental Husbandry Farm, *Sixth Report* (1971), pp 24–31.
9. See Audrey M. Williams, 'Wind Protection for Soil and Crops' in *Agriculture* (April 1972), pp 148–54; also P. C. Rickard, 'A New System of Wind Protection for Arable Crops' in the Arthur Rickwood Experimental Husbandry Farm, *Sixth Report* (1971), pp 32–6.
10. *CSPD*, Chas I, CLII, 84 (1629).

Acknowledgements

I AM deeply grateful for the assistance of the following institutions: the Bedford Borough Library, the British Museum, the Cambridge County Library, the Colman and Rye Local History Library, Norwich, the House of Lords Record Office, the King's Lynn Borough Library, the Norfolk Record Office, the Norris Library, St Ives, Huntingdon, the Public Record Office and the Squire Law Library, Cambridge. Above all I am indebted to the Bedfordshire County Library for their unflagging assistance in tracing rare books, to the Cambridge and Isle of Ely Record Office for their constant patience and courtesy during long hours spent working on their premises, and to the King's Lynn Conservancy Board and the G.O. and Welland and Nene River Divisions of the Anglian Water Authority for their generosity in making records available to me. I am grateful to the staff of the former Water Resources Board for advice on several points.

The following individuals answered specific queries or helped in other ways: Mr D. S. Akroyd, Deputy Director (Legal) of the Anglian Water Authority and Mr J. A. Maddison of the Engineer's Department, Mr D. Cowie of Binnie and Partners, Mr J. Davies, Curator of the Norris Library, St Ives, Huntingdon, Mr H. van Oosterom, Deputy Director (Rivers) of the Anglian Water Authority and Mr R. Wickens, Director of the Arthur Rickwood Experimental Husbandry Farm, Mepal. In particular I am indebted to Mr J. S. Bissett, Divisional Manager of the Great Ouse River Division, Anglian Water Authority, Mr M. W. Dymott of the Ministry of Agriculture, Fisheries and Food, and Mr T. A. Valentine, General Manager and Clerk of the King's Lynn Conservancy Board, who have shown a sustained interest in the work, and have been an unfailing source of encouragement and advice.

SOURCES OF ILLUSTRATIONS

Several individuals and organisations have generously assisted me in the search for photographs. The Anglian Water Authority has been of immense assistance and has provided plates 1a and 2a–6a. I am grateful to the *Lynn News and Advertiser* for permission to reproduce plates 1b and 6b and to Mr H. J. Mason for permission to use plates 7a–8a. Plate 8b is reproduced by kind permission of the Arthur Rickwood Experimental Husbandry Farm, Mepal.

Index

Abernethy, J., 222
Accretion on coast, 17, 207
Acts of Parliament mentioned in connection with:
Deeping Fen (1738), 137
Eau Brink Cut (1795), 151, 154
Enclosure prevention (1684), 184
Flood Protection (Great Ouse) (1949), 240
General Draining (1600), 56, 105
General Draining (1663), 81–2, 84, 94, 184
Haddenham Level (1727), 119
Holland Fen 1767), 206
Land Drainage (1920), 218
Land Drainage (1930), 218
Middle Level (1810), 159; (1844), 159–60; 1848), 160
Middle Level Separation (1864), 215
North Level (1753), 124
Pretended Act (1649), 73–4
Redmore, Waterden and Cawdle Fen (1738), 120
Tax Act (1667), 183
Tydd & Newton drainage (1773), 150
Waldersea drainage (1605–6), 56

Water Resources (1963), 243
Welland Outfall (1794), 137
Witham fens (1762), 139
Administrative problems, 46–7, 50–1, 81, 115–17, 121–5, 129, 141, 213–18, 245–7
Adventurers (undertakers), 49, 59, 61–2, 64–6, 69, 71, 77–8, 82–3, 85, 92, 105–6, 128, 130, 133
Adventurers' lands, 83–8, 107, 128, 183–44, 188–9, 191, 193, 197, 214
Aerial photography, 27–8
Agas, Ralph, 57
Agriculture, 10–11, 28, 34, 36–8, 51–2, 92–3, 140–2, 180–210, 251–7
Agricultural depressions, 154, 197–201, 210
Anglian Water Authority, 245–7
Anglo-Saxons, 11–12, 26–8, 30–2
Appold's Centrifugal pump, 173–4
Arthur Rickwood Experimental Husbandry Farm, Mepal, 254
Arundel, Earl of, 60, 78
Ashley, Henry, 146
Asparagus, 210
Atkyns, Richard, 44, 54, 59
Ayloffe, Sir William, 60–2

INDEX

Badeslade, Thomas, 101, 109, 112, 147
Banks, Sir Joseph, 177
Banks of rivers, their maintenance, 47, 79, 84, 96–100, 117–18, 177, 179–80, 224–6
Barley, 32, 37–8, 251, 256
Barnack, 35
Barrage schemes (Great Ouse), 227–8
   Wash, 247–8, 250
Baskerville, Thomas, 12
Bateman, J., 186
Beans, 140, 192, 194, 196, 207–8, 210
Bede, 11
Bedford, Bedfordshire, 93, 146, 181, 186, 189, 220
Bedford, Francis, 4th Earl of, 57–8, 62–7, 69, 71, 77–8, 105, 155
Bedford, William, 5th Earl (and 1st Duke) of, 64, 66, 73, 77, 87, 215
Bedford, Wriothesley, 3rd Duke of, 120
Bedford, 11th Duke of, 190
Bedford family, *see* Russell, House of
Bedford Level, 49, 58, 63–4, 69, 73, 77, 81–4, 88, 91, 94, 101–2, 107, 110, 113, 120–2, 125, 128–30, 135, 144, 183–4, 186–7, 189–90, 195, 197, 208, 210, 214–15
Bedford Level Corporation, 79–95, 99–101, 104–5, 107, 109–11, 113, 115–28, 149–50, 152–5, 160, 177–9, 183–4, 186, 188–9, 193, 195, 198, 213–15, 218
Bentham, James, 105, 127–9, 155, 185
Bevill's Leam, 68, 174
Bicker Haven, 17, 35

Binnie & Partners, 248
Black Death, 38, 46
Black sluice, 138, 175
Blythe, 56
Bonds, bondholders, 89–90, 179
Boston, Boston Haven, 30, 33, 36, 40, 56, 133, 135, 137–9, 142, 146–8, 154, 158, 180–1, 207–8, 220
Bottisham, 121–2, 162, 167–8, 186, 212
Bourne, Bourne Fen, 13, 34, 59, 133, 137, 236
Bradley, Humphrey, 58
Brandon, 13, 109, 189
British Transport Commission, 239
Burghley, Lord, 57, 58–9
Burnt Fen, 121, 127, 179
Burrell, Andrewes, 21, 72
Bury St Edmunds, 109

Cabbages, 194, 210
Callis, Robert, 48
Cam, river, 22, 60, 109, 121, 179, 228–9, 236
Cambridge, 15, 26, 69, 93, 109, 111–12, 127, 168, 180–1, 189, 197
   University, 61, 89
Cambridgeshire, 13, 41, 52, 59–60, 93, 151–2, 180, 186, 198, 201, 211, 220, 251–2
Camden, William, 25, 31, 45, 51, 207
Capital for draining, 57, 64–6, 77–8, 81, 89–91, 105–6, 119–20, 124, 153–5, 160, 179
Cardyke, 23–4, 29, 32, 73, 175
Carrots, 12, 210, 251–2
Casaubon, Isaac, 51
Catchment Boards, their foundation, 218–19
Catchwater drains, 23–4, 29, 73,

INDEX

Catchwater cont.—
135, 175–6, 180; *see* Cut-off Channel
Cattle, 11, 24, 28, 36–8, 43, 52, 54, 74, 93, 105, 107, 118, 127, 133, 136, 141–2, 181, 185, 202–5, 207–8, 253
Celery, 12, 210, 251–2
Centrifugal pumps, 173–4, 177, 211
Charles I, 62–3, 71–2, 81–2, 135
Chatteris, 33, 77, 159, 193
Chicheley, John, 116
Civil War, 66, 73, 95, 133, 135–6
Clarke, J. A., 169–71, 173
Claying the land, 194–5, 208, 256
Clough's Cross, 69, 157, 232
Coal, 168, 197, 212
Cobbett, William, 180
Cole, C. N., 90, 120, 152–3
Coleseed, 74, 92, 192, 194, 196, 208
Commissions of Sewers, 46–50, 60–3, 69, 71, 81, 83, 108, 129–30, 133, 136, 141, 202, 256
Common rights, 41, 57, 66, 104–6, 139, 185, 204; *see* Intercommoning
Commons and commoners, 36–7, 40, 43, 52, 57, 105–7, 184–6, 201–6, 252
Coode, Sir John, 216, 223
Corn, 12, 33, 37, 39, 74, 93, 107, 133, 140, 174, 180, 191–6, 198, 208–10
Cottenham, 107, 127
Cowbit Wash, 76, 231, 234
Cromwell, Oliver, 66, 73
Crop rotations, 184, 191–2, 194–6
Crowland, 11, 14, 27, 34, 36, 46, 51, 59, 69, 95, 124, 232, 234
  Abbey of, 9, 11, 33, 38
  Abbot of, 33, 43
Crowland Wash, 231, 234
Cut-off Channel, 103, 135, 229, 236, 240

Deeping Fen, 14, 32, 36, 43, 59, 61, 130, 133, 135–7, 142, 168, 172, 203–4, 206, 208
Defoe, Daniel, 23, 101–2, 111
Denver, Denver sluice, 59, 74–6, 103, 108–10, 112–13, 140, 146–8, 156, 167, 177, 222–3, 222–3, 225–9, 236–8, 240
Denver sluice commissioners, 218, 222
Devil's Dyke, 26–7
Diesel engines, 167, 211–13, 219
Dissolution of monasteries, 50–1
Ditches and drains, their maintenance, 33, 41–3, 46–7, 79, 84, 117, 255
Doddington, 34, 77, 186
Dodson, Colonel William, 24, 94–6, 99, 103, 151, 243
Dog-in-a-Doublet sluice, 224, 231
Domesday survey, 30, 32, 34–5
Doran, W. E., 225, 240
Downham (St John's) Eau, 76, 103, 123
Drought, 12–13, 24, 75, 94
Dugdale, Sir William, 26, 33–4, 39, 43, 55, 77, 130, 146
Dust storms, 255
Dutch, Dutchmen, 55, 58, 62, 66–7, 130
Dyke reeves, 42

Earith, 13, 25, 68, 74, 76, 109, 119, 179
East Anglia, 15, 28, 30, 245, 255
East Fen (Lincs), 13, 36, 40, 133, 136, 140, 142, 151, 174–7, 180, 202–5
Eau Brink commissioners, 155, 179, 214
Eau Brink Cut, 148, 151, 154–6, 159, 181, 221
Edmonds, Sir Clement, 54
Elizabeth I, 51, 55–6, 58, 105

Elstobb, William, 12, 104
Ely, 11–12, 14, 19, 31, 36, 45, 51, 68, 93, 110–13, 127–8, 160, 164, 168, 179–80, 184–6, 197–8, 225, 228, 236, 238, 240
Abbey of, 33
Bishop of, 42–5, 49, 61, 89
Cathedral of, 77, 100, 110, 238
Ely, Isle of, 11, 19, 31, 33, 36, 52, 56, 59–60, 64, 72–3, 93, 111–12, 193, 198, 253
Enclosure, 28, 37, 43, 69, 107, 184–6, 193, 204–8
Erosion, 13–14, 253–5
Expenditure on drainage works, 64, 77–8, 85, 88–9, 120, 177–8, 226, 242

Fascine work, 154, 158–9, 161, 227, 239–42
Feltwell, 19, 68, 113, 212
Fen Office, 88, 92, 102, 116, 183
Fish, fishers, fishing, 9–10, 12, 31, 34–5, 42–3, 106, 140, 195
Flax, 37, 74, 92, 208
Fleam Dyke, 26
Fleet (Lincs), 17, 33, 48
Floods, 21–3, 25, 29, 38–44, 51–3, 94, 99, 102, 110–13, 117, 119, 124, 126–7, 136–40, 152, 159–60, 163, 178, 221, 230–4
Fortrey, Samuel, 83, 93
Fosdyke, Fosdyke bridge, 158, 234
Fossatum Marisci, 40–1
'Free' lands, 183
French Wars, *see* Napoleonic Wars
Fruit-growing, 37, 201, 210
Fuller, Thomas, 78, 93

Gedney, 48, 53, 207
Gibb, Sir Alexander, 225, 227–8

Glacial period, 14–15
Glen river, 22, 33, 73, 129–30, 133, 135, 234, 236
Golborne, James, 127, 153
Gooch, William, 186, 191
Grand sluice, 139–40, 146–8, 158, 220
Grantham, R. F., 217, 221
Grazing, 10–11, 21, 32, 34, 36–7, 52, 72, 139, 141, 185, 196, 201, 207–8, 253
Great Ouse, river, 12, 14, 22, 25, 38–9, 41, 60, 68, 71, 74–6, 103, 108–10, 112, 119, 121, 129, 144, 146, 148, 151, 159–60, 167, 174, 178–9, 181, 215–19, 218, 221–9, 232, 236, 240, 248
Great Ouse Catchment Board, 218, 225, 228–9, 238–40
Great Ouse Flood Protection Scheme, 236–42
Great Ouse outfall, 54, 72–3, 76, 144–8, 154–6, 158, 220–2, 227–8, 248
Great Ouse River Board, 219, 225, 239–40, 242
Greatford Cut, 236
Grunty Fen, 185
Gunthorpe sluice, 156
Guthlac, St, 9, 11, 27, 186
Guyhirne, 41, 44, 68–9, 76, 135, 224, 231
Gyrwe, 31

Haddenham, Haddenham Level, 113, 119, 127, 187, 233
Hardwicke, Earl of, 155, 186, 215
Hatfield Chase, 62, 68
Head sluice, 240
Hermitage sluice, 109, 177, 179
Hobhole drain and sluice, 158, 176
Holbeach, 43, 48, 141, 207, 254
Holland, *see* Netherlands

INDEX

Holland (Lincs) and Holland Fens, 13, 36, 39–40, 45–7, 53, 124, 133, 135–7, 202, 206, 208, 232
Horsemills, 101
Horses, 11, 52, 54, 66, 118, 141, 181, 202–3, 208, 253
Horseshoe sluice, 57
Hundred Foot Engine, 168, 171–2
Hundred Foot river, 74–6, 103, 109–10, 112, 117–18, 147, 168, 171, 177–9, 220, 222, 227, 234, 238
Hundred Foot Wash commissioners, 179

Huntingdon, Huntingdonshire, 13, 37, 60, 69, 71–2, 146, 151, 173, 198, 220–1, 251

Ice Age, Glacial period, 14–15
Indenture of Fourteen Parts, 65
Ingulph, 39, 43
Intercommoning, 36–7, 40, 104, 204; see Commons; Common rights
Interest rates, 89, 120, 124, 153, 188
Internal drainage boards, 219
Invested land rolls, 113

James I, 56–7, 59, 61–2
Jenyns, John, 111
Jenyns, Roger, 116
Joliffe & Banks, 155–6
Jonas, S., 171, 180, 195

Kent, 66, 189
Kesteven, 40, 45
Kinderley, C., 148–9
Kinderley, N., 148
Kinderley's Cut, 149–50, 156

King's Lynn, 13, 26, 38–9, 53–4, 56, 76, 109, 112, 141, 146–8, 151, 154, 156, 220, 222, 227–8, 236, 239, 247
King's Lynn Conservancy Board, 238–40, 245
Kyme, Kyme Fen, 33, 133, 136

Labelye, Charles, 112, 148
Lakenheath, 13, 52, 113, 253
Landscape, evolution of, 14–17
Lark, river, 22, 73, 76, 103, 121, 179, 223, 228–9, 232, 236, 240
Leases, 190–1, 193, 196–7, 209
Lincoln, 13, 23, 29, 32, 133, 206, 220, 230
Lincoln, Earl of, 124
Lincolnshire, 11, 13–14, 17, 25, 31–5, 37, 40, 43, 47–8, 53–5, 59–60, 63, 72, 129–30, 135–6, 141–2, 144, 151, 171, 174, 176, 180–1, 202–3, 207–10, 245, 251, 254
Lindsey, Earl of, 136–7
Little Ouse, river, 22, 73, 76, 103, 121, 223, 228–9, 232, 236, 240
Littleport, Littleport Fen, 34–5, 45, 60, 86, 107, 168–9, 171, 179, 188, 197, 212, 225, 228
London, 35, 55–6, 59, 66, 88, 90, 92, 116, 141, 152–3, 181, 186, 189, 192, 195, 210
Londoners, 59
Long Sutton, 206–7
Lovell, Thomas, 59, 130

Lynn, see King's Lynn
Lynn Law, 63, 66–7, 69

MacDonald, Sir Murdock, & Partners, 228, 230, 236
Magdalen Bend, 222, 228–9, 236

Manchester, Earl of, 136
Manea, 19, 71, 112–13, 118, 163, 187
March, 59, 93–4, 118, 127, 193
March West Fen, 168, 171–2
Market gardening, 201, 210
Marsh reeves, 202
Marshland, *see* Norfolk Marshland
Matthew Paris, 38
Maud Foster drain and sluice, 158, 175
Maxey North drain, 234
Meadows, 36, 38, 43, 45, 67, 84
Mercia, 26, 30
Methwold, Methwold Fen, 52, 211–12, 153
Middle Fen, 121, 127, 164, 168
Middle Level, 73, 77, 120, 125, 156, 159–60, 163, 195, 214, 221
Middle Level commissioners, 173, 214
Middle Level drain and sluice, 159–60, 174
Mildenhall, 12–13, 109, 113
Mills, *see* Horsemills; Windmills
Monasteries, 32–3, 45–6, 50–1
Morton's Leam, 44–5, 68, 73, 76, 100, 103, 124–6, 135, 214, 231
Moxon, J. H. H., 178, 216, 223
Mustard, 118, 196, 207, 210, 256

Napoleonic Wars, 153, 168, 188, 191, 193, 197
Nar valley, 13
Navigation, 20–1, 23, 29, 56, 63, 79, 84–5, 94, 103, 108–10, 118, 127–9, 146, 149–50, 154–6, 181–2, 214, 223–4, 238–40, 245
Neale, Thomas, 112, 121, 163
Nene, river, 12, 14, 22, 25, 44, 59–60, 133, 135, 137, 144, 150, 168, 172, 216, 221, 223–4, 230–1, 248

Nene Catchment Board, 218, 223
Nene outfall, 54, 72, 108, 144–5, 148–50, 154, 156–8, 161, 181, 220
Nene Outfall Cut, 156, 181
Netherlands, 55, 57, 253
New Bedford river *see* Hundred Foot river
New South Eau, 69, 232
Nine Holes sluice, 179
Norfolk, 13–15, 25, 45, 60, 68, 72, 118, 142, 209, 211, 251–3
Norfolk Marshland, 19, 25, 36–7, 39–41, 44, 53–4, 102, 110, 129, 141, 159–60, 204, 206–7, 251
Norman Conquest, 11, 33, 36
North Forty Foot Drain, 138, 175
North Level, 73, 93, 107–8, 111, 119–20, 123–6, 149–50, 157, 167, 195, 214, 220, 232
North Level commissioners, 124–5, 157, 232
North Level Main Drain, 157, 167
Northampton, Northamptonshire, 13, 31, 60, 189, 223–4
Northey Gravels, 224

Old Bedford river, 68, 73–4, 76–7, 103, 111, 177–8, 227
Old West river, 179, 233
Opposition to drainage, 57, 59–61, 69, 104–10, 127–8, 133, 135, 149, 151, 154–5, 238–40
Ouse Cut (1830), 179
Outfall difficulties, 24–5, 54, 72, 103, 143–51, 160–1, 220, 248, 250
Outwell, 36, 41, 59
Over, Over Fen, 232–3

Paring and burning, 191–3, 208
Paupers' Cut, 156
Peakirk Drain, 69

Peat, peat fens, 12–13, 16–17, 19–21, 30, 32, 52, 66, 96, 99, 129, 191–4, 206, 251–5
Peat fires, 12–13, 193
Peat shrinkage, 16, 19, 88, 95–9, 104, 145, 172, 177, 251–4
Peterborough, 13, 25, 33, 44, 68, 76, 126, 154, 181, 185, 221, 223–4, 231
  Abbot of, 37
  Bishop of, 61
Peterborough Great and Little Fens, 69, 105, 133
Pigs, 37, 42, 117, 122, 202, 205
Pinchbeck, 168, 236
Pinchbeck engine, 171
Podike, New, 25, 44; Old, 44
Popham, Sir John, 57, 59, 67
Popham's Eau, 59, 76
Population, 28, 30, 38, 55, 93, 205
Potatoes, 12, 194, 201, 208, 210, 251
Preston, Sidney, 221, 224
Prices of land, 78, 113, 157–8, 186, 206, 210
Private drainage districts, 119–23, 214
Privy Council, 51, 58, 61, 71
Puddling, 179–80

Railways, 181–2
Rainfall, 22–3, 144, 230
Ramsey, 13–14, 32–3, 35, 37, 77, 121, 127
  Abbot of, 33, 45
Reeds, 11, 34–5, 51, 106, 117, 140, 202
Regional Water Authorities, 244–5, 247
Relief Channel, 103, 228–9, 236, 239–40
Rennie, John, 148, 162–3, 167–8, 175–6, 180
Rennie, Sir John, 158, 177, 222

Rents of fen land, 142, 163, 186, 198, 205–6, 210
Riots, at Ely and Littleport (1816), 197
River Authorities, 243–7
River banks, *see* Banks of rivers
River Boards, 219, 244
Roads, 20–1, 137, 151, 181
Roddons, 16
'Roman' banks, 26–7
Roman occupation, 23, 26–8, 35
Romans, 11, 17, 19, 23–4, 26–9, 31–2
Roswell Hill, 100
Russell, House of, 63–4, 74, 78, 83, 90, 130; *see* Bedford
Russell, Sir William, 57–8
Ruston, F. A., 159, 187

St Germans, *see* Wiggenhall St Germans
St Ives (Hunts), 69, 118, 222
St John's Eau, *see* Downham Eau
Salt marshes, 15, 17, 19, 53, 130, 207–8
Salt-pans, 32, 35–6
Salter's Lode, 68, 76, 109, 177
Sam's cut, 68
Sandy's Cut, 68
Sandys, Sir Miles, 77–8
Scoopwheels, 101–2, 167–8, 171–4, 211
Sea banks, 25–7, 40–2
Sea level, changes of, 15
Seven Holes sluice, 179
Sewers, *see* Commissions of Sewers
Sheep, 11, 36, 52, 54, 141–2, 171, 180–1, 185, 196, 202–5, 207–8, 253
Shire Drain, 69, 157
Silt lands, 15–20, 25, 28, 30, 32, 45, 52–3, 66, 129–30, 141, 251, 254

INDEX

Sixteen Foot Drain, 77, 121, 159
Skertchly, S. B. J., 12–13, 20, 24
Skirbeck, 30, 36
Smeaton, John, 164
Soham, Soham Mere, 34, 211, 228
Soil mixing, 254–5
South Forty Foot Drain, 135, 138
South Holland Main Drain, 137
South Level, 73–5, 103, 110, 112, 120–1, 125, 156, 195, 214–15, 221, 225–9, 234, 238, 240
South Level commissioners, 179, 214, 218
Spalding, 34, 36, 43, 54, 59, 76, 145–6, 154, 168, 171, 181, 207–8, 210, 223, 231, 234
   Monastery of, 33, 40
   Prior of, 33
Spalding Coronation Channel, 234
Stamford, 181, 221, 234
Stanground, Stanground sluice, 44, 100, 177
Staplewere Fen, 45
Steam engines, 162–74, 177, 211–13, 219
Stoke Ferry, 13, 109, 229
Stone, Thomas, 164, 203
Storage reservoirs in (Wash), 247–50
Stretham, 119, 185
Stretham engine, 168, 172
Stuntney, 19, 34
Suffolk, 13, 72, 142, 151, 192, 236, 245, 252, 256
Sugar-beet, 12, 251, 256
Sutton St Edmund engine, 167
Swaffham Bulbeck & Prior, 13, 19, 100, 121–2, 167, 212
Swavesey, 100, 107

Tail sluice, 240
Taxes for drainage works, 40–2, 47, 63, 78, 82, 86–8, 113, 123–5, 127–8, 133, 139, 155–6, 160, 183, 190, 198, 217, 219
Telford, Thomas, 155–6, 223
Ten Mile Bank engine, 167–8
Terrington, 36, 40–1, 53, 204, 208
Thetford, 108–9
Thomas, Sir Anthony, 60–2, 133
Thorney, Thorney estate, 19, 37, 51, 55, 57–8, 63–4, 93, 120, 186–8, 190–1, 198
   Abbey and Abbot of, 33, 45–6
Thornhaugh, Baron (Sir William Russell), 57–8
Tides, 22, 24–5, 39, 53, 74–6, 99, 108–9, 111–12, 140, 144–8, 158, 161, 220, 227–8, 234, 250
Tilney, 36, 38–9, 41
Tilney Smeeth, 36, 141, 204, 206–7
Tong's Drain, 76, 159–60
Training walls, see Fascine work
Turf-cutting, 34, 37, 196–7, 203
Turnips, 194, 196, 210
Tydd, 41, 48, 69, 102
Tydd pumping station, 224, 232

Ugg Mere, 23
Undertakers, see Adventurers
Upwell, 41, 44, 59, 118, 190

Vancouver, Charles, 151
Vermuyden, Sir Cornelius, 22, 62–3, 67–77, 84, 95, 99, 103, 125, 130, 135, 175, 183, 211, 222, 225, 229, 242
Vernatti, Sir Philibert, 130

Wages, wage inflation, 152–4
Waldersea, 168–70
Waldersea engine, 168, 171–2
Walker, James, 159

INDEX

Walpole, 36, 40–1
Walsoken, 36, 40–1, 53
Walton, 36, 40–1
Wash, the, 13–17, 22, 24–5, 30–1, 76, 103, 144–5, 152, 223, 227, 239–42, 247–50
Washes, washlands, 72, 76, 177–9, 196, 224–5, 229, 231–2, 234, 251
Water Resources Board, 248
Waterbeach, Waterbeach Level, 13, 119–20, 168
Welches Dam, 77
Well Creek, 59, 76, 111, 117, 159–60
Welland, river, 12, 14, 22, 32–3, 39, 43, 60, 76, 129–30, 133, 135, 137, 144, 158, 216, 218, 221, 223, 234–6
Welland Catchment Board, 218, 231, 234
Welland Major Improvement Scheme, 234–6
Welland outfall, 54, 72, 137–8, 144–5, 158, 161, 220, 234, 248
Wells, Samuel, 77, 111, 124–5, 150, 178, 215
Welmore Lake, 177–9, 225
Welney Wash, 178
West Fen (Lincs), 13, 36, 133, 136–7, 140, 142, 151, 174–5, 177, 180, 202–5
Westerdyke, Jan Barents, 67–8
Wheeler, W. H., 161, 171, 209, 216–17, 221

Whittlesey, 19, 64, 119, 121, 195, 197
Whittlesey Mere, 23, 68, 173–4
Wiggenhall St Germans, 36, 39–41, 45, 148, 159, 212, 229
Wildfowl, wildfowling, 9–11, 31, 34, 106, 140, 195
Wildmore Fen, 13, 36, 39, 136, 140, 142, 151, 174–5, 177, 180, 202–5
Willingham, 92, 107
Wind-breaks, 255–6
Windmills, 101–3, 121, 127, 137, 139, 144–5, 162–72, 211
Wisbech, 17, 20, 34, 41, 44, 48–9, 53–4, 56–8, 60, 69, 93, 108, 133, 135, 141, 145–6, 148–50, 154, 156, 167, 181, 189, 201, 207, 212, 223–4
Corporation, 150, 154
Wissey, river, 22, 73, 76, 103, 228–9, 232, 240
Witham, river, 12–14, 22, 32–3, 39, 129, 133, 136, 138–40, 144, 147, 158, 175, 208, 216, 218, 230, 248
Witham outfall, 135, 138, 144–5, 158–9, 161, 181, 220
Woodhouse Marsh Cut, 156, 181
World War I, 213
World War II, 213, 229, 231

York, Yorkshire, 29, 66, 181
Young, Arthur, 127, 141–2, 151, 151, 162, 164, 192, 203–10